RACING POST
ANNUAL 2013

Racing Post One Canada Square, London
E14 5AP. 020 7293 2001

THE IRISH
RACING POST
ANNUAL 2013

Irish Racing Post Suite 413,
The Capel Building, Mary's Abbey,
Dublin 7. 01 872 7250

Editor Nick Pulford
Art editor David Dew
Cover design Jay Vincent
Chief photographers Edward Whitaker,
Patrick McCann
Other photography Caroline Norris, Martin
Lynch, Getty, Mark Cranham
Picture editor David Cramphorn
Graphics Sarah Chubb, Dave Penzer, Mel
Shaw, Jay Vincent
Picture artworking Stefan Searle, Nigel
Jones, Jenny Robertshaw
Feature writers Graham Dench, Steve
Dennis, Alastair Down, Nicholas Godfrey,
David Jennings, Tom Kerr, Jessica Lamb, Lee
Mottershead, Jonathan Mullin, Julian Muscat,
Lewis Porteous, John Randall, Brough Scott,
Peter Thomas, Sam Walker
Contributors Paul Curtis, Dave Edwards,
Steve Mason, Peter Scargill

Advertisement Sales
Racing Post: One Canada Square, London
E14 5AP. 020 7293 2001
Cheryl Gunn, cheryl.gunn@racingpost.com,

Archant Dialogue Prospect House, Rouen
Road, Norwich, NR1 1RE. 01603 772554
Andy Grant, andy.grant@archantdialogue.co.uk
Kay Brown, kay.brown@archantdialogue.co.uk
Dean Brown, dean.brown@archantdialogue.
co.uk

Distribution/availability 01933 304858
help@racingpost.com

Published by Racing Post Books in 2012
Axis House, Compton, Newbury, Berkshire,
RG20 6NL. Copyright © Racing Post 2012

A catalogue record for this book is available
from the British Library.
ISBN 978-1-908216-25-0 [UK]
ISBN 978-1-908216-26-7 [Ireland]
Printed in Great Britain by Buxton Press

Every effort has been made to fulfil
requirements with regard to copyright material.
The author and publisher will be glad to rectify
any omissions at the earliest opportunity.

www.racingpost.com/shop

A golder amazing

GW00697110

2012 has been a golden year for sport and, while the Olympics took centre stage, racing shone brightly too. In this second edition of the Racing Post Annual, we bring you all the big names of an action-packed year that once again showcased racing as the king of sports.

We start with viewpoints from Graham Dench and John Randall, two of the Racing Post's foremost experts, on whether this is a golden age of racing. It's a valid question after a year in which we were privileged to witness the best horse on the planet, the most prolific winning machine in the history of jump racing, the best sprint mare of all time, the first novice chaser to produce the best performance of the Cheltenham Festival and the first mare to add the King George to Arc success – in short, Frankel, Big Buck's, Black Caviar, Sprinter Sacre and Danedream.

We also saw Camelot try and fail to become the first winner of the Triple Crown in Britain since Nijinsky. Despite his failure at Doncaster, he is symbolic of the recent move towards racing horses with a positive view of what they might achieve rather than the fear that their reputation or value will be diminished by defeat.

At least Camelot's connections were brave enough to go for the Triple Crown, just as the owners of Frankel, Black Caviar and Big Buck's were prepared to put winning runs on the line. It is worth remembering that, in the 1980s and 1990s, Frankel would probably have been retired to stud at the end of his three-year-old season after just nine races. Which means we would never have seen his two best performances on Racing Post Ratings in the Queen Anne at Royal Ascot and the International at York.

Whatever your view of how the current stars measure up to those of previous eras, the fact that we can make the comparison at all is largely down to the competitive spirit that has seeped back into the sport in recent years. Racing fans have been the biggest winners of all.

This has been a year of record-breaking feats. As well as the incredible winning sequence of Big Buck's, we had the achievements of Nicky Henderson and Quevega at the Cheltenham Festival, the closest finish in 173 years of the Grand National, Richard Hughes's seven-timer at Windsor, the fastest five furlongs of all time and a place in the history books for Dvinsky.

The Annual has all their stories, plus many others of remarkable triumph and some of sadness, such as the deaths of Lord Oaksey and Campbell Gillies and Tony McCoy's despair at the loss of his Cheltenham Gold Cup-winning partner Synchronised.

We hope this Annual is a fitting tribute to all of them.

Nick Pulford
Editor

BIG STORIES

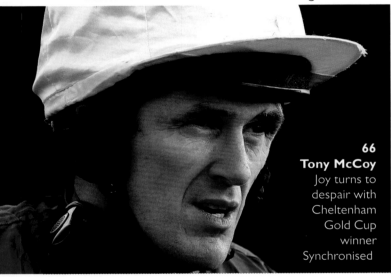

**66
Tony McCoy**
Joy turns to despair with Cheltenham Gold Cup winner Synchronised

Neptune Collonges
Page 50

FINAL FURLONG

STATISTICS

Black Caviar
Page 74

Richard Hughes
Page 84

Nicky Henderson
Page 94

Camelot
Page 26

'Whereas Sea The Stars kept us guessing as to how good he might be, Frankel left us in no doubt. He is responsible for the four highest RPRs ever recorded'
Frankel from every angle Page 12

'I told him to go carefully and pull him up if there were any problems. He said it was the most negative riding instruction he'd ever had'
John Hales Page 50

'This is my best lot of horses yet. I was with Fred Winter when he had that extraordinary team of legends – Bula, Pendil, Lanzarote, Midnight Court – and I'm very lucky to have the horses I've got now'
Nicky Henderson Page 94

'I've felt all along he's good. He did what he had to do at Cheltenham and I'm hoping there's more to come. It's a big comfort knowing he loves that hill'
Willie Mullins Page 106

'He doesn't need much downtime after a race, I just throw him out in a field and the next day he's charging around like a lunatic, bucking and kicking'
Keiran Burke Page 154

BOX OFFICE STARS

After another memorable
year on the Flat and over
jumps, two of the Racing
Post's leading experts
assess the claims to fame
of the headline acts

THOSE of us who became hooked on racing in the early 1970s have felt pretty smug about it for decades. There had surely never been a better time to become engrossed in our sport, and there probably never would be.

But then came Frankel. One swallow does not make a summer, but Frankel was not alone. It might be stretching things to suggest we are enjoying a spell to match the so-called golden age when in successive summers Nijinsky completed the Triple Crown, Mill Reef took the Derby, Eclipse, King George and Arc, and Brigadier Gerard won 17 of his 18 races. Yet there is no question that Flat racing has been blessed by some outstanding talents in recent years, and the latest season will go down as an exceptional one.

The sport was very different in the 1970s, as there were fewer horses and fewer races, racing was much more parochial and competition for attention in the sports pages and on television and radio was nowhere near so cut-throat. Make no mistake, though, Nijinsky, Mill Reef and Brigadier Gerard would have dominated any era.

Nijinsky's claim to greatness does not rest on the Triple Crown alone; in that same season he also won the Irish Derby and the King George, and he went down very narrowly in both the Arc and the Champion Stakes when past his best following a debilitating bout of ringworm.

Mill Reef also suffered two defeats, but he was increasingly impressive with each of his big three-year-old wins and he was an exceptionally talented two-year-old, when his effortless ten-length defeat of the classy Green God in the Gimcrack was one of the juvenile performances of the decade. He would surely have taken his tally of wins way past 12 but for serious injury only two races into his third season.

Brigadier Gerard, the horse with whom our latest champion is most frequently compared, beat Mill Reef in the 2,000 Guineas on the only occasion they met and went on to confirm himself as brilliant over a mile and a quarter as he was at a mile before stretching his stamina just far enough to win the King George on his only attempt at a mile and a half.

The good times were not over when Mill Reef and Brigadier Gerard were retired either, because over the next three years we were blessed with two outstanding fillies in Dahlia and Allez France, and the 'race of the century' between Grundy and Bustino at Ascot, plus a host of other highlights.

We have seen plenty of outstanding horses since then, of course, but it is rare indeed for racing to enjoy a spell like the current one. As recently as 2009 Sea The Stars was being hailed as the perfect example of the modern thoroughbred. Beaten only on his debut in a nine-race career that ended with an extraordinary performance in the Arc, in which he overcame all manner of traffic problems, Sea The Stars was celebrated for displaying all of the attributes we most desire in a racehorse, with an unsurpassed blend of speed, stamina and courage complemented by beautiful breeding, faultless conformation, a robust constitution and a superb temperament.

His style of racing did not lend itself to record-breaking performances and inflated ratings, but it was suggested at the time that we might never see his like again. Yet at the time of Sea The Stars' retirement Frankel was just ten months from making his racecourse debut and on the other side of the world Black Caviar was already four races into an unbeaten spree that in June 2012 was extended to 22 races with that dramatic Royal Ascot success.

Frankel did not show the versatility, stamina wise, of Sea The Stars, still less that of Nijinsky, Mill Reef or Brigadier Gerard, for his first 12 races were all

Leading lady Black Caviar is regarded as the best ever sprinter in Australia and she was too good for the Europeans even when she was below her best

at seven furlongs or a mile and his stamina was never stretched beyond the extended mile and a quarter of York's Juddmonte International, but not one of his predecessors could match him for the ruthless and overwhelming domination he exerted over his rivals time after time, and not one of them could match him for the sheer brilliance of his best performances or the eye-popping and scarcely believable manner in which he destroyed his rivals in his three signature performances, at Newmarket in the 2,000 Guineas, at Royal Ascot in the Queen Anne Stakes and at York in the International.

His Racing Post Rating of 143 is the best in the history of the service, which dates back to 1989. Timeform, which has been rating horses since shortly after the war, went even further with a provisional mark of 147, 2lb clear of Sea-Bird, its previous best, and 3lb ahead of Brigadier Gerard.

Putting Black Caviar's achievements into context is far harder from a European perspective, but in Australia, where they know a good sprinter when they see one, she is regarded the best ever, so we should count ourselves lucky that her connections were brave enough to send her to Royal Ascot, for she had little to prove in the Diamond Jubilee, with 11 impressive Group 1 wins to her name already.

Racing Post Ratings suggest she might have been as much as 11lb below her best at Ascot and, even without her jockey's

'None of Frankel's illustrious predecessors could match him for ruthless domination or for the sheer brilliance of his best performances'

Continues page 8

near disastrous error, she would not have won by far. Yet she was still too good for the best that Britain, Ireland and France could muster and her appearance contributed enormously to a memorable Royal Ascot.

Following his defeat by the unheralded Encke in the St Leger, some will argue Camelot has no place in any argument about whether recent seasons constitute another golden age, especially as there is a suspicion, to say the least, that he was merely the best of a bad lot when winning the 2,000 Guineas and Derby.

But while it's true there was no strength in depth among the 2012 crop of three-year-olds, Camelot won well at both Newmarket and Epsom, particularly when upped to a mile and a half for the first time on the latter track, and there are any number of possible explanations for his below-par performances in the all-important last leg of the Triple Crown and the Arc.

Anyway, it's perhaps enough that he was even risked there and indeed that he will be in training again at four. Just a few years ago the idea of going for the St Leger with a colt who had stallion potential like Camelot's would not have been contemplated and, nine times out of ten, nor would a four-year-old campaign.

Times change, though, and while it is a shame the Triple Crown eluded him we should be grateful the Ballydoyle team were prepared to take the chance and that the top horses in general now tend to be campaigned much less conservatively.

It might not yet be a golden age to compare with the one we enjoyed 40 years or so ago, but it has been a very long time since Flat racing fans have had it this good.

Golden greats *(from left to right)* Arkle, Brigadier Gerard and Nijinsky left indelible images during their stellar careers but the new generation is making a significant mark too

THE JUMPS
Words by **John Randall**

THE belief that jump racing has never had it so good has been validated by the recent exploits of Kauto Star, Big Buck's, Tony McCoy, Paul Nicholls and others. The best steeplechaser since Arkle, the greatest three-mile hurdler, the greatest jump jockey of all time and a uniquely dominant trainer have all contributed hugely to an era which future historians will surely describe as golden.

Kauto Star began the 2011-12 season already covered in honours and glory, and he added to them with his fourth victory in the Betfair Chase at Haydock and his fifth in the King George VI Chase, in both of which he beat reigning champion Long Run into second place.

Not only did he beat the record for the most wins in the King George that he had previously shared with Desert Orchid, but that Kempton win also turned out to be the best performance of the season over fences and therefore made him the champion (ie top-rated) chaser for the fourth time. That status was not affected by the Gold Cup, in which he was pulled up behind Synchronised.

No other jumper has been at the top for as long as Kauto Star, as his four titles spanned six seasons from 2006-07. He missed out in 2007-08, when his stablemates Master Minded and Denman were flattered to be rated above him, and in 2010-11, when he seemed a light of other days.

Only five-time champions Golden Miller, Prince Regent and Desert Orchid have been the top chaser more often but they gained their titles in consecutive seasons, so Kauto Star's six-year span of championships is unique.

Arkle in the 1960s set the standard by which all other jumpers are measured, and Kauto Star has clearly supplanted Desert Orchid as the greatest steeplechaser since that supreme champion.

His credentials rest on several criteria, in particular his rating, but also on his versatility, his record number of Grade 1 victories and his record prize-money, as well as his unique durability at the top.

Ratings are the best method of measuring greatness because they evaluate the only thing that really matters – quality of performance. Racing Post Ratings (RPRs) started in the 1988-89 season and on that scale Kauto Star (191) and Desert Orchid (189) have been the top chasers. Official ratings began with the first Anglo-Irish Jumps Classifications in 1999-2000 – after Desert Orchid's retirement – and Kauto Star's mark of 190 is the best.

Ratings are not perfect because they do not reward versatility or durability, but Kauto Star is unsurpassed on those two counts as well. The versatile French-bred proved a champion at both two miles and three miles by winning the Tingle Creek Chase and the King George in December 2006.

It is not just Kauto Star who has made the last few years a golden age of steeplechasing. Denman, the 2008 Gold Cup winner, and Master Minded, the Queen Mother Champion Chase victor in 2008 and 2009, were great champions by any standard, and Imperial Commander (2010) and Long Run

Continues page 10

(2011) triumphed in the Gold Cup with exceptional displays.

The mantle of greatness may settle next on Sprinter Sacre, the best novice chaser since Captain Christy when he won the Gold Cup in 1974. When he ran away with the Arkle Trophy in March, it was the first time ever that the best performance at the Cheltenham Festival was recorded in a novice chase.

Sprinter Sacre had the temerity to overshadow Big Buck's, who did not need to be at his best to notch a record fourth victory in the World Hurdle that consolidated his status as the greatest three-mile hurdler of all time. Among hurdlers who have excelled at three miles or further, Big Buck's is the greatest according to several criteria. The proof lies above all in his rating (RPR 178) but also in his world record of 17 consecutive wins over jumps and his run of four seasons as the champion (ie top-rated) hurdler, as well as his four World Hurdle victories.

Since RPRs started in 1988-89, Big Buck's (178) ranks second only to two-mile champion Istabraq (181) among all hurdlers over any distance. Next come four more stayers: Limestone Lad, Deano's Beeno, Baracouda and Iris's Gift, all on 176.

Big Buck's (174) is also second to Istabraq (186) on official ratings (ie since 1999-2000). Istabraq never ran beyond two miles and five furlongs and no three-mile hurdler of the past had anything like the form to challenge the claims of Big Buck's as the greatest of all time over that trip.

That excludes champions who excelled at staying trips short of three miles, in particular Night Nurse, who recorded the greatest single performance by any hurdler in the history of the sport when giving 6lb to Monksfield and running a famous dead-heat with him in the 2m5½f Templegate Hurdle at Aintree in 1977. It also excludes horses trained in France, where the local Champion Hurdle (Grande Course de Haies d'Auteuil) is run over 3m1½f.

In March, Big Buck's replaced Inglis Drever as the winningmost horse in World Hurdle history by taking the race for the fourth time and thus equalled the world record for the longest winning sequence over jumps. It was his 16th consecutive victory, matching the feat of triple Champion Hurdle winner Sir Ken between 1951 and 1953.

He broke the record when landing his fourth Liverpool Hurdle in April and now has in his sights the overall British record (Flat or jumps) of 21 consecutive wins by Meteor between 1786 and 1788.

Big Buck's has been the overall champion hurdler for the last four

seasons, a period of supremacy matched only by Istabraq and by Free Fare in the 1930s. If he were a two-miler he would be as revered as Istabraq but, because he is a stayer, he will never receive the credit he deserves.

Until the turn of the century nearly all the class and prestige in the hurdling division was concentrated at the minimum trip and stayers were very much the poor relations. Yet, in a remarkable reversal in trends, in the 12 seasons since Istabraq's reign ended, the overall champion hurdler has usually been a stayer.

The main reason for this sudden change is that the top three-mile hurdles have received a significant boost in prestige. When the Cheltenham Festival was expanded to four days in 2005, the Stayers' Hurdle was renamed the World Hurdle and became the centrepiece of the Thursday card. Other three-mile hurdles have been promoted to Grade 1 level, so that a coherent programme for the top stayers has evolved.

In the past, potential three-mile champions had little chance to show their talent and they were usually kept to two miles or were sent over fences – as Big Buck's was before his fortuitous Hennessy mishap in 2008.

The current golden age encompasses humans as well as horses, and Tony McCoy and Ruby Walsh are both contenders for the title 'greatest jump jockey of all time'. If records and statistics mean anything at all, McCoy is definitely the greatest, having been champion in Britain for the last 17 seasons and won more than 3,500 races, with a best score of 289 in 2001-02. His single-minded pursuit of perfection has enabled him to set standards previously unimaginable.

Photo call Big Buck's is the centre of attention for hordes of photographers and the packed stands at Cheltenham as he takes the final flight on his way to a historic fourth win in the World Hurdle

Yet Walsh is unrivalled for quality of winners. The eight-times Irish champion has been the regular rider of Kauto Star, Denman, Master Minded and Big Buck's, and has also won two Grand Nationals and a record 34 races at the Cheltenham Festival.

Another dual Grand National-winning jockey, Carl Llewellyn, sagely remarked in 2009: "The top ten or 15 are different class to when I was riding. Look back at the old videos, or when they show the archive stuff on TV – in their time those riders were brilliant, but now you just think 'Cor, were you really champion jockey?'"

Paul Nicholls has already proved himself one of the greatest jumps trainers of all time, and for quality in depth he has dominated the jumping scene in the last five years like no other trainer ever has – not even Vincent O'Brien in the early 1950s or Michael Dickinson in the early 1980s.

No-one else has had three great steeplechasers (Kauto Star, Denman, Master Minded) in his yard at the same time. Only Dickinson has ever matched, let alone surpassed, his 2008 feat of having the first three in the Gold Cup, and that maestro never had a champion hurdler – certainly not a great one like Big Buck's.

Nicholls was Britain's champion jumps trainer for the seventh consecutive season in 2011-12, having been second to Martin Pipe for the seven seasons before that. He may never dominate his rivals through sheer weight of numbers like Pipe did, but greatness is primarily about quality, not quantity, and in that respect he has contributed significantly to the current golden age.

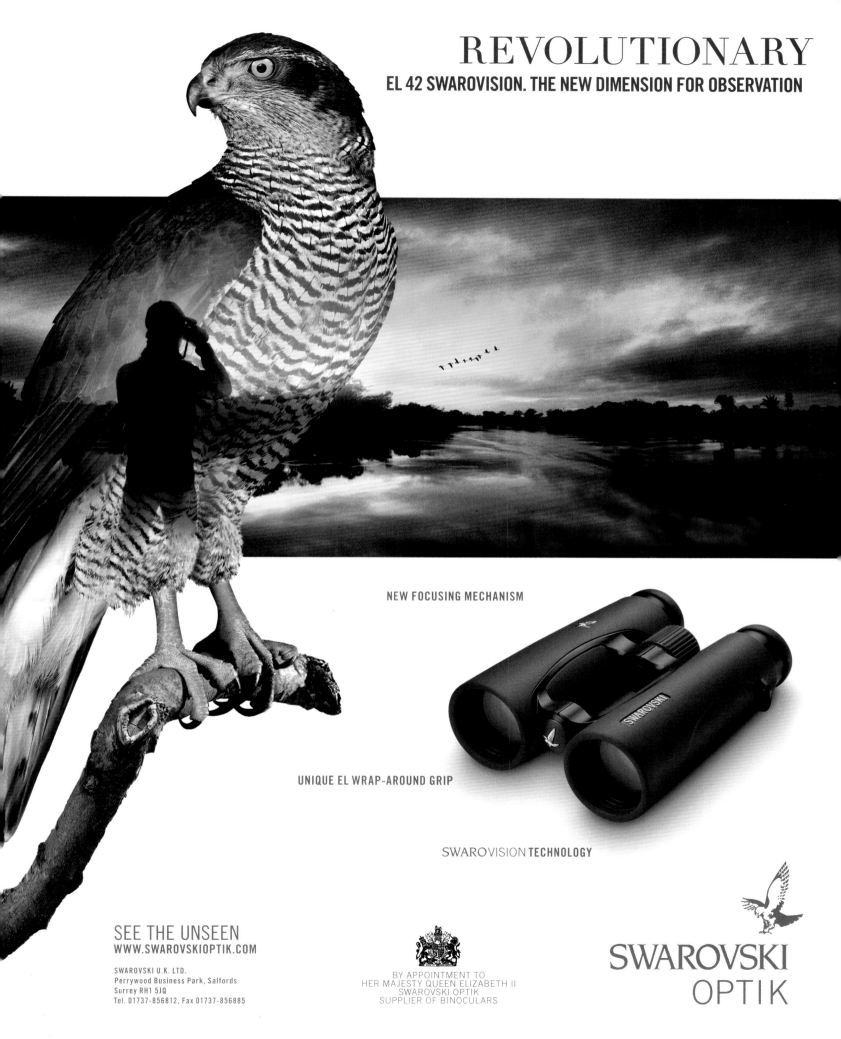

FRANKEL

PUTS THE REST IN THE SHADE

Sir Henry Cecil's
wonder horse
scaled new heights
in 2012 and by
the end he had
proved himself
a paragon of the
thoroughbred
down the ages

Words by **Brough Scott**

A S FRANKEL powered across the Ascot finishing line it was more than the perfect ending to an unbeaten three-season, 14-race career. It was final confirmation to these eyes that the animal we were watching was the finest thoroughbred that ever trod the turf. Four hundred years of selective breeding had not been in vain.

Those last few seconds of his racing life, as he swung off the rain-sodden Ascot bend and buckled down in pursuit of the already frantically ridden Nathaniel and Cirrus Des Aigles, amounted to Frankel's defining moment. We had long known how explosively exciting he was over shorter distances – in June on this very course he had clocked 10.58sec for the sixth furlong of the Queen Anne Stakes, a faster fraction than anything achieved by the five-furlong sprinters in the King's Stand half an hour later. We knew he had looked more impressive than ever when moving up to ten furlongs at York in August. But both of those performances had been in perfect conditions. These were the absolute opposite. This, for Frankel's place in greatness, was the ultimate question.

The whole purpose of horseracing is the asking of questions and as the days moved towards Ascot's final curtain

the queries grew shriller about whether Frankel could truly be ranked higher than all the great ones who had gone before. It was the giddiest and most glorious thought that there should be a current horse good enough even to be part of the discussion, but with Frankel there had been intimations of immortality from the very beginning. People first started to declare he was 'The Greatest' after his extraordinary ten-length demolition of the Royal Lodge field at Ascot in October 2010. Plenty more did so the following spring when he broke the 2,000 Guineas apart in such astonishing style, and by the time he took his unbeaten sequence to 11 by winning Royal Ascot's Queen Anne by 11 unbelievable lengths, the ratings experts were in raptures.

With Frankel's stamina proven at York it seemed almost curmudgeonly not to cede him the crown, yet in the week before the 2012 Champion Stakes I was happy to put the case against him, not because I didn't revel in all the excitement he had given us but because I wanted everyone to realise quite what the title of 'The Greatest' meant. It stated that what we were watching was superior to all the wonders who had gone before and, God help me, I had been blessed through age and good fortune to have seen more of those than most people.

One of the few splashes of colour in our Paddington home in 1940s and 1950s London was a magazine called The

Hold the front page
Frankel grabbed the headlines all season long

English Thoroughbred with pictures of the likes of Nimbus, Nearula, Aureole, Pinza, Crepello and upward to the astonishing Italian champion Ribot. He won the King George VI and Queen Elizabeth Stakes at Ascot as part of his unbeaten, 16-race career that included consecutive Prix de l'Arc de Triomphes, the second by six lengths still on the bit with six Classic winners trailing behind him. For no better reason than having been a nerdy youth I was aware of the heights Frankel needed to scale.

Race-riding and reporting experience brought me close to the more recent greats such as Nijinsky, Mill Reef, Brigadier Gerard, Dancing Brave and Sea The Stars, not forgetting the incredible Secretariat, whose record-breaking 1973 American Triple Crown has to be unquestionably the finest three races in five weeks that any horse will ever give. Secretariat, running only on left-handed dirt tracks and almost certainly with 'medication' that would fail a dope test over here, shows us the impossibility of comparison. But compare we wish to and compare we shall.

However much we lauded Frankel, the accolades were worthy only if we accepted what he had not done as he came to bow out at Ascot. His Dewhurst victory in October 2010 was not a match for the way Nijinsky sauntered home under Lester Piggott in 1969. He had never beaten a horse of the quality of

Mill Reef, as Brigadier Gerard did in that legendary 2,000 Guineas of 1971. As a three-year-old his versatility was never tested in the way Mill Reef's was when he won that season's Eclipse, King George and Arc, just as Dancing Brave was to in 1986, or in the way Sea The Stars went to a Group 1 contest every month for six months from 2,000 Guineas to Arc in his extraordinary summer of 2009.

Nijinsky, Dancing Brave and Sea The Stars did not campaign as four-year-olds and Mill Reef was able to run only twice at that age, but when Brigadier Gerard took his winning sequence to 15 it was by winning, albeit with a bit of a struggle, the 1972 King George over a mile and a half, a distance Frankel was never asked to attempt.

Yet when all those 'cons' were listed there was still something more than just a yearning that made you want to put Frankel above even the legends in the memory. I think it was the very sight of him.

Racehorses are all about movement. Standing still, Frankel was not as big or classically handsome as Brigadier Gerard or Sea The Stars, but even at the walk he was different. There was a stalk about the way he went, the hind legs coming up beneath him with the purpose of a predator, and when he launched into the canter his forelegs would lift up and reach forward so much more than a normal
Continues page 16

Perfect ending Frankel improved again as a four-year-old as he streaked (from left) through the Lockinge, Queen Anne, Sussex, International and Champion Stakes

HOW GOOD WAS HE? *Racing Post Ratings view*

FRANKEL'S position as the best racehorse in the history of Racing Post Ratings is beyond question, but his ability went a lot further than his headline figure of 143.

When he thrashed his rivals by 11 lengths in the Queen Anne Stakes at Royal Ascot, Frankel redefined what the modern thoroughbred might be capable of, but once wasn't enough for Frankel as he also turned the Juddmonte International in August into a rout. He was the first horse to rate above 140 on RPRs and it's hard not to think he's the best ever.

Ratings are a measure of individual performance in a particular race and as such don't reward consistency, yet Frankel is responsible for the four highest ratings ever recorded on RPRs with his two 143s and two at 139. That's an astonishing four times he bettered the form of our previous best turf horses, Daylami and Sea The Stars, who both rated 138.

Frankel is more Usain Bolt than Bob Beamon, who didn't jump beyond 8.22m after his world-record jump of 8.90m at the 1968 Olympics. Like Bolt, who has won both the 100m and 200m at the last two Olympics, Frankel showed sustained brilliance. What might have been his Bob Beamon moment in the 2,000 Guineas

was merely a prelude to even greater performances.

Only five other horses have attained ratings of 137 or above on Racing Post Ratings and none has achieved that mark, the unofficial 'high' of the modern era, more than once. Frankel ran to 137 or above an astonishing six times, dipping below 130 only once in the nine races stretching from his 2,000 Guineas through to his final start in the Champion Stakes. That makes eight individual 130+ performances, three more than the previous-best European tally of Dayjur.

Frankel's willingness to put distance between himself and his rivals certainly aided the accumulation of big figures, in contrast to an idler like Sea The Stars. Whereas Sea The Stars kept us guessing as to how good he might be, Frankel left us in no doubt. He's certainly the best we've seen, and most likely the best ever.

Frankel's best RPRs

143 2012 Queen Anne Stakes
143 2012 International Stakes
139 2012 Lockinge Stakes
139 2011 Queen Elizabeth II Stakes
138 2012 Sussex Stakes
137 2011 Sussex Stakes

horse that Shane Fetherstonhaugh, his diamond of an exercise rider, would tell of how he would have to position himself a full half-length further off than usual. And then when Tom Queally used to ask him to set down to run; ah, those are the memories.

THEY were also the answer to the questions which from birth are always asked, hopefully ever upward, of every racehorse who arrives in the game with Classic pretensions. By the time he came to answer our public queries he had been answering private ones with crushing affirmatives. He had been Juddmonte's No. 1 foal; luckily it was their turn to choose under a foal share arrangement with Coolmore, otherwise Frankel would have gone to Ballydoyle. He was their No. 1 yearling, which is why he was given the honour of carrying the name of the late Bobby Frankel and the inestimable advantage of being dispatched to the wisdom and diligence of Sir Henry Cecil and his team at Warren Place. As an unraced two-year-old he had left Prince Khalid's racing manager, Teddy Grimthorpe, and the rest ashen-faced by what he did on the Limekilns, which is why he was 7-4 favourite when he first appeared on a track that soggy August Friday evening at Newmarket two years ago and duly beat a well-touted John Gosden colt called Nathaniel by what looked a pretty comfortable half-length.

So there had already been plenty of talk about Frankel by the time I first clapped eyes on him at Doncaster a month later and, although he completely ran away with the race, the watcher's concentration was clouded by the stalls meltdown and withdrawal of the supposed Godolphin star Farhh (who, like Nathaniel, would reappear in the story), which left only two rivals for Frankel to flatten. Flatten them he did, beating the Gosden filly Rainbow Springs by an amazing 13 lengths, but while I remember thinking the lift of Frankel's stride was very impressive there was a tendency to dismiss the whole thing as a non-race despite Rainbow Springs' subsequent third in the Group 1 Prix Marcel Boussac at Longchamp.

No guilt is felt in hindsight, even if I did still play a bit of the doubter over Frankel's even more astonishing ten-length victory in the Royal Lodge. Again there was a small field, just five runners, and when Queally made his last-to-first move round the turn it was as if the brakes had failed and he had got the car stuck too high on cruise control. Bitter experience teaches that when something seems unbelievable on the racecourse, it usually is.

When Frankel put up rather a messy,

Continues page 18

HOW FAST WAS HE? *The Topspeed view*

A league of his own Frankel had ideal ground for his first run over ten furlongs at York and he scorched home by seven lengths to record the highest ever Topspeed figure

Frankel speed snapshots

Despite the manner of his victories the pick of his Topspeed timeline reads 136, 134, 132, 125, 124, 120 – numbers not usually associated with wide-margin, eased-down successes

With five furlongs left in the Juddmonte International at York he lagged 1.38sec behind the leader yet at the finish he was 1.15sec ahead of the runner-up

He clocked a lung-bursting 10.58sec (42.53mph) in the sixth furlong of the Queen Anne, faster than any split in the five-furlong King's Stand the same day

In the same race Turftrax data revealed he ripped 1.87sec out of high-class runner-up Excelebration in the final three furlongs

On the stopwatch his awesome 2,000 Guineas performance rated a massive 30lb better than any other performance that day

FRANKEL reached his peak in terms of speed with his incredible victory in the Juddmonte International at York. Quite simply, it was a performance par excellence.

In more than three decades of clocking racehorses, the best Topspeed figure before that amazing August day was the 132 recorded by Sea The Stars in the same race in 2009 and Frankel himself in the 2,000 Guineas. At York, Frankel went way beyond that to a staggering 136.

Arriving at that figure was not just about Frankel's performance. Form handicappers can assign a rating to a race studying just the particular race in question, but evaluating time performances is akin to doing a jigsaw, in that all the races at a race meeting have to fit. There has to be proportionality and balance to the card and for numerous reasons such symmetry is rarely possible.

On many occasions a modest horse punching above his weight downgrades a whole card, which can be frustrating but it is after all a time test, a measure of excellence against the clock.

At York, taking all the factors into account, Frankel was a study in

raw speed and power. Under ideal underfoot conditions, he stopped the clock at 2min 6.59sec, beating the extended ten-furlong par by 0.91sec. After Topspeed methodology was applied, he emerged with a ground-breaking 136.

He was renowned for brutal back-to-back mid-race 10.5sec fractions, but there was a subtle difference to this effort. More tractable as a four-year-old, he was in his comfort zone throughout and consequently produced a sustained finishing burst in the straight.

Five furlongs from home Frankel was seventh of the nine runners, having covered the distance to that point in 80.65sec, and trailed the leader Robin Hood (79.27sec) by 1.38sec. Four out he changed gear and splits of 11.34sec, 11.05sec, 11.45sec and 12.10sec destroyed the opposition.

That's the speed none of his rivals was able to live with; indeed, no other racehorse of the past 30 years has been able to deliver such exceptional figures. His final Topspeed of 134 in the Champion Stakes meant he had three of the four highest figures ever recorded (136, 134 and 132).

NORMAN COURT STUD

SIXTIES ICON

Galileo ex Love Divine (Diesis)

The Best Value Galileo Sire Standing in the UK
£8,500 1st Oct SLF
First crop includes: Group 2 and listed winner Chilworth Icon plus Cruck Realta & Effie B listed placed

WINKER WATSON

Piccolo ex Bonica (Rousillon)

£2,500 1st Oct SLF
Precocious two year old with first runners in 2013

Norman Court Stud, Rectory Hill, West Tytherley, Salisbury, Wiltshire SP5 1NF Tel: +44 (0)1794 340888
Stewart Bevan (Manager) Mobile: +44 (0)7790 218082
Tina Dawson (Nominations) Mobile: +44 (0)7776 165854 Email: tina.dawson@tdbloodstock.com

www.normancourtstud.com

THE GREATEST *The Racing Post Ratings view on his five races of 2012*

LOCKINGE

RPR VIEW An apparently straightforward reappearance in which Frankel confirmed himself the best horse in the world by dishing out a similar beating to Excelebration and Dubawi Gold – who had race fitness on their side – as in his Queen Elizabeth II Stakes success the previous October. It speaks volumes for Frankel's ability that such a performance could ever be considered routine, but this form at least matched his three-year-old RPR of 139+ with the strong impression that it wouldn't prove his limit.

QUEEN ANNE

RPR VIEW An astonishing display by Frankel, certainly his most visually impressive, as he romped to a scarcely believable 11-length thrashing of Excelebration, taking his form to a new high with an RPR of 143. He was the first horse to break the glass ceiling of the 140 mark and this performance cemented his position as the highest-rated horse since RPRs began. The most telling aspect of the race was the way Frankel took the more positively ridden Excelebration way out of his comfort zone.

SUSSEX

RPR VIEW His Royal Ascot performance scared away most serious opposition, with only Eclipse runner-up Farhh offering a serious form challenge in the field of four. With Farhh not at his best, Frankel seemed hardly extended to pull six lengths clear, a distance that could certainly have stretched by another couple of lengths had he not been eased. He returned an RPR of 138+, a head-in-chest figure for Frankel but one that still matched the pre-Frankel all-time high turf RPR set by Sea The Stars and Daylami.

INTERNATIONAL

RPR VIEW A first start beyond a mile for Frankel, but he was as impressive as ever in thrashing Farhh by seven lengths, with St Nicholas Abbey a close third and a yawning six lengths back to Twice Over. If there was anything left to prove this surely did so, as he was every bit as effective and superior as he had been over a mile. The winning margin may not have been as dramatic as at Royal Ascot, but this was a deeper race with three individual Group 1 winners in opposition and ranked alongside his Queen Anne romp with an RPR of 143.

---

hard-pulling and not nearly as spectacular performance in winning the Dewhurst, there was something of a relief to think there was no need to yield to all the hype just yet. What had he beaten anyway? Well, actually the Ascot runner-up Klammer won the Horris Hill on his only other start, while the third, Treasure Beach, won the Chester Vase and the Irish Derby and was inched out by Pour Moi and the whip-waving Mickael Barzalona at Epsom. And the Dewhurst second? Roderic O'Connor was to win the next season's Irish 2,000 Guineas.

But that's just the form book. The flesh is always more interesting and going to see Frankel at Newmarket in the spring became increasingly addictive. Warren Place is not a place for calling too many geese as swans but there was not much mistaking what they thought of this particular gosling. The morning sessions had been so geared towards not stirring Frankel to full intensity that there was

'He only ran as far off the pace as Queally could keep him and, when he moved, he stretched all the way. He did not just beat horses, he broke them'

a moment when Queally had to shake him up before putting Excelebration to the sword in the Greenham, but as the Guineas approached a huge sense of anticipation was building.

In the week before the Classic, Fetherstonhaugh confided (and rang back "please don't put it in the papers") that he thought something quite extraordinary might happen. On the Friday Henry took his massive hands off the wheel of his Mercedes and gave one of his famous rhetorical statements: "The pacemaker is drawn on the opposite side of the track but it doesn't matter, does it? I am just going to let him use his stride, that's

right, isn't it?" As if we would know. But history now does.

That 2,000 Guineas blew us away all right but almost to a fault and some thought Frankel might just have blown his mind as well. The scrambling, muddle-paced, muddle-tactics win in the St James's Palace raised more doubt and the stage was set for the famous Duel On The Downs with Canford Cliffs at Goodwood. It is worth remembering that was the last time Frankel supporters really thought they might have a showdown until Cirrus Des Aigles turned up for the Champion Stakes more than a year later.

The moment when Frankel opened up that day and Canford Cliffs cracked and hung left under the strain was one of the defining moments in the saga. All the earlier Frankel excitement was ablaze again. He had seemed much more tractable, albeit from the front, and Queally had calmly redeemed himself after getting some fearful stick for his

CHAMPION

RPR VIEW A small but select field included the highest-rated rival Frankel had faced in Cirrus Des Aigles, who had won the race in 2011 and was a proven mudlark. Frankel's final race wasn't his greatest in terms of figures, but it still added to his reputation as he ran out a convincing winner on soft ground despite the race not going to plan tactically. This final success still rated 136, a figure bettered on turf by only five others on RPRs, and it says a lot about Frankel that this level of performance could be considered below par.

One last look Ascot was packed on Champions Day for the 'I was there' moment of Frankel's 14th and final race

Ascot ride. The pair looked composure itself when they signed off with a four-length swatting of poor old Excelebration in the Queen Elizabeth II Stakes.

If not greater than the other legends, he had to be right up among them over a mile, although at the same stage of his career Brigadier Gerard had been unbeaten in ten races, having won the Sussex Stakes by five lengths, the Goodwood Mile by ten, the Queen Elizabeth II by eight and finished by taking the Champion Stakes over a mile and a quarter. Best of all, we were promised Frankel as a four-year-old. We would have time to tell.

THE thrill of a new season was that it would bring fresh questions and wider challenges on which judgement could be passed. The first was the durability question, which with high-mettled thoroughbreds is as much of mind as it is of matter. Many, Nijinsky being the most famous case, find the first gives before the second. Everything seemed all right with Frankel before his Newbury reappearance but it should be remembered that was just 12 months after his half-brother Bullet Train had completely dogged it at Newmarket before reverting to infinitely worthier work as pacemaker for his younger sibling.

Excelebration, fresh from a sizzling reappearance for his new trainer Aidan O'Brien, was back for another swing at Frankel. Would Frankel have his game together? Two furlongs out Queally asked his familiar question and, as I watched from the furlong pole, there was renewed greatness in the answer.

It reminded me what Frankel did differently. When asked to run it was not just one slingshot from the back, a race-winning move like Dancing Brave did at his best. Frankel ran only as far off the pace as Queally could keep him and when he moved he stretched all the way to the line as if he was pursuing a hare over the horizon.

He did not just beat other horses, he broke them. That day at Newbury he broke Excelebration yet again. I can see Frankel now, neck set straight, forelegs reaching out, those great quarters coming under and powering him forward like a greyhound. He was back and it looked as if he might be even better.

The confirmation, reflected in the ratings, came when Excelebration paid the price for taking on Frankel head to head in the Queen Anne. While the Ballydoyle challenger still finished second, he was 11 lengths adrift at the line. A case might still be made against Frankel for not having run over further than a mile, but it could not be said he was beating rubbish because when Excelebration was away from his nemesis he proved himself time after time at the highest level.

So, too, did Farhh, rehabilitated after **Continues page 20**

Continues page 20

his nervous breakdown that juvenile day at Doncaster and a half-length second to Nathaniel (remember him?) in the Eclipse before running a respectful six and seven lengths behind Frankel when runner-up in both the Sussex Stakes at Goodwood and the Juddmonte International at York.

That last event, of course, was Frankel's much-discussed first attempt at a mile and a quarter but, to be honest, trying to build up tension about this increased stamina test had become a fairly spurious pursuit. The horse's demeanour and his partnership with Queally had become much more secure, while his full-brother Noble Mission had just won the Gordon Stakes over a mile and a half. When Frankel cruised up to the Breeders' Cup Turf winner St Nicholas Abbey a quarter of a mile out, nobody could remember what the fuss had been about.

Judging by the way he drew clear over that extended ten furlongs in an extremely fast time, there's little doubt that on any reasonable ground Frankel could have stayed the Classic mile and a half. And, don't forget, he could definitely have beaten the sprinters at their own game. But, as the debates and the phone-ins rumbled on before Ascot, there was one thing we did not know. How would Frankel handle it if he had to get down and dirty against a really top horse in conditions that were really testing?

The beauty of this final Champion Stakes bow was that with Cirrus Des Aigles in the field we were about to find out. Frankel would be running on the slowest going he had encountered and against an opponent already proven as a top horse on any ground and an absolute machine in the very soft.

How magnificent was the contrast: the four-year-old, blue-blooded Frankel in his 14th and last race before retiring to the £100,000-a-time coupling life of a stallion, and Cirrus Des Aigles, the six-year-old gelding from the wrong side of the tracks who took six shots to win any race and even then it was only a minor event on the sand at Cagnes-sur-Mer.

But Cirrus Des Aigles' record now showed victory in 16 of his 45 races, including a record-time win in the 2011 Champion Stakes on good ground. On the three occasions he had been faced with heavy ground he had won by eight lengths, eight lengths and most recently by a crushing nine lengths at Longchamp. What's more, the crafty Olivier Peslier was in the saddle, just as he had been on the outsider Solemia in the Arc a fortnight earlier when he clawed back the Japanese favourite Orfevre as the ground took its toll. It would not be easy for Frankel.

On official ratings there was ten
Continues page 22

HOW DID HE DO IT?

Frankel clearly benefited from highly effective bio-mechanics, transferring energy into forward propulsion with minimum effort. His huge stride of 24 feet at full speed, compared with an average of 20-21 feet, was supported by unusually large feet. He must have a highly efficient cardiovascular system and probably an abnormally large heart (the average racehorse heart weighs 3.5-4kg but legendary Australian racehorse Phar Lap's was 6.35kg). In a race, a thoroughbred's heart will beat up to 240 times per minute, pumping at least 85 pints of blood around the body.

Frankel also benefited from a larger than normal spleen, which acts as a reservoir of red blood cells to transport oxygen to the muscles. This oxygen is supplied via the horse's lungs, which exhale and inhale 140 times a minute during a race, delivering 150 litres of air per second – amounting to 19,500 litres in the Champion Stakes. Frankel won so readily by maintaining between 130 and 140 strides per minute long after his rivals began to tire, clocking a top speed of 43.19mph at Goodwood in the summer (the norm for a five-furlong sprinter at the track is 40.5mph)

Mark Evans, of Channel 4's Inside Nature's Giants, says:
"With their huge hearts, cavernous lungs, self-doping spleens, built-in biceps catapults and light, long pogo-stick legs, all champion racehorses are extraordinary biological machines. But, as an equine athlete, Frankel is clearly in a class of his own."

WEIGHT
About 500kg

SHOE SIZE
Abnormally large – the equivalent of a 12-year-old boy wearing size 11 shoes

STRIDE LENGTH Covered 24ft per stride in full flight (the average racehorse covers about 21ft). Staggering mid-race sub-11sec fractions meant he covered the length of a cricket wicket each and every second

STRIDE FREQUENCY Between 130 and 140 strides per minute. Most horses lose stride frequency and stride length as they tire but Frankel maintained both for longer

BREATHING
Lungs exhale and inhale 140 times a minute, delivering 150 litres of air per second. That amounted to 19,500 litres in the Champion Stakes – about double the daily intake for a human adult

FUEL INTAKE
About 35,000 kilocalories per day. He was a bigger eater than any of his stablemates

OATS

HEART CAPACITY
240 beats per minute, pumping at least 85 pints of blood around the body

HEIGHT 163.8cm (16h ½in) from ground to shoulder

SPEED
Reached 43.19mph in the penultimate furlong of his second Sussex win. At that speed he was almost twice as fast as Usain Bolt

FACTS AND FIGURES

Date of birth
February 11, 2008

Height 163.8cm (16h ½in) from ground to shoulder

Weight At birth 123lb. Now about half a ton

Colour Bay, four white feet, star on forehead

Shoe size
7.5 in front, 7 behind

Diet Cecil's horses are fed on Canadian oats and hay (usually American). Frankel ate about 23lb of oats per day (more than any other horse in the yard) and had a preference for English hay. He also had corn, alfalfa chaff, bran, a feed supplement, calcium for his bones and the occasional carrot. Altogether about 35,000 kilocalories per day.

Race record
14 wins in 14 races

Group 1 wins 10

Rivals beaten 88

Racing Post Rating
143, the highest ever

Topspeed figure
136, the highest ever

Career earnings £2,998,302

Betting Odds-on in 13 of his 14 races – a £1 stake on all 14 wins would have made a profit of just £5.97

Aggregate winning margin
76 and a quarter lengths

Average winning margin
Almost five and a half lengths

Time spent racing
23min 24sec

pounds between them but if, as seemed likely, Cirrus Des Aigles was five pounds better in such conditions and Frankel were to run five pounds below his best – well, everyone could do the maths.

Not that anyone outside the opposition camps, nor any of those seeking confirmation of greatness, wanted such an outcome. But such thoughts were certainly there at Ascot and they added a special tension to the heroic sight of Cecil defying the ravages of chemotherapy to walk set-faced through the parade ring with the saddle under his arm.

We knew it was the last time we would see Frankel in all his majesty and so we feasted our eyes as Queally cantered him steadily back past the stands and down towards the ten-furlong starting gate. I had thought the sight of Mill Reef skimming across the Longchamp turf was the most perfect action I had seen on a racehorse, but the image of controlled power that emanated from Frankel that afternoon tops the lot.

When the stalls slammed open, however, it was reality that counted and for a few moments it looked as if Frankel was slightly out of gear, completely missing his kick out of the gate and needing urgent shoves from Queally to ensure he locked himself into race mode. In truth, all the other worries were in our imagination.

The fears flew around all right. Peslier had an awesome handful on Cirrus Des Aigles as he turned into the straight with Nathaniel hard at it beside him and Frankel with five lengths still to find. Queally was crouched but the reins were tight and the stride was sure as Frankel swept past Nathaniel and arrived to take Cirrus Des Aigles at the furlong pole. In such races the absolute moment of truth is what happens when the rider asks for extra and the horse has to dig deep and make it hurt.

This was Frankel's moment. Much bilge is said about "good horses being the same on any ground". Brigadier Gerard was a stone worse on bad ground and only courage got him through. Frankel needed courage here but he had the power and the class as well. There would be no ten-length routing but this final, tough yet decisive victory was his greatest too.

As he came back the big question returned and now the answer had to be in the affirmative. The horse we were looking at had long proved he was as fast as any of the other legends and now he had shown he could battle it out just as well. For me, after so many years searching for the ultimate thoroughbred, this really seemed to be the one.

Memories fade and the leaves are coming off the trees. But what a wonder we had with the horse they called Frankel.

THE VIEW FROM THE SADDLE *Tom Queally on his horse of a lifetime*

IT WAS clear Frankel was way above average from early on. When he won his maiden from Nathaniel he was very keen early on and I dropped him in, which isn't the usual way with Henry's. What was interesting was that, even in the soft ground, you could go both up and down the gears with him and there are not many you can do that with. He was playing with Nathaniel really.

At Doncaster next time, when he won by 13 lengths, he all but ran away with me – it was that unusual thing of being able to run with the choke out and still win.

So even at two I'd never ridden a horse with a will to win like him. As

a rule when they are that good and have a lot in hand they get there and just prick up their ears. But not him. He just seemed to eat away at the ground – he wanted to please you like anything.

I thought he would win the 2,000 Guineas. We had lots of plans beforehand but with the pacemaker drawn the other side we jumped and went. I knew we were going quick but if I had tried to go slower it would have broken his stride and upset him. It was very quick but he did it easier than any other horse and, while he is not over-big, he rode big and had this huge stride on him.

Royal Ascot this year was special. There was an element of demolition about it. A little after halfway he just opened up and won by 11 lengths.

The biggest job was getting him to the start. From day one I never gave him a decent canter to the start and the Lockinge was the only time he went to post down the middle of the course – it was always the rail.

I know Frankel very well and he knows me well enough. He's the best horse in the world – you get on and chat away to him, give him a pat and go to work. He's a kind horse, in his stable he's a gentleman, particularly when he's had his breakfast!

Graham Budd

AUCTIONS

IN ASSOCIATION WITH SOTHEBY'S

THE LEADING SPECIALIST AUCTIONEER OF SPORTING MEMORABILIA IN THE UK

All sales held at Sotheby's New Bond Street saleroom, London

Dick Francis first edition, first novel, with dust jacket

Graham Budd Auctions Ltd, PO Box 47519, London, N14 6XD
Tel: 020 8366 2525 E-Mail: gb@grahambuddauctions.co.uk
web: www.grahambuddauctions.co.uk

THE
BIGGER
PICTURE

Action at Hereford, where dark clouds gathered in July with the announcement that the course would close at the end of 2012. The venue, which has staged racing since 1771, is owned by Herefordshire County Council and run under a lease arrangement by the Reuben brothers' Arena/Northern group. The last long-established British racecourse to close was Stockton in 1981
EDWARD WHITAKER (RACINGPOST.COM/PHOTOS)

TRIPLE WHAMMY

Camelot won three Classics but a season that promised so much ultimately ended in disappointment with defeats in the St Leger and the Arc followed by a bout of colic

Words by **Julian Muscat**

FEW horses in the modern era have completed a season to such diverse reviews. Camelot was, to borrow the famous Churchillian view of Russia, a riddle wrapped in a mystery inside an enigma.

After a summer of dizzying achievement, Camelot's failure to complete the Triple Crown was a profound disappointment. To compound his St Leger reverse, the colt who had been victorious in the 2,000 Guineas, Derby and Irish Derby sank without trace in the Arc. It was a sorry end to a campaign that had started with Classic victory on each of his first three starts.

As the season ended there was no definitive answer to the question of Camelot's true merit. The apparent world-beater of midsummer was made to look leaden-footed by the time Frankie Dettori eased him down in the last 50 yards at Longchamp. As a result, there is much for Camelot to prove in 2013.

Continues page 28

LOST GENERATION *The figures that show Camelot and his fellow three-year-olds in a poor light*

RPR CHAMPION EUROPEAN 3YOs OF THE PAST DECADE

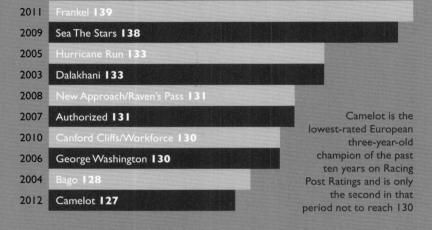

Year	Horse	RPR
2011	Frankel	139
2009	Sea The Stars	138
2005	Hurricane Run	133
2003	Dalakhani	133
2008	New Approach/Raven's Pass	131
2007	Authorized	131
2010	Canford Cliffs/Workforce	130
2006	George Washington	130
2004	Bago	128
2012	Camelot	127

Camelot is the lowest-rated European three-year-old champion of the past ten years on Racing Post Ratings and is only the second in that period not to reach 130

3YOs vs THE REST IN BRITISH AND IRISH OPEN-AGE GROUP 1 & 2 RACES

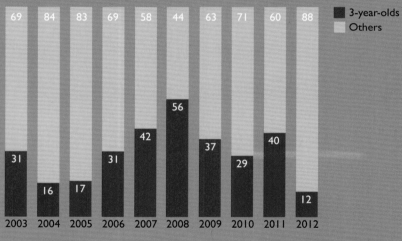

■ 3-year-olds
□ Others

	2003	2004	2005	2006	2007	2008	2009	2010	2011	2012
Others	69	84	83	69	58	44	63	71	60	88
3-year-olds	31	16	17	31	42	56	37	29	40	12

This graph compares the percentage of open-age Group 1 and 2 races in Britain and Ireland over the past ten years won by three-year-olds and horses of other ages. A higher proportion of deep purple in the bar indicates a good performance by the three-year-olds. Their best year was 2008, when they won 56 per cent of such races to outperform the other age groups. 2012 has been their worst year

He survived a colic scare in October, when he required surgery four days after his return from Longchamp, but that should have no bearing on the four-year-old campaign of a colt who has generated superlatives from discerning minds. He even received the ultimate compliment from the ultimate horseman in John Magnier. When part-owner Derrick Smith *(right)* visited Ballydoyle at the end of Camelot's juvenile campaign,

'You must get a picture of this horse in your mind because you'll never see a finer example than him'

the horse was brought before him.

"I don't know much about them," Smith reflected, "but John [Magnier] said to me: 'You are always asking what to look for in a horse. You must get a picture

of this one in your mind because you'll never see a finer example than him."

Smith visited Ballydoyle soon after Camelot had toyed with four opponents to win the Racing Post Trophy in October 2011, since when great expectations have stalked him. He was portentously named, too: Magnier's wife, Susan, had reserved the name some years earlier and waited for the right horse on which to bestow it.

The choice seemed particularly

THE RPR VIEW

Camelot was the best three-year-old in Europe in 2012, but that's not saying much. It was always going to be a tall order to follow the exceptional three-year-olds of 2011, including the great Frankel, but the class of 2012 didn't even come close to matching their feats.

Frankel's generation also included Danedream, Dream Ahead, Excelebration and Nathaniel, yet 2012 was largely devoid of star names and even Camelot's reputation was rather tarnished by defeats on his last two starts. He had appeared a potential superstar when he ran out an impressive winner of the Derby but by the end of the season, when he finished seventh in the Arc on his first foray into all-age company, he had become a disappointment.

Camelot's achievements in becoming only the third horse since Nijinsky to complete the 2,000 Guineas-Derby double – and the first since his great Ballydoyle predecessor to win the Guineas and both the Epsom and Irish Derbys – certainly stand historical comparison.

In truth, though, neither the Guineas nor the Irish Derby were strong renewals, with Camelot's Racing Post Rating of 121 in the Guineas the lowest since 2005. His five-length Derby victory was more striking and his RPR of 127 compares favourably with both the ten-year-average of 125 and the 124 Sea The Stars recorded at Epsom. At the same stage of their careers, then, Camelot was rated higher than Sea The Stars and was still unbeaten.

That's where the favourable comparison ends. The vast majority of Epsom winners go on to boost their ratings when tackling stronger opposition later in the year and it's by this measure that Sea The Stars is judged the best Derby winner (as opposed to having the best Derby-winning performance). His peak RPR of 138 left Camelot way behind.

There were mitigating factors for Camelot. He had valid excuses for his defeats on his last two starts and the disappointing performance of his contemporaries at the top end didn't help in attaining the 130+ figure that appeared within his grasp at Epsom.

This will be the first time there hasn't been a 130+ rated three-year-old since 2004, with Camelot set to be the lowest-rated European highweight ever on RPRs, a position that looks sure to be mirrored by the World Thoroughbred Rankings when the final figures are published in January 2013.

Words by Paul Curtis

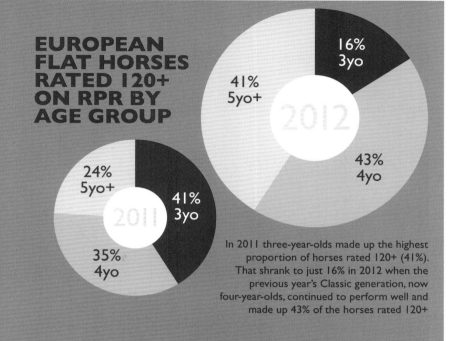

EUROPEAN FLAT HORSES RATED 120+ ON RPR BY AGE GROUP

2012
- 16% 3yo
- 41% 5yo+
- 43% 4yo

2011
- 24% 5yo+
- 41% 3yo
- 35% 4yo

In 2011 three-year-olds made up the highest proportion of horses rated 120+ (41%). That shrank to just 16% in 2012 when the previous year's Classic generation, now four-year-olds, continued to perform well and made up 43% of the horses rated 120+

83% Three-year-olds won 15 of the 18 Arcs (**83%**) up to 2011 but the best from that age group this year was Masterstroke in third place. It was only the third time in the past 25 years that no three-year-old finished in the first two

6 Until 2012, it had been **six** years since a three-year-old last failed to win at least one of Europe's Group 1 sprints. This year's blank was only the fifth in the past 20 years

2004 No three-year-old won a Group 1 in Britain in 2012 until The Fugue took the Nassau Stakes at Goodwood on August 4. It was the longest wait for a Group 1 winner since **2004**

120.8 The average Racing Post Rating of the top ten three-year-olds of 2012 is **120.8**, the lowest in the past decade and way behind the 127.4 achieved by Frankel's class of 2011. The previous low in the past decade was 124.5 in 2006

---

appropriate when Aidan O'Brien started asking Camelot some mild questions in March of his three-year-old season. He did so with trepidation. Bitter memories of St Nicholas Abbey played on his mind.

Two years earlier St Nicholas Abbey, another son of Montjeu, had been in a similar place. He looked like a Derby horse but, like Camelot, he had the speed to win the Racing Post Trophy at two. Yet the wheels came off when he

was prepared for the 2,000 Guineas. He finished sixth at Newmarket, leaving his Derby bid in tatters, and was not seen again for 11 months.

"Looking back, I think Aidan feels he was too hard on St Nicholas Abbey before the Guineas and he didn't want to do the same thing again," Smith related. "Aidan hadn't won the Derby for ten years and my feeling is that was the race he wanted

to win most of all. So the Guineas was a bonus for Camelot. He wasn't specifically trained for it."

It is some bonus to win a Classic in passing, but the build-up demanded Camelot should run. In mid-April, when all eyes were on the Craven meeting at Newmarket, Camelot turned heads in a gallop at Ballydoyle.

Come 2,000 Guineas day and **Continues page 30**

O'Brien was unconcerned by the big-race inexperience of his teenage son in the saddle. "However much I thought about the race, Joseph thought about it more," he said. "The horse had only run twice, so Joseph wanted to teach him well. He said to me if he was happy at halfway he'd start thinking about winning the race."

The trainer was in for a surprise when the father-and-son team walked the Rowley Mile on raceday. "We got halfway down the track when Joseph said to me: 'I'll be nearer the back than the front at this stage.' I was slightly worried, but I have learned to say nothing where Joseph's riding is concerned."

The jockey was true to his word. Having passed halfway among the backmarkers on the stands side, O'Brien engaged his mount at the two-furlong pole. At that point his path to the front was obstructed; he had decisions to make.

Having angled left, he then switched right and challenged between horses, switching his whip hand dextrously. Camelot hit the front and galloped strongly up the famous hill, in the end winning with greater authority than implicit in the neck margin over French Fifteen.

Camelot's victory augured well for the Derby: he'd needed every yard of the mile to suppress French Fifteen. In the process he lit a touch-paper that would glow with promise right through to the autumn. At that stage, nobody could have foreseen that the only outright Pattern winners among Camelot's 17 opponents at Newmarket would be Power, who beat many of the same rivals in the Irish 2,000 Guineas, and Caspar Netscher in the German equivalent.

It was a similar story with Camelot's victory at Epsom. While the galleries marvelled at his five-length dismissal of Main Sequence, with O'Brien as cool as you like in the saddle, they could not have known that the sole subsequent Pattern winner among the vanquished would be Thought Worthy – and that against fellow three-year-olds in the Great Voltigeur Stakes.

Those caveats would follow; at the time it was enough to marvel at Camelot's effortless supremacy. There was but a fleeting moment of anxiety in the Derby when the handsome bay, again restrained in rear, took a few strides to reach full velocity as the field completed its descent of Tattenham Corner.

"He lost his balance for a moment or two," Joseph O'Brien said. "It was just inexperience on only the fourth run of his life, and he'd run on straight tracks when he won at Doncaster and Newmarket. The gradients took him by surprise for a couple of strides. They wouldn't bother him at all if he went back to Epsom

again. I gave him a slap early in the straight and could feel what he had left. He quickened up really well after that."

Up in the grandstand, the colt's connections were in raptures. "I knew his work was out of this world before the race," Smith reflected. Nevertheless, he was apprehensive of O'Brien's inexperience around Epsom. "Earlier in the day Joseph rode St Nicholas Abbey to win the Coronation Cup for us by four and a half lengths," Smith recalled. "When I was leading him in I said to him: 'Let's hope Camelot does the same.' Joseph leaned towards me and whispered: 'He'll win easier, Mr Smith, he'll win easier.' That's confidence for you."

By the time Camelot added the Irish Derby to his bulging portfolio on June 30 he was all but committed to the Triple Crown. It was a close-run thing at the Curragh: both in the decision to run him on bottomless ground and in the race itself.

Once again, however, Camelot's struggle to fend off a relatively modest opponent in Born To Sea was lost within the mounting excitement that a 42-year drought without a Triple Crown winner was about to be slaked. Or so we thought.

FOR Camelot to revive a concept many felt was obsolete would have been a majestic achievement. He was pursuing a holy grail passed up by connections of Nashwan (1989) and Sea The Stars

Up close and personal
Joseph O'Brien and Camelot after the 2,000 Guineas, the first of their three Classic triumphs in a first half of the season that promised so much

(2009), both of whom had won the first two legs. But then Camelot had been singled out for high achievement from the day he was born.

He was foaled and raised at Highclere Stud, where proprietors John and Lady Carolyn Warren monitored his development with something approaching awe. "From his looks and general demeanour, it soon became obvious he was something special," remembers John Warren, as good a judge as there is of a young horse.

"It would have been fantastic to have been able to buy him. I discussed it with his owner [Sheikh Abdulla Bin Isa Al-Khalifa, who bred Camelot] and eventually he felt the only way to find out how much the horse was worth was to send him to the yearling sales."

Camelot aroused the same sensation in Coolmore's trusty talent-spotters when they first set eyes on him. So much so that when he came up for auction at the Tattersalls October Yearling Sales in 2010, they were determined to have him. At 525,000 guineas, the mission was duly accomplished.

"Coolmore puts a lot of work into looking at young horses all over Europe," Smith said. "For Demi [O'Byrne], Paul [Shanahan] and the team that go to the sales, Camelot had their best mark all the way through. Sometimes the grading changes from month to month, but not **Continues page 32**

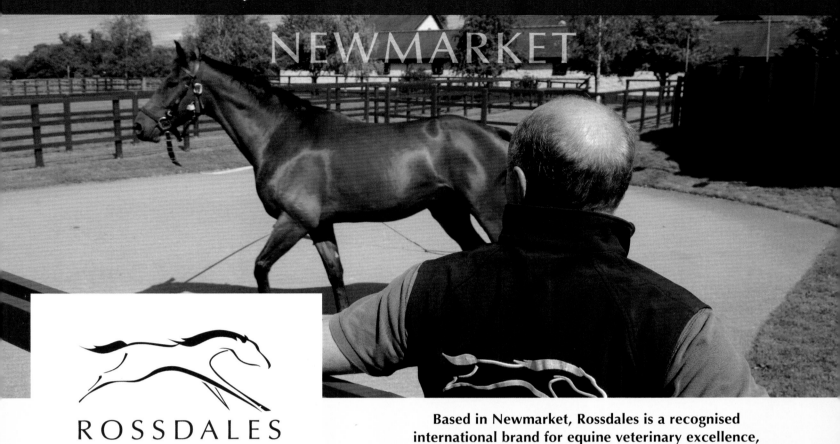

with him. He was always top of the class."

As St Leger day approached, mild hysteria accompanied Camelot's bid to the point where reason went west. Several theories have been aired for his defeat by Encke, not least Joseph O'Brien's ride, yet perhaps the primary cause was Camelot's ancestry. His stamina for the extended 14-furlong test was suspect. Although he is by Montjeu, his female family, of Classic middle-distance hue four generations back, has since been ushered towards speed by the use of Persepolis, Danehill and Kingmambo. The latter is broodmare sire of Camelot, whose dam, Tarfah, was best at nine furlongs.

The criticism levelled against Joseph O'Brien arose primarily from his persistence in probing the inside route up the long Doncaster straight. He was lured into a vacuum as gap after gap kept appearing, yet when the front-running Dartford fell away two furlongs out O'Brien was able to switch outside to launch his challenge.

Perhaps if he could ride the race again, O'Brien would deliver Camelot on the outside down the home straight. His mount certainly ran on after initially

Continues page 34

So near and yet so far
Camelot is beaten three-quarters of a length into second by Encke in the St Leger

BITTER END *Camelot on the wrong side of history*

FAR FROM making the Triple Crown fashionable, Camelot's St Leger reverse may serve to banish further attempts in the future. His quest could not have better amplified the gruelling nature of the assignment.

By the time Camelot headed to Doncaster the hype had overtaken reason. The St Leger is often seen as the softest of the Classics and, not least in the betting market, it seemed many had formed the view that he had only to turn up to win. Yet perhaps the 42 years that had elapsed since Nijinsky's Triple Crown had clouded minds to the difficulty of the feat he was attempting.

Nothing worth winning ever came easy. While one of the tests posed by the US Triple Crown is that it crams three races into five weeks, the British version demands the ability to perform at a high level in spring, summer and autumn from a mile to an extended mile and three-quarters.

That helps to explain why there have been so few Triple Crown winners since the phrase was coined on West Australian's sweep of the 2,000 Guineas, Derby and St Leger in 1853. In 159 subsequent years there have been 14 others, against ten winners of the 2,000 Guineas and Derby who failed in the St Leger. On that statistical evidence Camelot should have been a 4-6 chance at Doncaster, rather than a drifting 2-5 favourite.

There were just seven Triple Crown winners in the 20th century and since the second world war only Nijinsky has pulled off the feat. History is what prompted the Coolmore syndicate to target Camelot at the Triple Crown. John Magnier will have vivid memories of Nijinsky completing the sequence, and how the endeavour drained a colt who was trained by his father-in-law, Vincent O'Brien.

Five months is a long time to keep any thoroughbred, however brilliant, at his peak. Nijinsky's bubble burst spectacularly in the Arc but Camelot's didn't last that long. Far from reviving the Triple Crown concept, Camelot's fate may have consigned it to the vaults of history.

CAMELOT'S failure to clinch the Triple Crown also cost Aidan O'Brien the first clean sweep of the British Classics in the 198 years since the 1,000 Guineas, the youngest of the five Classics, was added to the roster.

As well as Camelot's victories in the 2,000 Guineas and Derby, O'Brien was also successful with Homecoming Queen in the 1,000 Guineas and Was in the Oaks. He became the first trainer to achieve the rare feat of winning four in one season since Henry Cecil in 1985.

O'Brien, who had a clean sweep of the Irish Classics in 2008, won two of his home Classics in 2012 – the Irish 2,000 Guineas with Power and the Irish Derby with Camelot.

By contrast, misfortune dogged O'Brien's raids on the French Classics. In the first of them, the French 1,000 Guineas, Up was drawn widest of all and beaten a length into second, while Furners Green was fatally injured after crossing the line in third in the French 2,000, beaten two short necks.

Luck was still against Ballydoyle in a rough French Derby, when Imperial Monarch was baulked and came eighth.

Although it seemed unlikely at the time, there would be another bitter pill to swallow at Doncaster.

CAMELOT was the tenth 2,000 Guineas and Derby winner to try and fail to complete the Triple Crown. The last before him was Cameronian in 1931 – since then the feat had been achieved twice, by Bahram in 1935 and Nijinsky in 1970.

In all, 25 Guineas and Derby winners have run in the St Leger, with 15 triumphing and ten beaten. Camelot followed Cotherstone and Ladas as only the third 2,000 Guineas and Derby winner to finish second in the St Leger.

Cotherstone in 1843, and not West Australian in 1853, should have been the first Triple Crown winner. He was an outstanding champion, winning the 2,000 Guineas and Derby decisively, and of all the failed Triple Crown candidates he went closest to winning the St Leger, being beaten only a head into second. He was far superior to his Doncaster conqueror Nutwith and the suspicion in those corrupt days was that his jockey got him beaten deliberately.

Ladas, in 1894, came within three-quarters of a length of winning the Triple Crown – the same margin by which Camelot was beaten. The winner was a filly, 50-1 shot Throstle.

failing to match Encke's kick just inside the two-furlong pole, and the way he clawed back a two-length deficit with a furlong remaining left many feeling he was not beaten by distance.

Yet focusing only on that visual snapshot produces a deceptive image of Camelot. The lack of acceleration he displayed in both the 2,000 Guineas and Derby was surely a more tell-tale sign. Once he was asked to race beyond his optimum trip, Camelot forfeited any ability to quicken.

Interestingly, Aidan O'Brien was in no doubt about Camelot's ideal distance in the wake of his Arc defeat. He put it at somewhere between a mile and ten furlongs, with the ability to sustain his talent over 12 furlongs, as he did in his two Derby wins.

It may also be that Camelot's draining effort in the Irish Derby bottomed him. His head carriage looked ungainly then, as it did at Doncaster, where he looked a tired horse at the finish. That would certainly explain his tame Arc showing, where he travelled supremely well for much of the race before finding nothing at all.

THE one bright spot in an anti-climactic autumn for Camelot was the announcement that he would stay in training. Although he will speak for himself in 2013, the argument is finely poised.

On one hand, many believe Camelot was infinitely better in midsummer, when he looked for all money like a horse on a roll. On the other, form experts maintain the form of his St Leger defeat corresponded with how he had fared against the horses he beat at Epsom. They have a point. Main Sequence, beaten five lengths in the Derby, finished four and three-quarter lengths behind Camelot at Doncaster. And Thought Worthy, more than 11 lengths behind Camelot at Epsom, finished just under 13 lengths adrift in the St Leger.

The moderate quality of Camelot's contemporaries suggests he did not achieve much in putting them to the sword, in which case there is a significant discrepancy between what Camelot shows at home and on the racecourse.

One man harbours no reservations about his status. In the aftermath of the Arc, Aidan O'Brien was happy to reiterate his belief that Camelot was the best horse to pass through his hands. "I have no doubt about that and you will see it for yourselves next season," he declared.

That was quite a statement, given the majestic racehorses who have graced Ballydoyle during O'Brien's time at its helm. Camelot still has a long way to go to get anywhere near the best of them.

MEA CULPA *O'Brien blames himself for getting it wrong with So You Think*

So You Think – with the same RPR of 127 as Camelot – was the best middle-distance older horse at Ballydoyle for the second year running, even though he had only two races in 2012 and was retired after winning the Prince of Wales's Stakes at Royal Ascot.

Yet, while the figures say the European version of So You Think was just as good as the dual Cox Plate winner who arrived with such fanfare from Australia, Aidan O'Brien wasn't satisfied.

So You Think's victory at Royal Ascot (*above*) was his sixth in 11 runs for O'Brien and his fifth

European Group 1 success. Twice for O'Brien he matched the best RPR of 129 he had earned in Australia and most of the time he was close to it, but the master of Ballydoyle was rather upset with himself for failing to get more out of the import.

After the Prince of Wales's, O'Brien said he had worked So You Think "too long, too hard and too often" in an appraisal that gave an insight into the trainer's continual quest for perfection, as well as an ability to admit he was wrong when son Joseph suggested easing up on the home work.

"All I can say to the Australian people is that I'm sorry I've made such a muck-up for so long," O'Brien said. "It took me a year and a half to learn how to train him properly. I've made a right dog's dinner of it up to now, but after I changed his work he began to quicken like he had never quickened before.

"If he was a lesser horse he probably wouldn't have survived what I've done to him. I was probably killing the horse by making him grind. I knew I had to change things. I'm learning to shut my mouth and listen."

THE CLASSICS
in pictures

1 Was and Seamie Heffernan win the Oaks at Epsom by a neck from Shirocco Star with The Fugue half a length behind in third

2 Encke storms home under Mickael Barzalona to foil Camelot's Triple Crown attempt in the St Leger

3 Photographers en masse at Epsom on Derby day

4 Homecoming Queen and Ryan Moore take the 1,000 Guineas by nine lengths

5 Derby day entertainment at the Curragh

6 Aidan O'Brien and owner Derrick Smith in the winner's enclosure at Newmarket after the 1,000 Guineas

7 Samitar takes the Irish 1,000 Guineas to give trainer Mick Channon and jockey Martin Harley their first major Classic

8 Royal Diamond (striped sleeves) charges home in the Irish St Leger, with the first four separated by a head, a short head and a neck

9 Beauty Parlour (Christophe Soumillon, centre) after winning the Poule d'Essai des Pouliches at Longchamp

10 Nathaniel Rothschild greets Great Heavens and William Buick after their victory in the Irish Oaks

11 Power and Joseph O'Brien win the Irish 2,000 Guineas

12 Lucayan (Stephane Pasquier, 9) snatches the Poule d'Essai des Poulains at Longchamp

Words by **Sam Walker**

RED LETTER DAYS

FOR nine days Frankel played kingmaker. His victory in the International at York in August gave his connections a choice of big races for his grand finale: would it be the British Champion Stakes, as had been the plan all along, or would he head to France for the Arc? It was an important question for team Frankel, for the superstar's adoring public and for the two competing racedays, which have become locked in battle to attract the best Flat horses of the year.

Whichever race was chosen for Frankel's final appearance would have a huge advantage over the other. After nine days of debate, the choice was made: it would be Ascot, as it had been in 2011 when Frankel lit up the first British Champions Day with his scintillating victory in the Queen Elizabeth II Stakes.

Simply by turning up Frankel would ensure the Champion Stakes had won the first round against the Arc. To win the second round he would have to produce the goods in the race itself.

THE MIDDLE-DISTANCE DIVISION

After losing Frankel, things only got worse for the Arc. A string of hard-luck stories saw Snow Fairy, Danedream and Nathaniel drop out of the Longchamp showpiece. Then the rains came. Pre-emptive excuses flooded in, including for the revised market leaders, Camelot and Orfevre. Longchamp needed an abrupt change in fortune for the race to secure a world-class winner – and they almost got it.

The French called the going 'collant', which translates as 'pantyhose' according to one usually reliable web source but essentially means gluey or holding. Orfevre had never encountered anything like it in Japan but when he swung into the straight pulling Christophe Soumillon's arms out, it seemed clear the ground that clung like a woman's undergarment was not going to stop him.

Japan's Triple Crown hero swept around the whole field and stormed into the lead, quickly going two lengths clear. Orfeve surged; the crowd roared; Longchamp officials must have smiled with relief. After all that bad luck they had found an exceptional winner. Unfortunately for them, there was one more twist to come.

After lugging right across the track, Orfeve seemed to pull himself up in front and 33-1 shot Solemia snatched the prize from his grasp. The filly became the joint-lowest-rated winner of the race in Racing Post Ratings history with a mark of 124. The average rating of the first four finishers – a useful indicator of a race's overall class – was a paltry 118.75.

With less than a fortnight between Arc day and Champions Day, competition is fierce between Europe's end-of-season championships. Which of the two days came out on top in 2012?

Defections and the terrible ground had taken their toll on the Arc.

For Frankel, at Ascot 13 days later, it was business as usual. Cirrus Des Aigles *(right)* – France's best horse but barred from the Arc because he is a gelding – went into the race as the second-best in the world according to RPRs and he had the soft ground he adores, but Frankel had too much class. The result was proof that Frankel is the perfect specimen of a racehorse and his success was a huge fillip for Champions Day's flagship event.

The 2012 match-up between the Champion Stakes and the Arc was no contest. With Frankel, Cirrus Des Aigles and Nathaniel in the line-up, the Champion would have struggled to turn up a poor result. As it happens the second and third ran to form and it produced one of the strongest results of the year with an RPR average for the first four that was 10lb higher than the Arc.

Prix de l'Arc de Triomphe (Winner's RPR 124, average RPR of first four 118.75)

Champion Stakes (Winner's RPR 137, average RPR of first four 128.75)

THE MILE DIVISION

The Queen Elizabeth II Stakes and the Prix de la Foret did not attract the world champion miler in 2012, because Frankel **Continues page 40**

Leading players Frankel and Solemia (top row); Sapphire and Ridasiyna (middle row); Rite Of Passage and Molly Malone

ran in the Champion Stakes, but the Ascot race secured his very able deputy.

Excelebration had lost all five meetings with Frankel by an average distance of five and a quarter lengths. But the horse who was continually put in his place by Frankel was better than everything else around – since his debut defeat in May 2010, Excelebration had won all eight starts in which Frankel did not run. He was a multiple Group 1 winner in his own right – perhaps a champion miler in another time – and on Champions Day he kicked it up a notch.

Excelebration had already defeated Cityscape and Elusive Kate in the Prix Jacques Le Marois in August and he extended his margin in October. It was an impressive display that confirmed his status as the clear second-best miler in the world behind the mighty Frankel with a career-best RPR of 131.

The Prix de la Foret has lower prize-money and a less traditional distance of seven furlongs, which means it will inevitably struggle to match the QE II in the long term. This year it was a long way behind with Gordon Lord Byron – likeable and progressive, but certainly not a champion miler – coming out on top by a length and a half with an RPR of 121.

Prix de la Foret (Winner's RPR 121, average RPR of first four 114.5)

Queen Elizabeth II Stakes (Winner's RPR 131, average RPR of first four 120.5)

THE STAYING DIVISION

Much like the weather, the staying division was consistently poor in 2012. By October no horse had managed to win two premier long-distance races and that opened the possibility of the Prix du Cadran or the Long Distance Cup crowning a champion. If any horse could win a second staying event, perhaps they would be the worthy champ – or perhaps we'd just get two more names for the hat.

Molly Malone was not on the divisional radar before the Cadran. Even after winning she barely registered, running to an RPR of just 112 for her two-and-a-half-length success over High Jinx (also 112) with seven lengths covering the first seven home.

'For traditional distaff events the best result is to unearth the next supermare – and one or both of the fillies' races might have done that in 2012'

That left Ascot as the last hope for a sense of order. Could the Long Distance Cup find the best horse in the staying ranks? With Rite Of Passage winning, it might just have, although this finish was even tighter than the Cadran and the ratings only marginally better.

At his best, Dermot Weld's winner landed the 2010 Ascot Gold Cup with an RPR of 122. He had a 17-month layoff to overcome on Champions Day and, with Aiken (116) and Askar Tau (115) finishing within a length, his winning effort was not evidence of a return to his best.

Prix du Cadran (Winner's RPR 112, average RPR of first four 111.5)

Long Distance Cup (Winner's RPR 117, average RPR of first four 115.25)

THE SPRINT DIVISION

Tired of feeling second-rate? Wish you could win a top-class race on your home turf? Fear not sprinters of Europe, October brings two opportunities to shine – and there's not an Aussie in sight.

When the leaves fall the fastest horses on the planet fly south for the winter, taking with them a cargo hold full of sprinting silverware. This year was no exception, with Black Caviar and Ortensia securing Group 1 wins before returning to the land of speed, while Little Bridge made sure the King's Stand Stakes once again went for export, this time to Hong Kong.

The Prix de l'Abbaye and British Champions Sprint may never crown a world champion sprinter but the fourth and fifth richest races in Europe offer much-needed sanctuary for the top local sprinters – and two chances to win a decent purse.

Wizz Kid was a worthy winner of the Abbaye. She's no Black Caviar, or even an Ortensia, but she's the fastest five-furlong

sprinter in Europe when the ground is on the easy side. She posted an RPR of 116 at Longchamp, with heavy-ground July Cup winner Mayson (119) battling well to finish a neck second. The first four at Longchamp had all proved themselves on soft ground – and the going might also have had a hand in the result at Ascot.

At Newcastle in June, Maarek had won a Group 3 in mud so deep that even Mayson couldn't handle it and, with the benefit of the stands rail, he ploughed through the soft going to land the Champions Sprint from Hawkeyethenoo.

The weakness of European sprints is often measured by how well the handicappers fared. Hawkeyethenoo, Sirius Prospect and Imperial Guest all hail from the 'handicapper' category and, in filling second, third and fourth at Ascot, they held the form well below the Group 1 level to which the race aspires.

Prix de l'Abbaye (Winner's RPR 116, average RPR of first four 115)

Champions Sprint (Winner's RPR 118, average RPR of first four 113.25)

THE FILLIES' DIVISION

Distaff races are a throwback to a bygone age. They were the days before Danedream and Black Caviar, the days before Snow Fairy and Moonlight Cloud, before Goldikova and Zenyatta. The new breed of supermares now compete against – and regularly beat – the very best colts. In America they tackle, and win, the Breeders' Cup Classic instead of the Ladies' Classic and in Europe they compete in, and win, the Arc.

For traditional distaff events like the Prix de l'Opera and the catchily titled Champions Day equivalent, the best result would be to unearth the next supermare, a filly ready to rise above the distaff ranks – and one or both might have done that in 2012.

The Prix de l'Opera saw a meeting of the best distaff players in Europe. Pretty Polly winner Izzi Top versus Falmouth winner Giofra versus 2011 Prix Vermeille winner Galikova, but all were eclipsed. The lightly raced Ridasiyna jumped right to the top of the pile – supermares excluded – with a dominant three-and-a-half-length win over Izzi Top that earned her an RPR of 121+. That took her to four wins in five races and, if she makes the expected improvement, she might well be too good to run in the 2013 Opera.

Sapphire was not quite so impressive in the Fillies' and Mares' Stakes at Ascot but she kept on stoutly for a decisive win, posting a career-best RPR of 118. The field was slightly weaker at Ascot than at

Kid's stuff Wizz Kid is not in the Aussie class but the Abbaye winner is the fastest five-furlong sprinter in Europe when the ground is on the easy side

Longchamp, but even so trainer Dermot Weld was thinking of an Arc bid with Sapphire in 2013.

Prix de l'Opera (Winner's RPR 121, average RPR of first four 114.75)

Fillies' and Mares' Stakes (Winner's RPR 118, average RPR of first four 112.5)

THE FUTURE

The decision to pit the Champion Stakes against the Arc was brave to say the least, but in 2012 there was no doubt Ascot had the best middle-distance race of the autumn.

Frankel was a key contributor to the success of both the first and second editions of Champions Day and without him the Champion Stakes may struggle to compete with the Arc in future, although the Ascot race will still have positives. It is run over the in-vogue distance of a mile and two furlongs and is less likely to produce the hard-luck stories commonly associated with the French race.

Perhaps the best selling point for Champions Day, however, is the 'day' element. Arc day is all about the one race. Prize-money for the Arc is ten times greater than for any other Group 1 at Longchamp on the first Sunday in October. By contrast Champions Day has at least one other race – the Queen Elizabeth II – with a strong history that acts as a respected and influential end-of-season championship. In the key areas of comparison, Ascot had a better line-up than Longchamp this year.

Adding two-year-old events for colts and fillies would be a major boost for Champions Day and in this regard Longchamp still leads the way, with Group 1s for both sexes. The problem for Champions Day organisers lies in the segregated nature of British racing, which means that snaring the Dewhurst, Racing Post Trophy or Fillies' Mile from another racecourse would require an epic feat of negotiation.

The mile division provides the real strength for Ascot, as Longchamp doesn't have a mile race. Seven furlongs will be forever considered an intermediate trip and, as such, the Prix de la Foret will never be specifically targeted with anything other than a seven-furlong specialist or a second-rate miler.

There will be tinkering from here. Champions Day is in its infancy and in flux; changes can be made for the better. On the other hand, a couple of strong years for Ascot will make Longchamp realise it has a legitimate rival.

In future it may be that the Arc remains the best race in Europe, while Champions Day wins the award for best overall day. This year, however, Ascot won hands down on both counts.

JAPANESE JINX *Orfevre pipped by Solemia*

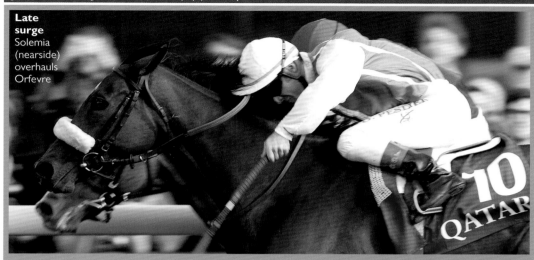

Late surge Solemia (nearside) overhauls Orfevre

THE seeds of Orfevre's dramatic bid to win the Qatar Prix de l'Arc de Triomphe for Japan were sown three decades ago when an insular racing nation started looking beyond its own shores for validation.

The precursor to a sensational defeat could be found closer to hand when Japan's 2011 Triple Crown winner tried to pull himself up in the back straight of a Grade 2 contest at Hanshin in March. Orfevre forfeited more than ten lengths before rounding virtually the entire field in a half-length defeat, at odds of 1-20. A remarkable display that came with an obvious warning: here was a horse as wayward as he was brilliant. It was a suggestion the colt's Arc performance would do little to dispel.

With no disrespect intended to French-trained longshot winner Solemia, the story of the world's richest turf race was at least as much about the vanquished Japanese raider. Even Solemia's rider Olivier Peslier admitted he thought he was riding for a place after catching sight of a light brown flash surging home on his outside. That chestnut-coloured blur was Orfevre, seemingly intent on succeeding where El Condor Pasa, Nakayama Festa and Deep Impact had failed so narrowly.

Somehow, it wasn't to be. As the Japan Racing Association's reporter put it: "Jubilant screams filled the air only to be choked abruptly into sobs and groans."

After producing an amazing turn of foot, Orfevre decided to mess about, veering across the track and colliding with the running rail close home as Solemia stayed on under the persistent Peslier, who claimed his fourth Arc victory by a neck.

Even the booking of Christophe Soumillon as Orfevre's rider – a break with the past strategy of using Japanese jockeys in the Arc – had not changed the run of bad luck. "It looked like it was a dream unfolding but in the end it was a catastrophe, a nightmare," Soumillon said. "We did everything right from a dreadful draw and I really thought history beckoned as we eased into the lead. When he hit the front I thought he had won."

In a sense, such an unlikely outcome was appropriate given the topsy-turvy unpredictability of the build-up to the Arc. In circumstances ranging from the mundane (Nathaniel's spiked temperature) to the unfortunate (Snow Fairy's injury) to the truly bizarre (the swamp fever that confined Danedream to Cologne), it seemed that every day another major contender fell by the wayside.

Japan's big hope at least got to the race, even if disappointment lay in wait again. "We believe that for most people in the racing world the Prix de l'Arc de Triomphe is the best race and we recognise that too," says Yuichi Goto, the JRA's London representative. "It is important for us to show Japanese horses in the major international races – we want to be recognised across the world, not just in Japan. The Arc is the most important race for that and 50 metres from the line at Longchamp everyone must have thought Orfevre was going to win."

As the tears came at Longchamp after an unfathomable defeat, trainer Yasutoshi Ikee was left questioning himself rather than his horse or his jockey, who stood accused of pressing the button a touch prematurely. "Second place is not sufficient – we came to win, it is a trainer's duty to win," said Ikee, who had a spell with Sir Michael Stoute in the late 1990s.

"I apologise to all Japan's fans. He had enough to win. He is a top-level horse and I think we proved a Japanese champion is on a par with the world's best. He finished far ahead of the French and English Derby winners, but this is a matter of win or lose and we have to win.

"He was able to run smoothly from the back as we had planned, but he got left out in front and was then marked and overtaken. For that to have happened shows my own skills are not yet on a par with the world's best. I am going to reassess things and I want to come back to win this magical race."

Ironically, it was a jockey who loves Japan – and is loved there in return – who dashed the nation's hopes. "Sometimes the jockey can make the difference," said Solemia's trainer Carlos Laffon-Parias. "I hoped she might get a place but this is much better. Olivier is the one who won the race."

It hardly needs pointing out again that Orfevre was the one who lost it.

Words by Nicholas Godfrey

ARC OF

Danedream led the way as the principals from the 2011 Arc mopped up a host of major prizes over middle distances

TRIUMPH

Words by **Nick Pulford**

AFTER Danedream had flashed home the 20-1 winner of the 2011 Arc, five lengths clear of a top-class field, 'surprise' was the favourite word of the headline writers as they drew an immediate conclusion about a race that had seen the unfashionable German-trained filly beat the 66-1 shot Shareta.

But the clock doesn't lie. As well as her winning margin – the fourth-biggest in Arc history, bettered only by three of the best winners of the race – Danedream had posted a race-record time of 2min 24.49sec. The ground was unusually fast for Longchamp on the first weekend of October, yet it was an incredible effort to run away from high-quality opponents at such speed and by such a distance. "Hugely impressive," said the Racing Post analysis of the race. "The acceleration to go clear was that of a truly top-class filly."

Andrasch Starke, Danedream's jockey, explains it in simple terms. "If you have a slow race, a lucky horse wins. If you have a fast pace, the best horse wins," he says. When he looked at the Arc result, Starke

was sure the headline writers had got it wrong. "There was no fake about the Arc. It wasn't a surprise result, not at all. There was a really strong pace and it was a record time. If you have a strong pace in a race like that, the strongest horses in the best condition will finish in front."

Within weeks, the form began to stack up. St Nicholas Abbey, beaten around six lengths into fifth place in the Arc, won the Breeders' Cup and then third-placed Snow Fairy took the Queen Elizabeth II Commemorative Cup in Japan for the second year running. Danedream herself was only sixth in the Japan Cup, but she had excuses: a bad draw, made worse by a hefty bump as she came out of the gates.

If the doubters judged that result with a self-satisfied 'I told you so', they were wrong. All across Europe, the best performers from the Arc were kept in training and put away in winter quarters. When they re-emerged in the spring of 2012, they would show exactly how good the Arc form was. Then there would be no doubts.

NOT all the Arc principals were sound and well, however. After her Japanese win, Snow Fairy had moved on to the

Fight to the finish
Danedream goes head to head with Nathaniel in the King George before edging a thriller by a nose.

Previous page (left to right)
Star fillies Snow Fairy, Danedream and Shareta; *(opposite page)* Shareta's trainer Alain de Royer-Dupre

big December meeting in Hong Kong – another place where she had won the year before – but had gone lame after a routine canter in the build-up to the Hong Kong Vase. The Ed Dunlop-trained filly was eventually found to have severe tendon damage that put her future in jeopardy. For her, it was going to be a long, hard road back to the racecourse.

Other trainers could plan more confidently for the 2012 season. Peter Schiergen earmarked four races for Danedream, including the King George VI and Queen Elizabeth Stakes at Ascot, before a return trip to Longchamp for her Arc defence; the principal aim of Alain de Royer-Dupre was to get a Group 1 win for Shareta and he was sure the best chance would come in high summer on her favoured fast ground; and Aidan O'Brien set his sights on Dubai with So You Think, the Arc fourth, and St Nicholas Abbey.

World Cup night was the next test of the Arc form and, while the Ballydoyle pair were beaten, St Nicholas Abbey produced his best performance yet to run Cirrus Des Aigles close in the Sheema Classic. On his return to Europe, St Nicholas Abbey surprisingly lost to

Every second counts

Danedream grabs the King George in the nick of time

Words by **Nick Pulford**

ANDRASCH STARKE had to think fast as he rounded the home turn on Danedream in the King George VI and Queen Elizabeth Stakes. Ahead of him were the leading pair of Brown Panther and Dunaden, while on his outside was William Buick, who had him neatly boxed in with Nathaniel.

The German jockey thought there might be a gap big enough for his little filly to squeeze through between Nathaniel and Brown Panther, but he wasn't sure. His brain was ticking and so was the clock: 35 seconds to the line and counting. The race hinged on Starke's next move.

"You have to make these decisions very quickly," Starke says. "It looked like there was a little gap, but I thought William Buick wanted to invite me into the gap and then close it on me. If Brown Panther or Nathaniel had moved just a little bit,

the gap would be closed. If I had to stop really hard, I would definitely have lost too much ground. So I had to wait for Nathaniel to move and then I had to move to the outside."

Ten more seconds had elapsed: only 25 seconds to the finish now, at the two-furlong pole, and Danedream was a length and a half down as Nathaniel drew alongside Brown Panther at the head of the race. Starke made sure Danedream was balanced and, with a furlong and a half to go, gave her two cracks of the whip. He was encouraged by her instant response but by now Nathaniel had grabbed the lead and the all-important far rail.

"At first I thought I would catch him," Starke says, "but I've watched a lot of races at Ascot and I know it's difficult to catch the leader when he has the rail. Nathaniel fought so hard that I started to think I wouldn't catch him."

At the furlong pole, Danedream

was still a length down. Twelve seconds left. Half a furlong out, the gap had halved but time was running out. Six seconds to go. Danedream was still closing but Nathaniel wasn't stopping. Three seconds to go, two, one . . .

"At the finish line I couldn't tell you I had won for sure, but sometimes you get the feeling that you've won by a nose or lost by a nose, and that day I thought maybe I'd just got the nose in front," Starke says.

Then he had cause to think again. "When I turned with my horse and heard the crowd screaming, I thought I must have been beaten. Then, when I cantered back, I saw my colours on the big screen and I suddenly thought maybe I'd won after all."

The photo-finish result had been announced by then and now all the screaming was coming from Starke as he punched the air in wild celebration. "It was an unbelievable

feeling," he says. "Honestly I was lucky to just get the nose in front but, fair enough, if I had got a clear run she would have won by one or two lengths."

Lucky? Starke does himself a disservice. This was a triumph that owed far more to judgement than luck.

Queen among kings

Danedream became the ninth horse to win both the King George and the Arc and the first filly to do so

Horse	King George	Arc
Ribot	1956	1955, 1956
Ballymoss	1958	1958
Mill Reef	1971	1971
Dancing Brave	1986	1986
Lammtarra	1995	1995
Montjeu	2000	1999
Hurricane Run	2006	2005
Dylan Thomas	2007	2007
Danedream	2012	2011

his stablemate Windsor Palace in a Group 3 contest, while Arc sixth Meandre was beaten on his seasonal reappearance.

The floodgates were about to open, however. In the space of just over four weeks, So You Think won the Tattersalls Gold Cup and Prince of Wales's Stakes before heading into early retirement, St Nicholas Abbey landed the Coronation Cup and Meandre took the Grand Prix de Saint-Cloud from Shareta. The 2011 Arc principals had won four of the first five all-age Group 1 races in Britain, Ireland and France run over ten furlongs or a mile and a half. Nobody doubted the form now.

THE Danedream camp were having doubts. Their filly had finished a hugely disappointing last of four behind Meandre in the Grand Prix de Saint-Cloud and they could not find an explanation. Having won a Group 2 at Baden-Baden on her reappearance, she had worked well before her trip to France but had gone out like a light early in the straight at Saint-Cloud.

German trainers tend to be cautious in targeting big overseas races and Schiergen started to have misgivings about going

for the King George, which was less than four weeks away. Starke played a big part in talking him round. "She was very disappointing at Saint-Cloud, she definitely had a very bad day," the jockey recalls. "It was nothing to do with the ground or the pace, because she was completely beaten by the time we came into the straight. She worked brilliantly before Saint-Cloud, that's what was so strange about the result.

"When she came back, she was just lying in her box and something was wrong with her. We put her away for a week and after that she started jumping around. I said to the trainer, 'Look, she's in the same form as before, you have the horse of a lifetime and you have to try the King George'."

Among those standing in the way was the 2011 King George winner, Nathaniel, who along with the ineligible gelding Cirrus Des Aigles was probably the best middle-distance performer not to have contested the previous year's Arc. St Nicholas Abbey

was there too, while the favourite was the Hardwicke Stakes winner Sea Moon. This was going to be a huge test for Danedream, who would have to answer one of the other doubts about the Arc form: the perceived influence of the weight-for-age allowance in favour of the three-year-olds.

Having received 11lb from the older males the previous October, Danedream carried only 3lb less than fellow four-year-old Nathaniel in the King George. The weight on her back was 9st 4lb, compared with 8st 8lb in the Arc. "It's more difficult for a four-year-old filly without the allowance and for a tiny, very thin filly like her it's doubly difficult with that weight," Starke says.

The race turned into a battle between Nathaniel and Danedream, "an unbelievable fight" in Starke's words. At the line there was just a nose in it, but the Arc form had come up trumps again: Danedream had become only the ninth horse to win both the King George and the Arc – and the first filly to do so.

OVER in France, Alain de Royer-Dupre was being rebuffed at every turn. The

Continues page 46

expected summer fast ground showed no sign of materialising for Shareta, who had been beaten three times on rain-softened going. The closest she had come to winning was a nose defeat in the Group 2 Prix Corrida by a little-known four-year-old filly called Solemia and that left the trainer even more frustrated.

"She was very unlucky in the Corrida and should have won comfortably," Royer-Dupre says. "She was kept in training because we thought she was capable of winning a Group 1. If she couldn't do that, it might not have been the right decision. What she really wants is a good pace and good ground. We ran her in the summer because we could be more certain she'd have her ground. That was one reason to choose York, along with the fact she'd always given the impression it was a course that would really suit her."

Shareta had good to firm ground in the Yorkshire Oaks but she also had high-class rivals, including Nassau Stakes winner The Fugue and Oaks one-two Was and Shirocco Star. Like Danedream, however, she showed plenty of fight to prevail in a tight finish by a neck from The Fugue. Her victory meant all of the first six in the 2011 Arc had subsequently won a Group 1 race and within four weeks she had done it again with an easier victory in the Prix Vermeille.

Four days before the Yorkshire Oaks, Snow Fairy had crossed the Channel in the other direction to make her comeback in the Prix Jean Romanet at Deauville. A course of laser treatment in Ireland, followed by six weeks of trotting at Jessica Harrington's yard, had helped nurse her back to health and the finishing touches had been three racecourse gallops at Newmarket, Lingfield and Sandown.

The comeback – one of the most amazing and heartwarming of recent years – was complete when she won by three-quarters of a length at Deauville. "I'm still going around in a bit of a daze," Dunlop said a few days later. "We've had loads of texts and emails and I'm proud of what I've done, proud of my staff, proud of my horse, and amazed that it's happened. If you'd seen her on December 7, you'd never have imagined she'd come out and win a Group 1 eight months later."

A Group 1 against her own sex was one thing, but everybody knows there are a group of 'Super Group 1' races that mean much more and one of those, the Irish Champion Stakes, was the next target for Snow Fairy. Ranged against her were Nathaniel and St Nicholas Abbey, the King George second and third, but they had to settle for the minor places again as Frankie Dettori drove Snow Fairy to victory by a length and a quarter.

Dunlop was speechless for a few

moments after Snow Fairy's stunning performance, which smashed the track record at Leopardstown. Once he had composed himself, he said: "She is the horse of a lifetime. To beat some of the best colts around and to take the track record after having a tendon injury, this has to be her best performance."

Nathaniel's trainer, John Gosden, had seen his colt beaten by the fillies in the King George and the Irish Champion and he offered his own words of praise. "Danedream and Snow Fairy are the best mares for years," he said. "It's tough giving mares like that weight." When Shareta added the Vermeille a week later, the 2011 Arc principals were cemented as the dominant force in British, Irish and French Group 1 races from a mile and a quarter to a mile and a half. At that point, in mid-September, their score stood at nine wins from 14 available races. To put further gloss on the figures, the nine wins had come from only ten races in that category contested by the first six from the 2011 Arc.

THAT was as good as it got. The next few weeks were laced with disappointment as first Snow Fairy, with heat in a foreleg after exercise, and then Danedream were ruled out of the Arc. An injury misfortune with Snow Fairy was nothing new, but Danedream's absence came in the most dramatic and luckless

Super mare Snow Fairy's amazing comeback from injury reaches its peak as she beats Nathaniel in the Irish Champion under Frankie Dettori

HOW THE 2011 ARC FORM WORKED OUT

Danedream 1st
Subsequent Group 1 wins: King George VI and Queen Elizabeth Stakes, Grosser Preis von Baden

Shareta 2nd
Yorkshire Oaks, Prix Vermeille

Snow Fairy 3rd
Queen Elizabeth II Cup, Prix Jean Romanet, Irish Champion Stakes

So You Think 4th
Tattersalls Gold Cup, Prince of Wales's Stakes

St Nicholas Abbey 5th
Breeders' Cup Turf, Coronation Cup

Meandre 6th
Grand Prix de Saint-Cloud, Grosser Preis von Berlin

circumstances when she was banned from travelling owing to a case of equine infectious anaemia (commonly known as swamp fever) near Schiergen's Cologne stable.

Danedream's trainer and jockey learned six days before the Arc that the Cologne training centre would go into quarantine lockdown to prevent any possibility of the disease spreading. Only two hours earlier Starke, who rarely rides the filly in work, had been on board for her final fast gallop. "Her work was as least as good as she had done before the King George," he says. "Then we heard about this case. I thought it couldn't be real. It was painful because we knew we wouldn't get the possibility again with a horse like that."

With Nathaniel also absent owing to a poor blood count, the Arc had lost three of its main players and much of its quality. The race lacked nothing in drama as Solemia collared Orfevre close home, but this time the tag of 'surprise winner' was hard to dispute. "The form does not look at all reliable," was the judgement of Racing Post analysis.

Even in the absence of Danedream and Snow Fairy, the previous year's Arc form hung heavy over the race – just as it had for most of the big middle-distance contests all season. It was hard to escape the conclusion that the outcome would have been very different if they had been at Longchamp.

DO YOU WANT MORE?

OWN & RACE IN FRANCE

MORE PRIZE MONEY

The Highest prize-money in Europe.
Group 1 in France : Up to €4,000,000 VS €1,566,265 in Great Britain.
Group 2 in France : Up to €400,000 VS €153,000 in Germany.
Group 3 in France : A minimum of €80,000 VS €47,500 in Ireland.

source: European Pattern Races 2012 - 2011 figures

MORE PREMIUMS

Besides of prize money, amazing owners' premiums.
+75 % for a 2 yo | +63 % for a 3 yo | +48 % for a 4 yo and up.

MORE RACES

172 racecourses offering a rich and diversified program for all type of horses.
4,776 flat races, 2,210 jump races.

source: France Galop 2010 figures

MORE INCENTIVES

French Racing
& Breeding Committee

France, where racing makes sense

www.FRBC.net
contact us!

THE
BIGGER
PICTURE

The sun shines on the Killarney August
Festival as the leaders jump the fourth fence
in the Diarmuid Cronin Electrical Mares
Beginners Chase. The race was won easily
by the Philip Dempsey-trained Jacksonslady
PATRICK McCANN (RACINGPOST.COM/PHOTOS)

ON THE NOSE

Neptune Collonges triumphed by the narrowest margin in Grand National history but only after months of soul-searching by owner John Hales and his family

Words by **Nick Pulford**

AN hour before the Grand National, John Hales was close to tears. The brave face he had kept all day crumpled as he was interviewed by Lydia Hislop on Racing UK and his voice crackled with the emotion that is always close to the surface where Hales and his horses are concerned. "I'm sorry," he said several times as he struggled to hold himself together enough to talk about his National hopes for Neptune Collonges. Several times Hislop had to put a comforting hand on his arm: "Everybody understands," she told him.

Once-a-year viewers on BBC might not have appreciated Hales's difficulty, but the insider audience on Racing UK knew very well he was in a dark place. This was Aintree, the scene of the blackest day in Hales's 20 years as a leading owner

in jump racing. In April 1998, One Man – the flamboyant grey who was the best horse to carry Hales's yellow and white colours with the red star – had been killed in action on the Mildmay course. Fourteen years had passed, but the pain had not.

Now here he was, back at Aintree with another much-loved grey. He had never blamed Aintree in any way for the tragic accident that befell One Man and his horses had run there several times since – even in the National – but this was different somehow. Neptune Collonges – 'Nipper' to Hales, his wife Pat and daughter Lisa – was just one race from retirement after seven years of honourable service. Did that one race really have to be in the National with all its risk, real or perceived? It was a question the family had wrestled with for months.

Two hundred miles away, at the David Broome Event Centre in South Wales, **Continues page 52**

Lisa Hales was taking part in a show jumping competition. It was her interest in horses from a young age that led her father into ownership and she now runs a show jumping yard on the family farm in Shropshire. Even for this accomplished horsewoman, who knows only too well the fragility of horses in a training and competitive environment, the nerves were frayed.

"I have been back to Aintree since One Man died, but I didn't want to go this time. If anything bad happened I didn't want to be there," she says. "I'd had lots of invites from friends to go and watch the race with them, but I wanted to keep busy. I had a few to ride that day. I fell off the first one, I've had him six years and never fallen off him in my life, but I just didn't have my mind on the job. It wasn't going too well."

She had left her father in no doubt about her feelings, even right up to the moment he left for Aintree. "I told him on the Thursday that if Nipper didn't come home, then he shouldn't either. So I think he was under quite a lot of pressure." She can laugh about it now, because everything turned out so well, but the fears and the tension were all too serious as the family debated whether to send their beloved Nipper to Aintree.

THE CRUNCH came after the Grand National Trial at Haydock in February. Neptune Collonges, carrying top weight on heavy ground, ran a cracker to chase down Giles Cross to a neck after a gruelling three and a half miles. In everything but the result, it was a portent of what was to come at Aintree. Hales, however, was caught between his family's worries about the National and the belief that Neptune Collonges and trainer Paul Nicholls should be allowed to do their jobs. Racehorses are there to race, after all.

"Paul had been training Neptune all season with the Grand National in mind but I knew it was a taboo subject in the family," he says. "I genuinely believed we would retire him at Haydock – he hadn't run badly up to then but was showing signs he'd had enough. But he came out full of enthusiasm, he ploughed through the mud, he loved it. Paul came on the phone and said, 'That was awesome'. I thought, 'Oh dear, I've got a problem now'.

"The family had a meeting. My view was he'd earned the right to go, to bow

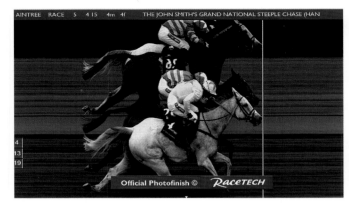

out at the top in the greatest steeplechase. My wife was 50-50 at best. She said she would go but she wasn't looking forward to it. My daughter said, 'Dad, you'd better bring him home safe and sound'. Talk about pressure."

It was almost too much for Hales, as that emotional appearance on Racing UK showed. As well as the instructions Nicholls gave Daryl Jacob, Hales had some words of his own for Neptune Collonges' jockey. "I told him to go carefully and pull up if there were any problems. Daryl told me later it was the most negative riding instruction he'd ever had."

The clock ticked slowly to 4.15pm and then there was a ten-minute delay after the false start when Synchronised ditched Tony McCoy and ran loose. Hales, a nervous race watcher at the best of times, had taken himself off on his own to a spot near the winning post, while his wife stood in front of the stands with Nicholls. As the race finally got under way, he says, the dream of winning wasn't in his mind.

"All I ever considered was his safety. I was on walkabout, glancing up at the screen, half watching it, listening to the

Caught on camera
The photo-finish shows Neptune Collonges a nose in front of Sunnyhillboy at the end of a race in which Daryl Jacob plotted a skilful course over the tricky fences

The National on Betfair

Neptune Collonges		Sunnyhillboy
43	Pre-race	25
75	In-running high	
1.3	Run-in	1.03
6	At the line	1.2
1.2	Freeze-frame	6

Neptune Collonges was matched at an in-running high of 75 and never traded at shorter than 1.3 on his way to winning the Grand National, while runner-up Sunnyhillboy was as low as 1.03 on the run-in.

Even after crossing the line, Sunnyhillboy was hot favourite at 1.2 and Neptune Collonges was trading as a big outsider at 6. But the odds switched around completely when the freeze-frame was shown on TV and shortly afterwards Neptune Collonges was declared the winner by a nose.

commentary. When he came past me first time round, he was eighth and I thought, 'That's a lovely position, now jump carefully and we'll take you home'."

But on the second circuit the old grey's stamina, fighting spirit and, ultimately, his class came to the fore. Stealthily, he crept into contention and as they crossed the Melling Road for the final time, with two to jump, he was at the tail of a leading group of eight. If it had been a level-weights race, his chance would have been obvious but he was carrying 11st 6lb while most of those around him had no more than 11st. No winner since Red Rum had carried more than 11st 5lb and, as JP McManus's colours came away from the last in front with Sunnyhillboy, another gallant defeat looked in prospect.

"My biggest joy was when he jumped the last; I knew he was safe then," Hales says. "He was fourth coming over the last and it still never dawned on me he could Continues page 54

Lycetts – We know your world.

At Lycetts we offer expert, impartial advice to cover all your bloodstock, equine property and liability insurance requirements, in addition to a wealth of products for farm, estate, high value property, commercial insurance and financial planning.

For further information and advice contact:

Camilla Baker on 01638 676 700
The Coach House,168 High Street, Newmarket, Suffolk CB8 9AQ.
Email: newmarket@lycetts.co.uk

Charlotte Alexander on 01672 512 512
1 Stables Court, The Parade, Marlborough, Wiltshire SN8 1NP.
Email: marlborough@lycetts.co.uk

Offices throughout the UK and in Ireland.
Visit our website at www.lycetts.co.uk

Lycetts

We know your world

Insurance services for bloodstock • private clients • farm & estate • commercial • financial planning

win the race. After four and a half miles it was a tough ask to run down JP's horse giving him 15lb. I was almost in line with the finish and from my angle I couldn't tell who'd won, it was impossible. I was still walking about, listening out for the result of the photo-finish. When it was announced, I went into a state of shock."

Down in South Wales, Lisa had watched the race with mounting excitement. "I watched it in the horsebox, there were three of us. I wanted to see it, but I didn't want too many people around." Panic set in on the hell-for-leather run to the first fence – "Nipper wasn't going very quick, he was taking his time," she can joke now – and hardly let up for the next nine minutes.

"The normal fences were okay, but Becher's and The Chair were a bit of a worry," she says. "When they jumped Becher's the second time and he was about sixth, I started to get a bit excited. When they jumped the last I thought, 'He's going to be third, oh that's brilliant, what a performance.' Then I started to think he might be second, and when he began to gain on Sunnyhillboy I was screaming at the TV. I couldn't quite believe it."

And, of course, the tears flowed again. Tears of joy and relief. Neptune Collonges had crowned his career with a National victory that will live long in the memory and, quite probably, in the record books. Most importantly, the grey son of Dom Alco was going home to Shropshire to live out his days with Azertyuiop and Noland, two more retired stars from the Hales firmament.

Not everyone was so lucky. The National claimed the lives of Synchronised and According To Pete, two public favourites from different ends of the ownership spectrum, and Hales knew that hollow, wretched feeling only too well. JP McManus, having lost Synchronised and finished so close with Sunnyhillboy, congratulated the winning owner as he left the rostrum after the trophy presentation. "It speaks volumes for the man that he came up to me in the moment when he'd just lost the horse that won the Gold Cup for him," Hales says. "We shook hands and it was a very moving moment. I'd lost One Man there and I knew exactly how he felt."

WITH all the pre-race worries dispersed, Hales was overwhelmed by the reaction of racing fans from far and wide to the National triumph. The first inkling came at the traditional post-National victory parade, which took place in Ditcheat the morning after a very long night before. "That was one of the most wonderful things that happened. We couldn't believe it, there were thousands there and they'd

'I didn't have a clue who had won'

The look said so much. Relief, elation and, above all, gratitude to a lost friend and mentor. When the result of the closest finish in Grand National history was announced, Daryl Jacob raised his hands to the sky and said a little prayer to Kieran Kelly, the jump jockey who had helped Jacob through difficult early days in his career. Aged just 25, Kelly was killed in a fall at Kilbeggan in 2003 but, while he is gone, he is not forgotten.

"He's always there, I always see him," says Jacob, 29, who was still a teenager and had recently moved to England when Kelly was killed. "I've got pictures of Kieran in my house, in my car, everywhere. He was one of my best-ever friends. He looked after me in Ireland and he made me come over to England. He's a massive influence on my career."

To think of others even in a moment of personal triumph is typical of Jacob. In the Aintree weighing room he was quick to give a consolatory hug to Richie McLernon, who was on the wrong side of the National photo-finish. Later, as others went to celebrate his victory on Neptune Collonges, the Grand National-winning jockey was at the hospital bedside of Noel Fehily, another close friend, who had broken his leg in a National fall. Losing Kelly has taught him to value friendship above all else.

'We couldn't believe it, there were thousands there and they'd come from all over the country, it wasn't just the village turning out'

come from all over the country, it wasn't just the village turning out.

"I can't believe the difference between winning at the Cheltenham Festival and winning the Grand National. I had letters from China, Australia, America, all over the world. The big difference is that Cheltenham is for the professionals – jockeys, trainers, owners, even the professional racegoers if you like. But

the Grand National belongs to the public. Every factory, every office, has a sweepstake and it's something that's built into the fabric of this country."

The Grand National prize-money has been spent already – a little on a room dedicated solely to the Grand National at Hales's home and considerably more on two promising young jumpers. Following the retirements of Neptune Collonges and Noland, who also bowed out at Aintree on National day, Hales looked to replenish his stock. The majority went on Fascino Rustico, who had been an impressive winner of a Carlisle bumper that worked out well. He cost £310,000 at the Brightwells Cheltenham sale in April and is now with Nicholls.

"Like Kieran, Noel has been a massive part of my career. He's taught me an awful lot since I came over. Best friends are hard to come by and when you've got them you've got to make sure you keep that friendship well."

Jacob has learned, too, to grasp every opportunity, having turned his career around after the self-doubt and boozing of his youth. That's what prompted him to take up the position as number two for Paul Nicholls – a decision that paid off spectacularly in his first season at Ditcheat.

He knew he would get rides on top-class horses and in return he gave Neptune Collonges a top-class ride in the National, saving ground on the brave man's inside-to-middle route and skilfully avoiding the trouble around him.

"I went through the race in quite a lot of detail and I studied the horses I wanted to follow and which ones I didn't, where I wanted to be at certain points of the race," he says. "But to be fair to the horse he did everything for me and in the last two furlongs, when I really needed him to knuckle down, he answered every call. He did all the hard work, I just sat there.

"Jumping the last I still thought I had a chance, but then Richie's horse quickened away and got three lengths on me. I was hoping and praying he was going to come back to me, because I knew my horse had no more pace to go after him. Richie's horse tied up a little bit and my horse, being the strong stayer he is, just kept grinding it out.

"It was so tight I didn't have a clue who had won. It was on the nod and it was so hard to tell who was up and who was down."

Just as impressive as his National success was the Graded-race double at Sandown on the final day of the season. With confidence coursing in his veins, he gave great rides to old lag Tidal Bay in the Bet365 Gold Cup and exciting novice Sanctuaire in the Celebration Chase. That left him with 83 winners – up from his previous best of 56 the season before.

All in all, a job well done.

'I had a great ride, he was brilliant'

The old adage says nobody remembers the runner-up. Who, in years to come, will be able to name Richie McLernon as the jockey who was beaten a nose on Sunnyhillboy in the closest finish in Grand National history?

For a few fleeting moments, the biggest spotlight in racing was on McLernon but ultimately, after an agonising wait for the photo-finish, he was left in the shadows as the fame and glory went to Daryl Jacob and Neptune Collonges. The opportunity may never come knocking again and Lambourn trainer Jamie Osborne surely voiced the unspoken thoughts of many when he tweeted: "Will Richie McLernon ever get over that one?"

According to the jockey, it took less time than you might imagine to jolt him out of his disappointment. Synchronised, a stablemate of Sunnyhillboy at Jonjo O'Neill's yard, had died out on the track and the shattering news consumed McLernon's thoughts.

"When the result was called out, it was gut-wrenching, but the news on Synchronised was terrible – that hit me much harder," he says. "It was a big loss to the yard and everyone there. I rode Synchronised a lot when he was a young

horse and he was lovely. You get to know these horses, you become attached to them, you form a bond. It takes a long time to get over it. Finishing second, you can always go back and try again."

McLernon, 26, says "it just wasn't to be" in the National. "A lot of things went through my head – What if I'd done this? What if I'd done that? – but you can't change it now. I had a great ride, he was brilliant. When I got near the water jump I could feel the other horse coming. Sunny's only a little lad and Neptune Collonges was a big horse beside him, but he gave his all."

At least McLernon had the consolation of a first Cheltenham Festival winner the previous month, when Alfie Sherrin took the JLT Specialty Handicap Chase. "That was a great day. Mr O'Neill was confident he'd run a good race. The horses were in good form and I knew the drying ground would help him, so I expected him to run well. Winning was a great feeling. You graft all year for those four days at Cheltenham, that's what it's all about. To get a winner was extra special."

And, as we all know, everyone remembers the winners.

Then, four days later, a phone call from bloodstock agent Anthony Bromley led to a second purchase. "He said, 'You're not going to believe this John, but a grey in France by Dom Alco has just trotted up by 12 lengths in his first chase at Auteuil. I don't think he's a Kauto Star or an Azertyuiop in terms of his speed, but he's very impressive over a longer distance.'"

Hales didn't hesitate. "That's what I want," he says. "The only big race left I want to win is the Gold Cup. So I bought him." He's called Unioniste and is also in training with Nicholls.

Neptune Collonges paid for those two additions to the Hales portfolio, but now there is a more altruistic side to his earning potential. As a National

winner, with the added unusual features of being a grey and the narrowest victor in the history of the race, he is much in demand and is likely to remain so for years to come. The beneficiary is Alder Hey children's hospital in Liverpool, as Hales explains.

"Wherever he goes, to parades or cricket matches or whatever, I don't ask for a penny in expenses. Instead I ask them to make a cheque out to Alder Hey hospital. So what we're using Nipper for now is for charity."

Hales wouldn't agree that Liverpool owed his family something after all the heartache. But Aintree and Neptune Collonges gave them so much on that grand April day.

Grand legacy
Hales has bought two promising young horses, Fascino Rustico and Unioniste, out of his National winnings

THE
BIGGER
PICTURE

Richie McGrath parts company with Stopped Out at the third-last in an eventful beginners' chase at Catterick in February. Five runners started the race but the only finisher was the Evan Williams-trained Bruslini, who scored at 7-2
JOHN GROSSICK (RACINGPOST.COM/PHOTOS)

TOUGH
AT THE TOP

Paul Nicholls won the Grand National and Champion Hurdle for the first time as he completed a seventh consecutive season as champion jumps trainer. But it was far from easy

Words by **Tom Kerr**

ON A cold and damp Grand National day at Aintree in April, Paul Nicholls did something he has done only very rarely in his career. He held up his hands and admitted defeat. Oscar Whisky had just won the Aintree Hurdle for his old friend and rival Nicky Henderson, and with that surely the trainers' championship had been taken out of the hands of the man who for six unbroken years had ruled the roost of British jump racing.

"I just said 'I wave the white flag, that's it, you beat us'," Nicholls recalls. Yet it was no mathematical certainty and just under two hours later the white flag hastily tumbled down as Neptune Collonges got his nose in front of Sunnyhillboy to give Nicholls his first Grand National victory. With its riches came a seventh trainers' championship, a prize that had hung in the balance during a titanic title battle over the winter.

Nicholls, although so well acquainted with jump racing success he may well be listed as its next of kin, was palpably ecstatic. "It's blown Nicky Henderson out of the water now," he said, a comment that reflected both the importance of the title to him and the struggle it had been to complete the seven-timer in a season with more ups and downs than an express elevator.

Two months before that day of high drama at Aintree, Nicholls received the news any trainer preparing for Cheltenham must dread. The one thing, totally beyond anyone's control, that can destroy the work of an entire year – the horses were coughing, and the festival was just around the corner.

"It was the first time really that we've been hit at the wrong time and we had these horses coughing at the end of February right through to the middle of March," he says. "It was frustrating, and we didn't go into Cheltenham this year with the horses in top form."

While some yards might close ranks at such a development, Nicholls responded with customary openness and declared

Continues page 60

the setback to the world. It has come to be expected of Nicholls that he shares news of the yard with a candour rarely found in racing, and as a consequence of his transparency and his success he is perhaps the single most scrutinised practitioner of the sport in history.

"When you're dealing with horses like Big Buck's and Kauto, and when you've had Denman and Master Minded, you're going to have the media scrutiny because they're public horses," Nicholls says. "We try to be honest and upfront when we have a problem and it's better than not saying anything. When you've got a big string of horses there's no point covering things up, you've just got to be forward and say, 'look we're struggling'."

To any neutral observer the Nicholls team did struggle at Cheltenham. The record shows a litany of disappointments and mishaps: Al Ferof blundered and lost his chance in the Arkle, Pearl Swan fell at the decisive moment of the Triumph, Kauto Stone didn't make it past the first in the Champion Chase. And, most disappointingly of all, at the end of a fairytale season Kauto Star was pulled up in the Gold Cup.

At the time Nicholls bemoaned the fact that "anything that could go wrong did go wrong", although in retrospect he describes it as "a good Cheltenham". For most other trainers, of course, landmark wins with Rock On Ruby and Big Buck's would have constituted a great festival, but Nicholls sets high standards. In the year he celebrated his 50th birthday by ticking off the final two major races missing from his collection – the Champion Hurdle with Rock On Ruby and later the Grand National with Neptune Collonges – he was as driven as ever.

After the most testing of seasons, Nicholls is proud of the way the team pulled together to keep the stable on top. Delegation may be vital in an operation that stretches across three yards but, make no mistake, the principles of the man at the top permeate all the way down.

Much was made of Rock On Ruby being handled by Nicholls' protégé Harry Fry at the Seaborough satellite yard in Dorset but Nicholls, typically straight-talking, is keen to point out it was no flag of convenience that his name appeared alongside the Champion Hurdle winner. "Harry's learned it my way," he says. "We all work together and it's good for Team Ditcheat to win these big races. It's a team thing."

By the time the festival tour moved on to Aintree, Nicholls was just about the hottest trainer around with a 56 per cent strike-rate in the fortnight before the Grand National meeting. His lead
Continues page 62

ROUGH LUCK *The fall that brought Kauto Star down to earth*

Sad end Ruby Walsh and Nicholls' assistant Dan Skelton with Kauto Star after he was pulled up in the Gold Cup

Friday, February 24, 2012 is a day that will live with Paul Nicholls for a long time. With two and a half weeks to go to Cheltenham, each day was becoming vital for his festival hopefuls but this should have been a routine morning for Kauto Star as he stepped into the schooling ring at Ditcheat. It was something he had done countless times before and, even at the age of 12, he was in the form of his life after a historic fifth King George VI Chase triumph on his latest outing.

What happened next shocked Nicholls to the core. Kauto Star, described by Ruby Walsh as "incredible" in his schooling at home, had done everything right until the final fence of the session. But this time he met it wrong and crashed to the floor in what Nicholls admitted was a "pretty awful fall".

While the old warrior had recovered quickly from problems in the past, this time he did not. He was sound after the fall but clearly very sore and not his usual self. His participation in the Cheltenham Gold Cup hung in the balance until the eve of the festival, when he was finally given the go-ahead after another schooling session at Ditcheat. This time it was not awful but "awesome", in Nicholls' words.

With four days to the Gold Cup, his fans could get excited again about the prospect of another historic moment as he sought to join the ranks of triple Gold Cup winners and become the first to do it in non-consecutive years. Sadly, it was not to be.

Early in the Gold Cup it became clear the effects of the fall were still with Kauto Star. He jumped poorly and over-extended himself at the water jump. Realising his mount had no more to give, Ruby Walsh pulled up before halfway. In response, the vast Cheltenham crowd broke out in spontaneous applause that went on and on. It was a fitting tribute to a magnificent champion.

Yet for Nicholls, the what-ifs of the race are hard to bear. "One of the hardest things of the season and probably of my career was that schooling fall, it was a real blow," he says. "Up until the point he fell we thought we had a massive chance in the Gold Cup. You've just got to look at the form of the race and think where he would have been among that lot if he'd been at his best. It's just so unfortunate he had that fall at the wrong time. I look back and wish I hadn't run him, but I was looking for any reason not to run him – veterinary-wise or otherwise – and everything seemed to be right."

It was a disappointing conclusion to what had been, until that fateful Friday at Ditcheat, a triumphant campaign. The previous season, the crown appeared to have passed to Long Run, five years Kauto Star's junior, but the old king refused to abdicate. He beat Long Run by eight lengths in the Betfair Chase at Haydock and then, even more memorably, by a length and a quarter in the King George. "Awesome, just awesome," Nicholls says with relish. "He was as impressive as ever at Kempton. Haydock was phenomenal and I didn't think that could be bettered, but then he went and won the King George for the fifth time. What he did in those two runs astounded me."

Kauto Star may have failed to win back the Gold Cup but he did what nobody had expected him to do and finished the 2011-12 season, once again, as the highest-rated jumps horse in training. At an age when many have to be content with duelling for nostalgic glory in hunter chases, Kauto Star was still reaching for the stars. Even for a trainer like Nicholls, who has seen many of the best chasers of our age pass through his hands, the experience of being associated with such a horse is almost overwhelming.

"It's a once-in-a-lifetime thing," he says. "You have the Denmans and the Master Mindeds – brilliant, brilliant horses – but Kauto's record is phenomenal. I feel incredibly lucky and privileged. He's done it all."

Pair makes a full house

Paul Nicholls is already one of the greatest jumps trainers of all time and in 2011-12, on his way to becoming champion for the seventh season in a row, he achieved two more important milestones.

Having won the Cheltenham Gold Cup on four occasions, Nicholls finally landed the other two biggest jumps races in the calendar when Neptune Collonges won the Grand National and Rock On Ruby took the Champion Hurdle.

That made Nicholls only the 11th trainer in history to win all three races and, apart from Kim Bailey (who was the last to complete the full set in 1995), he is the only active trainer to have done so.

Vincent O'Brien leads the way for most wins in the Grand National, Gold Cup and Champion Hurdle with ten, but Nicholls now has six and is alongside Nicky Henderson in joint-seventh in that list. Two more wins would put him joint-second with Fred Rimell and within striking distance of O'Brien.

An eighth title would put him joint-second with Fred Winter in the all-time list but still a long way behind Martin Pipe's 15 championships.

Nicholls has few big races left on his 'to do' list. He has won nine of the 12 Grade 1 races at the Cheltenham Festival (missing are the Neptune Novices' Hurdle, Albert Bartlett Novices' Hurdle and Champion Bumper) and most of the big handicaps in the jumps calendar. The Irish Grand National is the only one of the major Nationals he has yet to win.

Moneyspinners *(clockwise from top left)* Big Buck's, Silviniaco Conti, Sanctuaire, Rock On Ruby, Zarkandar and Tidal Bay collectively contributed £900,000 to Nicholls' title-winning total

over Nicky Henderson in the trainers' championship was a slender £13,000 but Big Buck's got him off to a flying start in the first race of the meeting, the Liverpool Hurdle, with a record-breaking 17th consecutive win. With a total of three winners on the first two days, Aintree was already more successful for Nicholls than Cheltenham had been, yet there was no let-up from Henderson either.

The Lambourn trainer took the lead after winning the first three races on Grand National day, with Simonsig, Sprinter Sacre and Oscar Whisky, and that left Nicholls needing a big hit in the Grand National, the Spanish treasure fleet of the jumps season. He was far from confident, however, after 52 unsuccessful runners in the race. He had saddled a second, a third and a fourth but never the winner.

"We'd half given up because things hadn't gone our way in the past," he says. "We felt we had a bit of a chance with Neptune Collonges. He stayed, he had class, he'd run some good Gold Cups, but we never really imagined he'd win. We thought he'd run nicely. We'd been so unlucky in Nationals that I almost discounted winning."

In a race of high drama that was partially overshadowed by the deaths of two horses, including Cheltenham Gold Cup winner Synchronised, Neptune Collonges finally plugged the biggest hole in Nicholls' incredible record. Obsession with the risk factor of the National detracted from what was a brilliant race and the closest finish in National history, but for Nicholls there was unbridled joy at the result.

"There were eight or nine in a line coming to the second-last, that's what you want to see in a race like that, and it was a brilliant race for everyone involved with us. I still can't believe we've done it and I still watch it nearly every day. It's a unique race, it's more public, different from the Cheltenham Festival, and it's an honour to have won it."

In the end, the Grand National did not decide the title race; it just made the run-in more comfortable for Nicholls. He would have won anyway, if only narrowly, because of another amazing triumph on the final day of the season when that

National treasure First prize of £547,267 for Neptune Collonges in the Grand National finally saw off the challenge of Nicky Henderson in the battle for the trainers' championship

old warrior Tidal Bay, after more than two years without a victory, produced a splendid weight-carrying performance to land the Bet365 Gold Cup at Sandown.

There would have been something fitting about Tidal Bay being the horse to have won it for Nicholls, as with his quirks and troubles he could have served as a passable metaphor for his trainer's season. Against all the odds, after all the ups and downs, Nicholls was champion for a seventh season in a row. It is clearly a title he has not learned to take for granted but, with jump racing's biggest prizes remorselessly struck off, all he can do now is defend the summit from all challengers.

"I never thought 20 years ago when I started that I'd win one trainers' championship, never mind seven. I know how incredibly lucky I've been and I really do appreciate that," he says. "It's hard getting to the top. Once you're there it's just as hard, if not harder, to stay there. But we relish a challenge and we will rise to it. I always look forward, not back."

If he had cared to, Nicholls could reflect with pride on another memorable season, but his sights were set on the far horizon. Once the dark clouds of early spring drifted away, the view from Ditcheat was mighty fine.

'It's hard getting to the top. Once you're there it's just as hard, if not harder, to stay there. But we relish a challenge and we will rise to it'

THE BIGGER PICTURE

Matt Sheppard, who trains in the grounds of Eastnor Castle in Herefordshire, takes smart handicap chaser Ikorodu Road (left) for exercise with stablemate Big Robert, ridden by the trainer's son Stan
DAVID DEW (RACINGPOST.COM/PHOTOS)

'I cried. I was in a mess. I went straight home, didn't ride for days and just stayed in the house'

Tony McCoy went from joy to despair with Synchronised, the Cheltenham Gold Cup winner who was struck down in the cruellest fashion at Aintree

Words by **Alastair Down**

BY TRADITION the best party of Cheltenham Festival week is held in the weighing room on the evening of the Gold Cup. The intense pressure of the meeting is lifted at last, there are triumphs for some jockeys to celebrate and disappointments to be dulled by others, with bucketloads of champagne provided by the man who

rode the most important winner of the season earlier in the day. In 2012 that man was AP, who had triumphed for JP on Synchronised.

Tony McCoy was delighted that his wife Chanelle, his dad, brothers and sisters were at Cheltenham to enjoy the moment but there was someone missing – so he sent for his daughter Eve, 4, who was driven up by the nanny to join the party on course.

"Eve made me have a running race with her round the paddock," McCoy

recalls. "It was a reminder what the most important thing was and it wasn't winning the Gold Cup. As far as she is concerned I am there to entertain her and she is not bothered by anything else."

Synchronised's Cheltenham triumph was a joyful occasion on many levels: the festival crowd is bonded to AP and it was a first Gold Cup success for jump racing's biggest benefactor, JP McManus, and as a trainer for Jonjo O'Neill, who had

won as a jockey with Alverton in 1979 and in perhaps the most dramatic renewal in the race's history on Dawn Run in 1986.

Until the 2011-12 season, Synchronised had been a handicapper; a high-class one with victories in the Welsh and Midlands Nationals but a handicapper nonetheless. After two runs in handicap hurdles, however, Synchronised was pitched into Grade 1 company in the Lexus Chase
Continues page 68

at Leopardstown's Christmas meeting and, although the ground was not as soft as he likes, he powered clear for a decisive victory. That put the Gold Cup firmly on the agenda.

"I was quietly impressed by the way he won the Lexus," McCoy says. "He quickened up well and I told Kieren McManus [JP's son] afterwards he was a good thing to be in the first three at Cheltenham as only Kauto Star or Long Run could have won the Lexus the way he did.

"I never sat on him between the Lexus and Cheltenham, but about two weeks before the Gold Cup Jonjo suddenly began to get excited about the horse – you could tell by the way he was talking. He is a brilliant trainer and God only knows how he found those three winners in three good races at this year's meeting.

"Coming to the Friday I was very happy despite the fact I hadn't ridden a winner because if I am riding well and doing nothing wrong it doesn't get me down like it used to years ago. I felt it was going to be my day. After Alderwood won the County, I convinced myself Synchronised was going to win and I wasn't dreaming."

McCoy had to work hard to make it come true, as Synchronised made a series of mistakes and struggled to go the pace. "People don't realise the Gold Cup is the most gruelling race of all. Horses might be able to do it over three miles round the likes of Kempton but three and a quarter in the Gold Cup is completely different. And it was made for Synchronised because with him you just felt him warming up and hanging on in there as things got harder.

"It was important to keep him in touch early and, although I started him in a good position, by the time we were down by the water jump first time he was flat to the boards and finding it tough. But he never gave up.

"On the final circuit at the fence at the top of the hill I pulled him to the outside and he really picked up. But that was too far from home, so I let him run back in between them and pop. He got in deep to the third-last but rounding the bend, although he had plenty of ground to make up, I knew it would be close."

Still it was far from easy. McCoy was pushing away in fifth place, six lengths behind a group of four – Time For Rupert, The Giant Bolster, Long Run and Burton Port. "Going to two out Synchronised was flat to the boards but getting closer and closer," he says. "Between the last two I just knew he was going to win and after the last he was gone, just getting going to be honest."

The champion had won the Gold Cup

before, on Mr Mulligan in 1997, but this one gave him particular pleasure. "It's the pinnacle of the sport. The Grand National may have a wider profile but from a racing man's point of view you want to win the Gold Cup. JP had never won the race and Synchronised's dam was the first winner I ever rode for him. I get on very well with JP, although we don't always agree. I must have driven him mad sometimes. He's like me – he always thinks he's right whereas I know I'm right. I feel great pride wearing his colours."

THE joy of the Gold Cup is in McCoy's face as he relives that day, which makes the events at Aintree all the harder to bear. The Gold Cup-Grand National double was last achieved by Golden Miller in 1934 but Synchronised was 7lb well-in compared with his BHA rating and, four weeks after the
Continues page 70

King of the hill McCoy after winning the Gold Cup with Synchronised (above) and on Alderwood in the County Hurdle

McCoy had 199 winners in 2011-12, 90 less than his seasonal record of 289 but still comfortably enough to win his 17th consecutive championship by 46 from perennial runner-up Richard Johnson. Having missed a crucial month of the season just after Christmas, McCoy had 100 fewer rides than Johnson but had a 27 per cent strike-rate that was bettered only by Barry Geraghty (29%) among the top 50 jockeys. The trainer who provided the champion with most winners, including Cheltenham Gold Cup winner Synchronised, was Jonjo O'Neill with 58.

McCoy's biggest wins in 2011-12

Synchronised
Gold Cup, Cheltenham

Synchronised
Lexus Chase, Leopardstown

Alderwood
County Hurdle, Cheltenham

Alderwood
Champion Novice Hurdle, Punchestown

Binocular
Christmas Hurdle, Kempton

A man for all courses

McCoy had ten or more winners at seven different courses – the next best in Britain or Ireland were Barry Geraghty and Davy Russell at three courses. Almost half of McCoy's total winners came at those seven courses: Worcester 17, Newton Abbot 16, Uttoxeter 16, Bangor 13, Ffos Las 12, Southwell 11, Leicester 10

Fairyhouse
LEADING THE FIELD

Fairyhouse Fixtures 2013

Tuesday 1st January NH
Wednesday 9th January NH
Sunday 20th January NH
Saturday 2nd February NH
Saturday 23rd February NH

Easter Festival
Sunday 31st March NH
Monday 1st April NH
Tuesday 2nd April NH

Tuesday 16th April NH
Wednesday 5th June F (E)
Wednesday 12th June F (E)

Wednesday 3rd July F (E)
Sunday 14th July F
Monday 23rd September F
Saturday 12th October NH
Wednesday 6th November NH
Wednesday 20th November NH

Premier Jump Racing Weekend
Saturday 30th November NH
Sunday 1st December NH

Saturday 14th December NH

Fairyhouse Membership 2013

Adult €160, OAP €110, Couple rate €280, Joint Fairyhouse & Navan €240, Partner rate* €280
Groups of 10+ €140 plus one free membership, Owner €130

*Both applying members should reside at same postal address

Membership Benefits:

• Free entry to all 20 fixtures • Special partner rate with Navan racecourse • Reserved car parking • Access to members lounge •
• Reciprocal days to other tracks in both Ireland and the UK • Members trips and lots more •

www.fairyhouse.ie
Fairyhouse Racecourse Ratoath County Meath Ireland
Tel: 00353 (0)18256 167 Email: info@fairyhouse.ie

Gold Cup, he was in good form. The National bid was on.

"After Synchronised had won the Lexus he was apparently a bit quiet but after the Gold Cup he seemed better than ever in his life," McCoy says. "And in the back of everyone's mind, having won a Welsh National and a Midlands National over four miles-plus, was the idea that he was a National horse."

Fate intervened in the most cruel way. Synchronised fell at Becher's Brook on the first circuit and, after galloping on riderless as McCoy got up from the turf, he suffered a hind-leg fracture at the 11th fence and was put down. The shattering news took some time to filter through and, when it did, it cast a dark shadow over the incredible finish fought out by Neptune Collonges and Sunnyhillboy, one of McManus's other three runners.

I recall with total clarity standing in the winner's enclosure after the result was announced with John Hales and other connections of Neptune Collonges in rhapsodies. A few feet away to my left stood the entire McManus clan looking crestfallen at Sunnyhillboy being beaten a nose.

Then a friend tugged my arm and, gesturing towards the McManus family, said: "I don't like the look of this." News had reached them of events on course and they stood stricken with shock. It was as bleak an on-course moment as I can ever remember.

"The sad thing was that he jumped the six fences well but then just knuckled over on landing," McCoy says. "I saw him gallop off and said to a mate down at the fence, 'I'm feeling sore but the horse is all right and that's what matters.'

"As I was in the car going back to the weighing room it came over the radio that he had been seriously injured. I cried, to be honest. I was in a mess and plenty sore in the ambulance room and when JP came in to see me I was still crying. I went straight home, didn't ride for days and just stayed in the house. The circumstances of how it happened hit me hard – one minute the horse was okay and then he got injured running loose.

"At the end of the day sport is all about trying to do things that haven't been done before. Noreen McManus had bred Synchronised and he was as much a part of the family as a horse could be. If Synchronised was a boxer you'd never get in the ring with him as he never knew when he'd had enough. He was as hard as nails but something about him was very likeable. He was like me – he wasn't much to look at but he stuck at it."

OVER the past year McCoy has had to stick at it through some horrendous falls. His mental control of physical pain

Top dogs McCoy celebrates his 17th title with Irish champion Davy Russell at Punchestown

borders on the freakish but on a couple of occasions last season he really was suffering – or "sore" as he tends to say.

"The fall that got me was at Taunton at the end of December when Laudatory came down on top of me," he says. "I broke seven ribs and punctured a lung. The doctor wanted to put me on a stretcher but I said: 'No, because it makes me look dead and I'm not dead.'

"I had some gas and air and walked to the ambulance. But when I'd been in the ambulance room for ten or 15 minutes I was finding it hard to breathe and told the doctor I was struggling. At the hospital in Taunton I had an MRI scan, which revealed the rib and lung damage.

"I rode again on the 27th or 28th of January but I was very sore and should have given it more time. It never really healed and then I had the fall from Darlan in the Betfair Hurdle at Newbury. But I rode in the bumper as I really liked the horse and would rather be sore than watch someone else on it."

I watched the Betfair alongside McCoy's old mate John Francome, not a man given to over-dramatising events. When Darlan fell, he said simply: "He could be dead." McCoy looked disturbingly pale when he got back to the stands and nobody else would have ridden again that afternoon. But two hours later he drove Shutthefrontdoor home to win the bumper by a short head. Sometimes with McCoy you don't know whether to cheer or try to have him locked up.

"I appreciate everything much more these days, whereas I used to worry about the numbers and that there might be no

more good days. I don't want not to ride horses, although I know I can't go on forever. The only time I really lost it last season was when there was a newspaper headline saying I couldn't take the falls anymore. That made me really mad."

Even after 17 consecutive titles, and at the age of 38, McCoy still has the numbers on his mind. He would like to reach 4,000 winners, he says, and he knows exactly how far he is from his target. Then, with a big grin, he adds: "I might be one winner out there – but I don't think so!"

Magic in the genes

The great Sadler's Wells produced winners of virtually every major Flat race during his illustrious stud career and Synchronised's victory added the Cheltenham Gold Cup to the roll of honour, which already included Istabraq's Champion Hurdle hat-trick.

The dam was something special, too, as far as Tony McCoy and JP McManus were concerned. Mayasta, who foaled Synchronised in 2003, had seven years earlier been the first winner ridden by McCoy wearing his future patron's green and gold hooped silks.

Little did either man know where it would lead them all these years later.

King Jonjo the fourth

Jonjo O'Neill joined an exclusive club that now has four members by adding Gold Cup victory as a trainer to his pair of wins as a jockey on Alverton (1979) and Dawn Run (1986).

The others to win the race in both roles are Danny Morgan (Morse Code in 1938 as a jockey and Roddy Owen in 1959 as a trainer), Pat Taaffe (who rode Arkle to his hat-trick in 1964-66 and also won on Fort Leney in 1968 before training 1974 winner Captain Christy) and Fred Winter (a winning rider on Saffron Tartan in 1961 and Mandarin in 1962 and the trainer of 1978 winner Midnight Court).

THE BIGGER PICTURE

The runners burst from the stalls
in a seven-furlong nursery at Lingfield
in September
EDWARD WHITAKER (RACINGPOST.COM/PHOTOS)

HEART STOPPING

Words by **Nicholas Godfrey**

Australia's darling Black Caviar led the overseas domination of Europe's big sprints but only after a disastrous end to her remarkable journey was averted at the last moment

WINNING ugly, the Americans call it. That moment when a great team or an individual performs below their best but still, somehow, manages to come out on top. It happened to Frankel at Royal Ascot in 2011, when the 20-1 shot Zoffany came uncomfortably close to him, and this year it was the turn of Black Caviar.

What mattered most was that the 'Wonder from Down Under', like Frankel, was able to remain unbeaten despite a below-par performance at Royal Ascot but, boy, was it close. Many expected a procession for Australia's sprint queen when she was sent out of the gates a 1-6 shot for the Diamond Jubilee Stakes against 13 seemingly overmatched rivals. Instead the race turned into a mad scramble for the line.

As she encountered an uphill finish for the first time in her flawless racing life, Black Caviar seemed to be feeling the burden of hyperbole just as surely as if she had been handed an extra stone of lead to hang from her saddle. But then it must be hard to run with the weight of half the world on your shoulders – or at least the expectations of a continent. "More or less the whole of antipodean London is coming," Ascot officials had told us, while back at home thousands watched live on a big screen in chilly Federation Square, Melbourne's equivalent of Trafalgar Square, at 12.45am local time.

Peter Moody, the mare's trainer, had done his best to manage expectations – "I would love nothing more than to see her come out and win by ten or 11 lengths, but we're not going to put on a show just for the Poms" – and perhaps jockey Luke Nolen had taken those words to heart more than was strictly necessary.

As the line neared and the sizeable

Aussie support at Ascot roared her on, it was clear Black Caviar wasn't going to notch her 22nd straight win in spectacular fashion – but she was going to win. Then, unaccountably, Nolen stopped riding 80 yards out. The hopes of a nation – and a dream for her owners that had been more than a year in the making – hung by a thread

NICK SMITH, Ascot's head of international racing, knew Black Caviar would be a big draw at the royal meeting. She was top of his wish list even before her winning streak went into double figures and he had quietly harboured hopes of enticing the Black Caviar team in 2011, having spoken to the owners in February that year during his annual 'recruitment' trip down under. The owners are a sporting bunch, a syndicate of ten friends and relatives put together

The morning after How the Racing Post reported Black Caviar's dramatic win

over a few beers on a boating holiday on the Murray River, which divides Victoria and New South Wales. They range from a lawyer, a doctor and an accountant to a husband-and-wife team of potato farmers, a social worker and a grandmother. Several were sold on the idea of Royal Ascot immediately. "I did think there was a slight chance when I spoke to them after the Lightning Stakes that year," Smith recalls.

Moody, however, was going to take some convincing and he quickly put the kibosh on the idea. "I'd imagine they had a pretty short conversation," Smith says. "But you couldn't say Pete was anti coming to England altogether as he'd been here before with Magnus. Actually, Pete told me later he wouldn't be bringing Black Caviar that year but they'd win anyway with her stablemate Hinchinbrook."

So Royal Ascot went ahead in 2011 minus Black Caviar – and, for that matter, minus the injured Hinchinbrook. In the meantime, Black Caviar continued to showcase her talents by winning Group 1 races for fun at home, easily mastering anything thrown at her in Melbourne, Sydney and Brisbane. She was similarly unflustered at the beginning of her five-year-old campaign and by the time the Lightning Stakes came along at Flemington in February 2012 Smith was confident he had got his girl second time around. "We didn't have to work hard," he says. "After she won the Lightning Stakes again it was a done deal as long as she didn't have a setback. They had decided they were going to do it – the only question was whether she went to Dubai first."

Moody, who had always seemed lukewarm about Royal Ascot, was by now coming around to the idea of "kicking some Pommie butt", although he still had some reservations. "The travel does worry me," said Melbourne's leading trainer, a big boy from the Queensland bush, as he contemplated an incredible journey. "It is daunting – it's certainly exciting but I'd be lying if I said I wasn't a little bit tentative, a bit nervous about it all. It is strange that we have to travel three-quarters of the way around the world to race inferior opposition for inferior prize-money so she can stamp her greatness."

You could see his point. Only the most one-eyed xenophobe, safe in their myopic outlook that nothing matters unless it happens in Blighty, could quibble with Black Caviar's achievements before she was sent on her travels. Every inch a superstar, the racehorse with "the neck of a duchess and the arse of a cook" (according to the legendary

Close call Black Caviar (nearside) just holds on in a desperate finish by a head from Moonlight Cloud (far side) and Restiadargent

Bart Cummings) had fully earned her iconic status in Australia, where she is a household name. "If I had everyone come and pat her and charged $5 for a photo, I would be a millionaire in a week," Moody said.

Australian visitors to Royal Ascot are nothing new. Since Choisir's ground-breaking twin triumphs in 2003, Takeover Target, Miss Andretti and Scenic Blast had all delivered famous victories for the southern hemisphere. This, however, was something different. Never had any equine visitor to Britain created such excitement as Black Caviar, whose autumn campaign at home was geared entirely towards getting her to Britain in the best possible shape. Previous Australian triumphs may have given the impression that there was nothing to it, but nothing could be further from the **Continues page 76** truth. Meticulous planning and no small expense would be needed to keep Black Caviar in tip-top condition at the end of an Australian season that had seen her race, on average, once a month for the previous eight months.

"It is a very arduous trip, much more so than the Breeders' Cup for European horses," Smith says. "That's only a seven- or eight-hour trip to the east coast, or maybe 12 to the west coast, whereas this was at least 30 hours from Australia with a couple of stops in Singapore and Amsterdam."

Based on two horses sharing a flight to America, the cost of a Breeders' Cup trip might be about £10,000 per horse; the entire cost of Black Caviar's three-week stay in Britain was an estimated £60,000, although Ascot is known to contribute about 50 per cent of the expenses for top international horses. There might not be the same assistance for a Wagga-Wagga

Continues page 78

Panic over
Trainer Peter Moody (right), assistant trainer Tony Haydon and jockey Luke Nolen

BLACK CAVIAR *The facts and figures*

Her syndicate owners blew their budget to buy her. Having planned to spend no more than A$125,000 (£78,000), she cost A$210,000 (£132,000) at the Inglis Melbourne Premier yearling sale in 2008

Her racing colours, designed by the daughter of syndicate member Gary Wilkie, reflect her name: salmon pink with black spots to represent the caviar roe

She has been sent off favourite for each of her 22 races, starting at odds-on for the last 21

Her best Racing Post Rating is 133 – the highest achieved by a filly or mare; at Royal Ascot she fell to 122, her lowest in Group 1 company

She is unbeaten in 22 consecutive races, equalling the record for an Australian-trained horse

Each of her last 19 victories has been a Group race, including 12 Group 1 events

Her height is 16.2 hands (164.6cm)

She weighs about 575kg – more than the average steeplechaser

She loves swimming and going to the beach

She has her own range of merchandise, from T-shirts and baseball caps to ties and keyrings

Only once before Royal Ascot had she won by less than a length, having scored by just three-quarters of a length on her fourth start in September 2009, when she stumbled at the start in Group 2 company at Flemington; she tore muscles in her chest that day and was off for four months afterwards. She won by a head at Ascot

Acclaimed Australian poet Rupert McCall has penned a five-stanza tribute entitled Of Caviar In Black, originally published in Brisbane's City North News

As well as her website, profits from which are donated to the Olivia Newton-John cancer centre, you can follow Black Caviar on Facebook, you can tweet with her on Twitter (@blackcaviar2006) or you can email her at blackcaviar@blackcaviar.net. au

Among the celebrities to have been granted an audience with Black Caviar before she visited Royal Ascot was athlete Sally Pearson, who went on to win gold in the 100m hurdles at the London Olympics

Australia's human athletes are compared to her, not the other way round. Anna Meares, who beat Victoria Pendleton to win cycling sprint gold in the velodrome, was acclaimed as 'Black Caviar on wheels'

Estimates go as high as 10,000 of the number of Australians and New Zealanders who attended Royal Ascot for the Diamond Jubilee Stakes

handicap winner whose connections fancy a tilt at the Britannia.

From the turn of the year, all roads led to Berkshire for Black Caviar. Possible trips to Hong Kong and Dubai for lavishly endowed prizes were ruled out; in retrospect, even her first victory over seven furlongs at Caulfield in February reads as a shrewd tactical move from Moody to see if she would be able to handle the stiff six furlongs at Ascot.

A short break after the Lightning Stakes preceded a couple of bloodless Group 1 victories in Adelaide two weeks apart at Morphettville. The target at Royal Ascot would be the Diamond Jubilee rather than the King's Stand, where her Aussie compatriots have a stellar record, and it was to be a one-race smash-and-grab raid, Moody having vetoed the idea of a summer-long visit. Fanciful suggestions of a titanic clash with Frankel, maybe at Goodwood in the Sussex Stakes, were never more than pie in the sky, readily dismissed by both camps.

Black Caviar's journey from Australia was unremarkable apart from her outlandish travelling garb: a specially designed Lycra suit, custom-made to aid blood flow during the flight. As robust-looking as she is, Black Caviar remains essentially a fragile animal, prone to muscle tears early in her career, so it must have been with a deal of relief to her connections that she exited the plane in one piece.

Although she arrived a couple of weeks before the race, all the serious work had been done at home and she did little more than stretch her legs while housed at Abington Place Stables on Newmarket's Bury Road. Moody and Nolen arrived much later, not in time even for a special press conference nine days before the Diamond Jubilee, where Black Caviar was the focus of attention at 5am in the morning as she did a light canter on the all-weather. In Moody's absence, stable manager Jeff O'Connor voiced a warning to Black Caviar's rivals. "She's rock-hard fit and she's ready to go," he said. "We're not here to be beaten, that's for sure."

There were questions, however. The weather wasn't playing ball, the wettest June on record ensuring Black Caviar would be racing on the softest ground she had ever encountered. The aura of Australian invincibility in sprints was dented by a lacklustre display from her compatriot Ortensia in the King's Stand. Then there was the shadow of Frankel, who added to the pressure by stamping his authority on the meeting in the very first race with his sensational 11-length victory in the Queen Anne Stakes.

Duly impressed, Moody nevertheless kept on in mischievous mood. "We all **Continues page 80**

Summer of love

Devotion and dedication lay behind Ortensia's amazing Nunthorpe triumph

Words by **Nick Pulford**

IT'S a familiar story: twenty-something Australian, single, looking for adventure, travels to England intending to stay for a few weeks and ends up sticking around for six months. The difference for Leah Gavranich, the Aussie who set up home in Newmarket for the summer, was that she wasn't a lone traveller.

Gavranich's companion was Ortensia, the less heralded of the two Australian sprint mares who travelled to Britain in search of Group 1 glory. The six-year-old mare achieved that goal with a Nunthorpe Stakes victory that, in its own way, was just as memorable as Black Caviar's nerve-jangling Golden Jubilee success.

Ortensia's story was remarkable even before her visit to Britain. She had been retired the previous year after a solid career with Tony Noonan but her owners then decided on another roll of the dice by switching her to Paul Messara's stable. The move paid off with a career-first Group 1 win at Ascot (the Perth version) and then there was nothing to lose.

The first port of call for Ortensia and Gavranich, a travelling groom for Messara, was Dubai. They took another Group 1 victory in the Al Quoz Sprint on World Cup night and, a week later, landed in Britain.

From April to October, based at Jane Chapple-Hyam's yard in Newmarket, Ortensia and Gavranich were inseparable. "I haven't had a day off," said Gavranich shortly before her return trip to Australia. "She's ridden seven days a week and I've been by her side every morning and afternoon."

Messara flew in for all but one of Ortensia's races and was in regular contact with Gavranich, who relayed information to him gathered from a helmet cam and a tracking device that measured speed, distance, heart rate and recovery. Just as important was Gavranich's intuitive bond with the mare.

"Me and her are similar – we don't really like a lot of people," Gavranich said. "She can be very standoffish but if you've got a relationship with her, she'll let you pretty much do anything with her."

At first it seemed as if things wouldn't work out. Ortensia's first run was in the King's Stand Stakes at Royal Ascot, where she boiled over before the race and was only ninth, and then the heavy ground was against her in the July Cup. Fourth place at Newmarket wasn't too bad in the circumstances, however, and Messara decided to extend her stay.

Glorious Goodwood was the next destination and this time, with conditions in her favour, Ortensia showed her true form by winning the Group 2 King George Stakes. That victory capped a memorable week for Gavranich. "I had my birthday here," she said. "I was 26 on July 31 and the next day my mare turned seven on southern hemisphere time. We shared our birthdays and then on the Friday she won at Goodwood."

Gavranich's devotion to Ortensia was evident as much as ever that week. "I just had a quiet dinner for my birthday," she said. "I'm not one to go out and party when I know I've got to get up and ride my horse at six in the morning."

Ortensia had momentum now, as well as a fast-developing special relationship with William Buick that was to reach a spectacular peak in the Nunthorpe at York. She was outpaced in the early stages but Buick didn't panic and, having switched to the far side, he conjured an amazing finish from the willing mare. Ortensia got up close home to win by a neck from Spirit Quartz, who had also been runner-up at Goodwood.

"At York she came from an impossible position," Gavranich said. "If she's on song, she's very good, but if something goes wrong it really goes wrong. She hit her peak at York, I don't think you'd see her better than that."

She went wrong again in the Haydock Sprint Cup but, as with her Ascot and Newmarket defeats, there was a reason. This time she was found to have an inch-long cut to her fetlock after the race, which explains why she was a well-beaten 12th.

Gavranich left with only good memories. "I gave up a lot to be with her, but opportunities like this don't come around very often. It's been six months, but it feels like a few weeks, it doesn't feel that long at all."

For that incredible display at York alone, it was all worth it.

 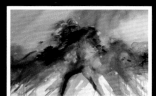  

saw the best local horse Frankel win here on Tuesday, but he's never going to leave the UK, his owners will never take him away from home," he said. "This mare's owners have had the balls to put her on a plane and travel halfway around the world. That is something phenomenal. Imagine having something this good and sharing it with the rest of the world."

WHAT the world saw in the last 80 yards of the Diamond Jubilee Stakes was dramatic and, for her many fans at Ascot and back home in Australia, heart-stopping. Nolen, who had ridden her to 18 of her 21 victories, has always played down his role in the Black Caviar story, claiming he was "just lucky to be in the right place at the right time", but for a few anguished seconds he must have felt like the wrong man at the wrong time. When he stopped riding, with the winning post almost within touching distance, the result was in serious doubt for the first time since Black Caviar's trip to Royal Ascot had been first mooted.

French-trained rivals Moonlight Cloud and Restiadargent challenged strongly as Nolen, realising his error, desperately chucked the reins at Black Caviar. The mare lengthened again, clawing her way to the line in the last four or five strides, but she and Moonlight Cloud could not be separated as they flashed past the post to a cacophony of noise from the stands. The photo-finish showed Black Caviar had got home by the most dramatic of heads. There is no official winning margin called 'skin of the teeth'.

Ashen-faced, Nolen performed a memorable mea culpa. He had little alternative, having jeopardised Black Caviar's place in the pantheon with his own bid for racing's hall of infamy. "Relief is the first emotion," the jockey admitted. "I think my heart has only just started again – it was pilot error but I got away with it. I probably underestimated the testing track here. She'd had enough and I just let her idle and that big engine throttled right down." Then, in a quote destined to go down in racing history, he added: "I shit myself duly!"

Nolen continued: "It's unfortunate because we're going to talk more about my brain-fade than the horse's fantastic effort. Her determination got her there. She's now 22 from 22 and that's what it should be about – it would have been a travesty if she had got beat because of pilot error. I let her coast. It was an error every apprentice is taught not to do but I got away with it, thank God."

Nolen was looking at a 42-day suspension if he hadn't got away with it, but Moody refused to criticise his jockey. ''I believe she was probably out on her feet a furlong and a half out," he said.

Little piece of history Danny Shum leads in Little Bridge, the first Hong Kong horse to win at Ascot

'The photo showed Black Caviar had got home by the most dramatic of heads. There is no official winning margin called "skin of the teeth"'

"Only her grit and ability got her home. Luke was trying to look after her and, while he nearly got caught short, he got the job done."

Clearly she hadn't performed anywhere close to her optimum level and Racing Post Ratings said it was her worst run in a Group 1 race. Truth to tell, she didn't look great in the parade ring: a bit hairy, even to untrained eyes. "I was talking to serious paddock watchers and they thought she was over the top," recalls Smith, who was as relieved as her connections that she got over the line.

"She was Australia's horse but she became our horse," he says. "So much was hanging on her running at the meeting.

In the run-up, every time the phone rang from Newmarket I was in a panic in case something had gone wrong and, while it was a great week, it would have been a bit flat at the end if she had been beaten in those circumstances. It's bittersweet because you'd love to see the owners jumping up and down and all they could have been thinking was relief that they'd got away with it. We all know she wasn't at her best and it wasn't a good ride but it was pretty dramatic all the same."

It wasn't the dominant performance many had expected, nothing to compare with what Frankel had produced at the start of the week, but her connections insisted there were no regrets. "We never expect dominance – we never ask her for dominance," Moody said. "You've only got to win by a quarter of an inch."

Neil Werrett, the mare's managing part-owner, agreed. "That's what we were prepared to win by and she got the job done. I don't think anyone has regretted bringing the horse here. We've met the Queen and the horse got a pat

Mission accomplished

Little Bridge's triumph in the King's Stand put Hong Kong trainer Danny Shum in the spotlight

Words by **Nick Pulford**

LITTLE BRIDGE is the most popular horse in Hong Kong – it's official and everything after an end-of-season public vote – but he wasn't the most celebrated winner at Royal Ascot when he took the King's Stand Stakes ahead of leading British hope Bated Breath and better-fancied overseas challengers. "A solitary, echoing holler amid a crescendo of utter silence," was how the Racing Post reported the reaction to his victory.

Black Caviar garnered nearly all the attention among the overseas raiding party on Royal Ascot and Little Bridge, along with his little-known trainer Danny Shum, went virtually unnoticed as they quietly went about their business in Newmarket during final preparations for the King's Stand. But, make no mistake, this was a raid as well planned and executed as any in recent years.

To understand how Shum went from Hong Kong to Royal Ascot success with his first overseas runner, it is necessary to go back 40 years to an intrepid 18-hour journey from the relative backwater of Singapore to the United States. The target for Malaysian-born trainer Ivan Allan was the Washington DC International and, although the trip ended in misfortune when the Lester Piggott-ridden Jumbo Jet was brought down by a fallen horse at halfway while in a promising position, it

was still one of the more remarkable stories in the pioneering days of international racing.

Allan, best known in Britain as the owner of 1984 St Leger winner Commanche Run, did not stop there. He plundered Hong Kong's big prizes from Singapore and, after setting up base in Hong Kong, went further afield. In 2000 he became the first Hong Kong trainer to win an overseas Group 1 when high-class miler Fairy King Prawn scored in Japan and in other years he had near-misses in the Japan Cup and Dubai Duty Free.

At Allan's side for most of the Hong Kong years was Shum, the trusted right-hand man who oversaw the preparation of the Allan raiders on their foreign trips and knew exactly what to do when he sent Little Bridge for the King's Stand. He wasn't testing the water; he was determined to make a big splash. "I had this planned for quite a long time because I love Britain. It is a fantastic country for horseracing. To win there was a dream for me."

Shum, 52, who started training in his own right in 2003, had waited patiently for the right horse to send overseas and, as Royal Ascot approached, he was sure Little Bridge was the one.

Under orders from the Hong Kong Jockey Club not to spend more than two weeks away from his commitments at home, Shum arrived in Newmarket a week after Little Bridge and took the reins, literally, to ride him in his crucial final pieces

of work. "I worked him on the Al Bahathri gallop four days before the race and he did so well that when the jockey arrived in England I told him, 'He's better than you thought. He's improving and he's got a very good chance.'"

With Zac Purton, the jockey, Shum walked the course at Ascot the day before the King's Stand. A week earlier, he had taken Little Bridge there to familiarise him with the track. It wasn't new to the trainer, as he had been to Ascot with Allan-trained runners, but he was leaving nothing to chance. He did his research on Little Bridge's rivals and talked through the race with Purton.

"All the speed horses, all the good horses, were close to him. That was good because he likes a fast-run race," Shum says. "We talked about how the race might develop, but it was a surprise that he was the first to break when they jumped out. I was worried then he had no cover, but he was so fresh and well it didn't matter."

Having taken a lead from Tangerine Trees, Purton struck for home a furlong out and held off Bated Breath by three-quarters of a length. Although Cape Of Good Hope had landed the Golden Jubilee in 2005 when the royal meeting was held at York, Little Bridge was the first Hong Kong-trained horse to win on the hallowed Ascot turf.

Allan, Shum's mentor, tried and failed in that quest, but Shum had done it at the first attempt.

from the Queen, so if this was the end, she's ended on a high. I'm sure many owners would love to be living the dream of owning and winning at Ascot. Unfortunately, England didn't see the best of Black Caviar. At the same time, we're very thankful she won."

The question left hanging in the air after Royal Ascot was whether Black Caviar had run her last race – a scenario that looked all the more probable when it emerged she had been injured during the race, sustaining soft-tissue damage. She had suffered similar problems before, but Moody said it was the worst he had seen her after a race. Soon after she returned home to Melbourne, the trainer ruled out the spring carnival, saying she would not be ready to race until after the turn of the year, if at all.

Whatever the future holds, Black Caviar's place in racing history is assured and, while the Diamond Jubilee was not her best race, it was in many ways the most memorable. She came, we saw and she conquered – but only just.

Greatness already assured

BRITISH racegoers may not have seen the best of Black Caviar but she is nothing short of a phenomenon and, having grabbed a slice of racing history with the longest winning streak ever seen at the major metropolitan city-centre tracks, she equalled the overall mark for an Australian-trained horse with her 22nd victory in the Diamond Jubilee Stakes at Royal Ascot. Racing's answer to Don Bradman thereby matched the 22-win record held by Miss Petty and Sava Jet, who both raced only at low-grade Queensland bush tracks.

Black Caviar, the highest-rated filly or mare in the history of Racing Post Ratings, was world champion sprinter in both 2010 and 2011 and will be again in the World Thoroughbred Rankings for 2012. Injuries restricted her to just five starts in her first two seasons before she earned her place in racing folklore at four and five with a series of breathtaking

victories in Australia. Eight wins as a four-year-old in 2010-11 were followed by eight more in 2011-12, as shec clocked up 11 Group 1 wins at various tracks in four different Australian states over those two seasons.

In March 2011 she first achieved her highest RPR of 133 with an electrifying weight-carrying performance in the Newmarket Handicap. That rating, hit for a second time the same year in the TJ Smith Stakes at Randwick, is the best RPR for a sprinter since Dayjur's 136 in 1990. Racing Post historian John Randall says she is the best female sprinter of all time and Australasia's greatest ever filly or mare over any distance.

By the time of the Diamond Jubilee, her official mark of 132 meant she theoretically had a full stone in hand of 118-rated Moonlight Cloud, her closest Royal Ascot rival. Which, as it turned out, was just as well.

ROYAL ASCOT
in pictures

1 Patriotic fervour was hard to miss in Diamond Jubilee year

2 The John Gosden-trained Fallen For You lands the Coronation Stakes

3 Estimate becomes the first royal winner at the meeting since 2008 with victory in the Queen's Vase

4 The Queen with Sir Michael Stoute (left), Estimate's trainer, and her racing adviser John Warren

5 Big hats were still in — even if fascinators, mini-skirts, midriffs and cravats were out under the strict new dress code

6 Frankie Dettori celebrates his Gold Cup triumph on Colour Vision

7 Thomas Chippendale leads a King Edward VII Stakes one-two for Sir

Henry Cecil ahead of Frankel's full-brother Noble Mission

8 Adam Kirby and Reckless Abandon after the jockey's first Royal Ascot success in the Norfolk Stakes

9 William Buick after his fifth winner of the meeting, Camborne in the Duke of Edinburgh Handicap, but he was pipped to the jockeys' award by Ryan Moore

10 The field flashes past the grandstand in the Ascot Stakes

11 Princess Highway wins the Ribblesdale Stakes, in the week her owner-breeder Walter Haefner died at the age of 101

12 Ryan Moore takes the Britannia on 6-1 favourite Fast Or Free

13 Black Caviar fever takes hold on the final day

31 RIDES, **SEVEN** RACE MEETINGS, **FIVE** WINNERS, **ONE** SUSPENSION, **983** MILES TRAVELLED, **SIX** MORNINGS ON THE GALLOPS, **TWO** ROUNDS OF GOLF, **30** MINI-CHOCOLATE BARS . . .

. . . seven days on the title trail with top Flat jockey Richard Hughes in July Cup week, one of the busiest of the racing year

Words by **Lee Mottershead**
Pictures by **Edward Whitaker**

Monday

THE WEEK starts as the previous one started and the next one will start as well. For Richard Hughes, every week and almost every day starts this way. The alarm clock sounds, the jockey stirs, out of bed, into a pair of jeans and down to Herridge. Until he stops being a jockey, this is how his days will always start.

Herridge, with its long, tree-lined drive, acres of gallops, a trainer's house

and, on this July Monday, 180 horses, is a regular and favourite haunt of the man they call Hughesie. Less than a ten-minute drive from his own home, it is where his father-in-law Richard Hannon lives and trains. There is a second yard a stone's throw away at East Everleigh, but Herridge is where Hughes is happiest. This morning, though, the almost unfailingly chirpy jockey has reason to be a little bit despondent.

Life itself is grand. Hughes got back the previous evening from a weekend in Hastings spent glamping – upmarket camping to the uninitiated

– during which he got to spend some valuable family time with wife Lizzie, four-year-old son Harvey and two-year-old daughter Phoebe. "We had a great time," Hughes says. "In the morning Harvey went off to get some wood, then when he got back we put the stove on and made bacon and a big pot of scrambled eggs. After that we went off to the beach. I skipped lunch and had four 99s instead. I would sacrifice most food for ice cream."

Now, though, is not the time for ice cream, nor indeed is it ice cream weather. The skies overhead

threaten rain. More rain. It has rained, seemingly incessantly, for weeks. Flat racing has repeatedly been staged on ground more accustomed to winter jumping and, like turf tracks up and down the land, Hannon's gallops are saturated.

Prior to setting foot on the sodden land, 40 of Hannon's Herridge inmates circle a warm-up ring. Janoub Nibras, a short-head winner of a two-runner race when 1-7 at Kempton last time, gets a smack down the shoulder from his rider, Elvis Singh. It makes no difference **Continues page 86**

Continues page 86

as seconds later the errant juvenile whips round, causing Singh to be nearly dislodged and Hughes to immediately take note. "He's fresh," he says from a standing position. "If he runs in a nursery this week, he'll win." Elsewhere in the group of 40 someone sings the old Fleetwood Mac line 'Thunder only happens when it's raining', which seems somehow timely, and Hughes prepares to be legged up on an unraced two-year-old named Colmar Kid, whose racing career is expected to begin at Newbury on Friday.

Hughes takes Colmar Kid first up an uphill all-weather gallop before directing him on to another part of Hannon's property, a vast expanse of green grass in the middle of which are sets of small marker poles, laid out as a channel for galloping horses. Colmar Kid goes in the right place and goes quite quickly, much to the delight of Herridge head lad Tony Gorman. "He's very nice," Gorman says. "Everything about him is nice."

Hughes expects to be riding Colmar Kid at Newbury on Friday. Quite what Hughes will be riding on Saturday, and indeed where, is unclear. Owing to Newmarket's desire to stage the July Cup on a Saturday, the card is now positioned in a slot that also includes York's John Smith's Cup and, for one year only, the Weatherbys Super Sprint at Newbury. For Hannon and Hughes, this is not in the least bit helpful, for while the reigning champion trainer makes few forays to York outside the Dante and Ebor festivals, Newbury and Newmarket are both happy hunting grounds.

"It's a bloody cock-up and it's all Newmarket's fault," says Hannon, cigarette in one hand, cup of coffee in the other. Any moment now, his racing secretary will supplement Sheikh Fahad's Strong Suit for the July Cup, whose principal supporting race, the Superlative Stakes, could play host to Coventry Stakes runner-up Olympic Glory. At Newbury, however, Hannon will be represented by his usual large quota of runners in the Super Sprint, while one of the stable's most promising first-season inmates, Toronado, is a possible runner in the card's opening race.

"Do you know where you're going yet?" asks Hannon. "Wherever Toronado runs," says Hughes, surprisingly unequivocal. "We'll run him at Newbury then," says Hannon, whose son and heir, Richard junior, is just yards away handing out cups of tea and coffee to visiting owners and a Racing Post journalist.

"You'll be able to go on to Salisbury's evening meeting if you ride at Newbury," Hannon notes. Hughes replies by saying he is not yet sure whether he will ride at Salisbury. "The Queen's got a runner,

you'll be going," insists Hannon, firm and clear, his response a reminder of who is boss.

For now, the uncertainty continues. Thank heavens, then, for the certainty that on Mondays in the summer Hughes knows how he will spend the afternoon and evening. The afternoon is all about playing golf. The evening is all about riding at Windsor. As he begins to wheel his golf trolley towards the clubhouse of Tidworth Garrison Golf Club his mobile rings. It is Sir Alex Ferguson,

'Hughes is successful at the golf but less so at Windsor. Eurytheus fails to fire. The same applies to Hughes's other mounts. Most unusually, he returns home from a Monday night at Windsor barren'

owner of Eurystheus, one of Hughes's Windsor mounts. Hughes says something optimistic to Ferguson before meeting up with fellow jockey and Hannon stalwart Pat Dobbs for 18 holes. Hughes is successful at the golf but less so at Windsor. Eurytheus fails to fire. The same applies to Hughes's other mounts. Most unusually, he returns home from a Monday night at Windsor barren.

Tuesday

"The problem is that our horses, as a rule, tend not to like soft ground," explains Hughes as he waits to say hello to his still-to-be chosen mount during Tuesday morning's first lot.

That indifference to the ground perhaps explains why the runner-up to Paul Hanagan in the 2010 jockeys' championship is enduring an unusually fruitless period. Since riding four winners on Saturday, June 30, nine days have

passed and Hughes has not ridden a single winner. Nine days will become ten as, with no afternoon action south of Wolverhampton, the Wiltshire-based rider has opted to take an afternoon off. Not, however, a morning off.

"Get a lead, get a lead," shouts Gorman as another huge batch of horses circles round waiting to be let loose on the all-weather gallop. Instructions are dished out to those who need to be instructed. "You stay out here and just walk and trot," he tells an Indian rider, who is then informed his mount "has just been castrated".

Very much still in possession of all his attributes is Olympic Glory, on whom Hughes does his first bit of riding that day. As he gets off, a concerned expression takes over his face. "He didn't go well," Hughes says. A little later a good reason for the indifferent performance becomes apparent when Julie Wood's potential

star is found to be ever so slightly but ever so definitely lame. A question mark suddenly hangs over his participation at Newmarket.

As for Hughes's participation at Newmarket, a plan has been hatched. The Darley July Cup is due to be run at 2.40pm, one hour after the Superlative. The Weatherbys Super Sprint is not off until 3.50pm. The gap between the two feature races is hardly huge but it's one that can be bridged with the help of an aeroplane. Luckily, Hannon has one at his disposal.

The dash between two tracks will make for a busy afternoon but at least it makes riding at the two meetings possible. So, it seems, until Hughes arrives at Sunningdale, scene of his latest 18 holes. A phone call tells him Newmarket has changed the time of the July Cup to 3.20pm.

Thank heavens for the golf.

All in a day's work – and play Hughes at the Herridge yard of Richard Hannon, in the saddle on the juvenile Colmar Kid on his way to the gallops and in his workout, and out on the golf course

Wednesday

No golf today. Hughes is returning to his role as a jockey, a role in which he could badly do with a winner. Not that the drought is bothering him even with ground to make up in the championship.

"I'd say it would play on some people's minds but not mine," Hughes says. "Whatever trainer is sending out the most winners, his jockey will be riding the most winners. Richard hasn't been sending out his usual number of winners because the ground hasn't been suiting our horses. Things will change."

There are plenty of chances for things to change at Lingfield but the early omens aren't good. In the card's opening race Hughes finishes seventh of nine. In the second event, a one-mile-one-furlong handicap, he partners a 58-rated filly called Authoritarian, who goes in close pursuit of leader Eightfold all the

Continues page 88

way down the straight. It looks from the stands as though she is sure to go past but, despite considerable urging from the saddle, does not. For his part in her head defeat, Hughes receives around seven per cent of the £503.25 second prize and a two-day whip ban. The former annoys him. The latter does not.

"I stepped over the mark," he admits. "She needed a smack after only three furlongs and was fully off the bridle early in the straight. I hit her 11 times in the space of three furlongs and knew I had passed my limit, so I put my stick down and sacrificed the race. That was the most annoying aspect of the incident. If you get suspended for misuse of the whip you at least want to have the consolation of having won. I didn't but I also didn't have any reason to be critical of the stewards' decision. It would have been very hard for the stewards not to ban me. I was probably a little complacent."

Hughes's next three mounts are all beaten. Mollyow, at 47 one of the lowest-rated animals Hughes will ride all year, is touched off in the two-miler. Thirty minutes later he finishes third of four on an evens favourite. His last 30 rides have all been defeated. There the drought ends. Jack Of Diamonds, evens favourite for a sprint maiden run amid thunder, lightning and pouring rain, gets off the mark and gets his rider back among the winners.

So bad is the lightning during the finale that officials decide it would not be safe to use starting stalls. "The weather's driving us all bonkers," says Hughes on his way out of the racecourse. "We started the day with the turf track nearly riding good. Eddie Ahern and I were sat in the weighing room and agreed that if the sun had kept shining the ground would have dried out to good to firm. After 15 minutes' rain it was bordering on heavy."

Hughes has less reason to complain

than Ahern. Both had planned to ride at Kempton's evening meeting. Hughes makes it there, but Ahern doesn't. He barely makes it out of Lingfield. "Eddie's car got stuck in water leaving the track," Hughes explains.

This summertime, the living is not so easy.

Thursday

Hughes is back on a roll at just the right time. The previous night he made it two winners on the day when taking Kempton's nightcap on Noel Quinlan's heavily punted Abriachan.

"I can imagine Noel watched the closing stages of the race with a smile on his face," Hughes says. "He rang me earlier in the day and said that, although he realised this was the 9.20 race on a Wednesday night and it might not be the most important thing in the world for me, it was very important to him. He asked me if I knew what he meant. I told him that I did indeed."

Hughes rarely fails to understand what people mean. With Hannon, however, there is never a chance of not grasping his meaning and his antagonism towards Newmarket is clear on this first day of the track's July festival.

Before leaving for the races, Hannon's son Richard jnr directs proceedings on the gallops, where a team of Argentinian polo players has come to watch. "She

Home comforts Hughes relaxes in the bath; wife Lizzie with their children Harvey and Phoebe

would do you for polo," says Hannon jnr as a nimble juvenile filly speeds past. "Mind, she'd cost you £300,000." Not long after, Hughes sets off to Newmarket. He doesn't expect to ride a winner and does not, although the stable is successful with Alhebayeb in the Group 2 July Stakes. The colt is the first Group winner Hannon has trained for Hamdan Al Maktoum. Understandably, but unfortunately for the yard's stable jockey, Hamdan's retained rider Paul Hanagan – Hughes's nemesis in the epic championship battle of 2010 – has first pick of all the owner's horses.

It proves to be an expensive day. Hughes flies to Newmarket and then on to the evening fixture at Epsom. That's £800 in travel costs with no winners to eat into the amount coughed up. Fortunately, a long day ends with very little spent on food. There was yoghurt for breakfast, then a little coffee and chocolate at home before leaving (the Hughes family fridge is full of chocolate). More chocolate was nibbled through the afternoon but, boosting the quality of the rider's diet, Matty the tea boy made him a chicken salad sandwich at Epsom, which he ate on the way home. After a cup of tea in the kitchen he went to bed.

"When you're as busy as hell you don't think about food," he says.

Just as well really.

Friday

Hughes was faced with a difficult choice in the Cherry Hinton Stakes. Hannon's two runners both have obvious chances. City Image won a Listed race over the course and distance on her previous start, while Maureen could not have been more impressive when getting off the mark first time out. It's a tough call. He thinks

Continues page 90

'It proves to be an expensive day. Hughes flies to Newmarket and then on to the evening fixture at Epsom. That's £800 in travel costs with no winners to eat into the amount coughed up'

Jockey Club Estates

Newmarket Training Grounds
"Centre of Excellence"

The Jockey Club
1750

• 2500 (1000 ha) acres • 19 miles (31 km) of all weather gallops • 50 miles (80 km) of turf gallops incl. 5 peat moss gallops and a watered gallop • Turf and all weather schooling facilities • 2 trotting rings • 6 lunging rings • 6 out of 10 previous Oaks winners have been trained in Newmarket.

It is our passion and purpose to provide the finest facilities in the world for the training of Thoroughbred racehorses. Keep your horses close to some of the world's leading equine facilities, including veterinary and research centres, farriers, Tattersalls, Newmarket Racecourses and more. Open 365 days a year and maintained by a skilled and dedicated team of professional gallopsmen.

Watch our new DVD on your smart phone or on our website, or email us your postal address and we will send you a free copy.

Contact info: Phone: +44 (0) 1638 664151
Email: estates@thejockeyclub.co.uk • Twitter: @NewmarketGallop
www.jockeyclubestates.co.uk

Jockey Club Rooms

The Jockey Club Rooms sits in its own immaculate lawned and walled gardens, in the very heart of Newmarket, offering a perfect and tranquil setting for your Wedding Day.

Wedding Parties are offered exclusivity of the "Rooms" for their entire stay and in addition complimentary use of our Bridal Suite. With a dedicated Wedding Planning Team supported by our House Butlers, the Jockey Club Rooms offers a truly unique and memorable experience.

Tel: 01638 663101 Fax: 01638 664170
Jockey Club Rooms, 101 High Street, Newmarket, Suffolk, CB8 8JL
Email: info@jockeyclubrooms.co.uk **Web:** www.jockeyclubrooms.co.uk **twitter** **facebook**

Jockey Club Rooms

long and hard, but on the basis that he can't decide between the two he decides to ride neither and goes to Newbury instead.

The reason for his choice of destination is not entirely linked to confusion over the Cherry Hinton duo. A handful of Hannon's owners were brought into the yard by Hughes, the owners of unraced two-year-old Montiridge representing some of that number. Hughes is a fan of Montiridge in Newbury's seven-furlong maiden but he also wants to ride the likeable Colmar Kid in the same race. At first the maiden looks likely to divide, which is good, but then not enough horses are declared and it doesn't, which is bad. Hughes picks Montiridge, who not surprisingly starts a shorter price than Colmar Kid, but as confirmation that the stablemate is also well regarded he is backed from a morning high of 20-1 into 8-1. He disappoints but Montiridge copes well with the desperate ground and wins easily against more experienced horses.

"I really wanted to ride Montiridge," Hughes says. "The lads who own him were among those who helped me fly around the country when I was chasing Paul Hanagan in the 2010 championship. When I saw the horse for the first time as a yearling I told them he would be a good one for them to buy. I spoke to them on Tuesday and told them we would run at Newbury, but I warned them that on heavy ground against horses who had run well already, he would need to be something special to win. I knew he was a good horse but to win in those circumstances he must be really good."

It turns out to be a profitable day for Hughes as he also lands the six-furlong fillies' maiden on Amberley Heights. Although the first to admit when he has ridden a bad race, he is also prepared to acknowledge a very good ride. This was one of those.

"She's a grand little filly but we thought she would need the run," he says. "I must have been 12 lengths off at halfway but I nursed her into it and managed to get her to win. There are some races you win

when you don't necessarily think you were on the best horse, and this was one of those occasions."

Hughes is happy and leaves Newbury having ridden well and made some good decisions. Maureen does better than City Image but finds one too good at Newmarket. The journey home from Newbury is shorter as well.

Saturday

The soft ground has been enough to prevent Toronado running at Newbury and enough to force the abandonment of Salisbury's evening card but not enough to stop the fast-ground lover Strong Suit taking up his supplementary entry in the Darley July Cup. Hughes is off to Newmarket.

On conditions he knows Strong Suit will hate, the stable jockey does not expect much from Sheikh Fahad's colt and has written as much in his weekly Racing Post column. He is also not sure what to expect from Olympic Glory given that the juvenile was lame earlier in the week.

Both perform better than expectations. Olympic Glory travels smoothly through the

Continues page 92

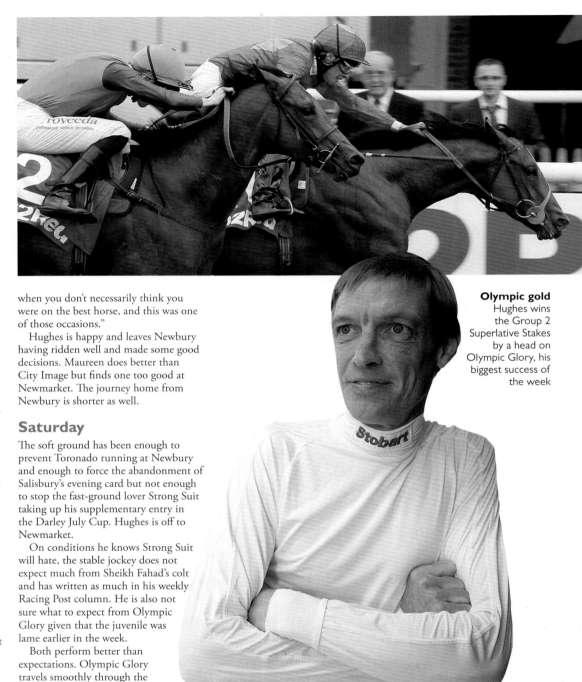

Olympic gold
Hughes wins the Group 2 Superlative Stakes by a head on Olympic Glory, his biggest success of the week

---

Richard Hughes was making rapid strides in the British Flat jockeys' championship by midsummer – but only after conceding a significant head start to his rivals when he was handed a 50-day ban during his winter riding stint in India.

In a wide-open year Hughes knew this was his best chance of a first title – "I'd love to taste how it feels," he said in his Racing Post column – and

he was on the back foot immediately.

The suspension was the result of an arcane rule that does not exist in Britain – whereby jockeys in India are required to ride to the trainer's instructions – and Hughes fought a long battle to have the decision overturned or at least not to have it applied in Britain.

The BHA stood by its obligation to uphold bans imposed in other racing

jurisdictions, however, and Hughes had to sit out the first month of the championship.

Ryan Moore, Paul Hanagan and the other main contenders were all well into double figures by the time Hughes resumed on May 1, although the poor weather in April had limited the damage to his title hopes.

At the end of July Cup week, Hughes was 18 behind the

pace-setting Moore and starting to hit top gear. The wheel of fortune turned his way when Moore broke his wrist in a fall in August, although Hughes had almost caught up by that stage and was already odds-on for the title.

By September, with no other challenger in sight, some bookmakers felt confident enough to declare Hughes the winner and pay out early. They were proved right.

EXPERIENCE THRILLING RACING

at our racecourses across the UK

With over 500 racedays to choose from throughout the year, you'll find a great day out whatever the occasion.

Racing & Leisure Group

www.arenaracingcompany.co.uk

T: 0207 802 5120   **E:** info@arenaracingcompany.co.uk

BATH ■ BRIGHTON ■ CHEPSTOW ■ DONCASTER ■ FFOS LAS ■ FOLKESTONE ■ FONTWELL PARK ■ GREAT YARMOUTH ■ HEREFORD
LINGFIELD PARK ■ NEWCASTLE ■ ROYAL WINDSOR ■ SEDGEFIELD ■ SOUTHWELL ■ UTTOXETER ■ WOLVERHAMPTON ■ WORCESTER

Arena Racing Corporation Limited. Registered in England and Wales No. 00857819. Registered office: Millbank Tower, 21-24 Millbank, London, SW1P 4QP

Group 2 Superlative Stakes but, having cruised into the lead, begins to run out of puff up the final hill. He runs like a horse who is not quite cherry ripe, which he isn't, but he still wins. Strong Suit is only eighth but goes well enough for long enough to convince the man on top that sprinting could be his game.

Reflecting on his day, Hughes says: "I rode Olympic Glory on Tuesday morning and told the boss I wasn't happy with the way he moved. We brought him in and it was obvious he wasn't 100 per cent sound. The farrier had a look at him and found a corn on his foot. He had three days off but we declared him hoping he would come good and he did.

"With Strong Suit we decided we had already supplemented him, so there wasn't much to lose by running. We know he can't go on soft ground but at halfway I was going so well I had take a pull. When I let him down he got stuck in the Dip, but we've learned he's definitely quick enough for six furlongs."

Any Saturday on which you win a Group 2 is a good Saturday but the victory of Olympic Glory and the defeat of Strong Suit highlight to Hughes that, while injuries can be overcome, the weather cannot.

Sunday

Lizzie Hughes, like any Flat jockey's wife, sees precious little of her husband in the summer. She does, therefore, insist on one rule. If Richard is not riding on a Sunday, it becomes a family day, which means no golf. Hughes does not seek to wriggle out of the rule, for the time spent with Harvey and Phoebe is the time he enjoys most.

On this Sunday he spends it with Harvey, Phoebe and at least 40 others, all of them squeezed into the vast kitchen ruled and run by Hannon's wife Jo. It's a Hannon family get-together, organised to celebrate a trip home from their emigrated daughter Clare and her husband Martin.

In between talking to the various members of the Hannon clan and their friends, Hughes catches a glimpse of an occasional bit of golf on TV – it's only bending the rules – before wrapping up his week with a trip to Andover to attend a meeting of Alcoholics Anonymous.

He will attend more such meetings over the weeks ahead. It's part of his routine, just like mornings on the gallops, afternoons and evenings on the racecourse, family days, rounds of golf, chocolate and hot baths.

This was a week in the life of Richard Hughes. For much of the year it could have been any week. He would not have it any other way.

AND THEN THIS HAPPENED . . . *Hughes's own version of the magnificent seven*

A PLACE IN HISTORY

Hughes became only the second jockey in British racing history to win seven races on one card. The other, of course, was Frankie Dettori with his Magnificent Seven at Ascot on September 28, 1996.

Dettori won every race on one of the biggest cards of the year, including the Queen Elizabeth II Stakes on Mark Of Esteem. Hughes's feat does not really compare, not only because it took place at a low-grade meeting but also because he rode one loser on the eight-race Windsor card.

The world record for the most wins on one card is nine by Eddie Castro at Calder, Florida, on June 4, 2005.

HUGHES'S SUPER SEVEN

Pivotal Movement (picture 1)
Trainer: Richard Hannon 13-8jf

East Texas Red (picture 2) Richard Hannon 5-2f

Embankment (picture 3) Amanda Perrett 7-1

Magic Secret (picture 4) Jeremy Gask 4-1f

Links Drive Lady (picture 5) Dean Ivory 5-2f

Duke Of Clarence (picture 6) Richard Hannon 7-4f

Mama Quilla (picture 7) William Haggas 15-8f

Cumulative odds 10,168-1

Windsor wonderland

THE two events were almost exactly a year apart, but on both occasions Richard Hughes left the racing world stunned.

On the evening of October 13, 2011, the Racing Post's website ran a story that rocked racing. 'Richard Hughes quits in protest at new whip rules' was the headline to an article that reported how one of the sport's most successful riders was resolved to ending his career unless the BHA amended strict new whip regulations that had resulted in him receiving a controversial suspension at Kempton. Amid talk of strike action, the BHA listened, the regulations were amended and Hughes resumed a career that peaked in the most glorious fashion on October 15, 2012.

The venue was not Ascot but nearby Windsor, and it was not Frankie but Hughesie, yet the number was still seven and the outcome every bit as magnificent.

Hughes had long believed he might one day go through a six-race Monday evening at Windsor unbeaten. "I always thought it was possible," he reflected later. "Whenever I go to Windsor I expect to win the juvenile maiden for Richard Hannon, so that's normally one in the bank, but there's often a claimer or a seller on the card and we struggle to find horses for those."

The October 15 fixture at Windsor was in the afternoon and, with his first championship already as good as won, Hughes did not quite go through the card. Nor did he win six races; he won seven.

As per his prediction, he landed the juvenile maiden for Hannon. The winner's name was Pivotal Movement, who started a clean sweep of the first five races for Hughes. It was then that Ryan Moore, a little weary having flown in that day from Canada, left Windsor racecourse earlier than expected having told his good friend, at that stage minus a ride in the concluding race, that he could take his place on the finale's warm favourite.

That made going through the card possible. Defeat in the sixth race scuppered that hope but success in the seventh left Hughes, unruffled and in no way nervous, on the brink of achieving something only Frankie Dettori had previously managed in Britain. Aboard the William Haggas-trained Mama Quilla he duly did it, triggering numerous interviews, countless autographs and a few well-earned bags of crisps and the odd glass of cola down the pub.

"Twelve months ago people were desperate to talk to me, but not for very positive reasons," Hughes wrote in his Racing Post column that Saturday. "On this occasion, being in the news has been so much more enjoyable. Everything has changed and entirely for the better."

Words by Lee Mottershead

SEVEN
IS A MAGIC NUMBER

Nicky Henderson was the dominant force as a select band of jump racing's finest put themselves in the history books at the 2012 Cheltenham Festival

Words by **Steve Dennis**

I T'S a favourite party game: name the Magnificent Seven. There's always one that eludes recollection – Yul Brynner, Steve McQueen, Charles Bronson and Robert Vaughn are easy, James Coburn not far behind them, Horst Buchholz a gift for the once-bitten. But that's only six; he may have been magnificent but for some reason Brad Dexter seems to slip easily through memory's sieve.

Not so the 'other' Magnificent Seven, not if you ask Nicky Henderson. He rattles them off: Sprinter Sacre, Finian's Rainbow, Riverside Theatre, Bobs Worth, Simonsig, Bellvano, Une Artiste, only the last of those flirting momentarily with Brad Dexter territory before taking her place alongside the others. Henderson had a very good Cheltenham Festival in 2012; you might say magnificent.

"Every year I begin by saying I'd settle for one winner, because everyone knows how difficult it is to win any race at the festival," says Henderson, 61, whose first victory at the big meeting was the

Continues page 96

Henderson set three Cheltenham Festival records – for the most wins in a career, a year, and a day

He has now had 46 career wins at the meeting, beating Fulke Walwyn's record of 40 (1946-1986)

He won seven races in 2012, beating Paul Nicholls' record of five in 2009

He won four races on the Wednesday – no trainer had ever had more than a hat-trick

HENDERSON'S MAGNIFICENT SEVEN

Sprinter Sacre (8-11f) storms to victory in the Arkle Chase, seven lengths clear of Cue Card

Simonsig (2-1f) is another seven-length novice winner as he impresses in the Neptune Hurdle

Bobs Worth (9-2) comes back to his best with victory in the RSA Chase by two and a half lengths

Finian's Rainbow (4-1) outbattles Sizing Europe by a length and a quarter in the Champion Chase

Une Artiste (40-1) makes it four on the Wednesday with victory in the Fred Winter Hurdle

Riverside Theatre (7-2f) takes the Ryanair Chase by half a length to deny Albertas Run a hat-trick

Bellvano (20-1) lands the Grand Annual Chase, named in honour of Henderson's father Johnny

Champion Hurdle with See You Then in 1985.

"The year before, it took us until the Thursday to get on the board, so nothing about it is guaranteed. Saying that, last season there were a couple of horses who we expected to run very well, so we were hopeful. I always think it's important to get something on the first day, just to settle all the nerves – Darlan ran a great race to be runner-up in the opener and then we had Sprinter Sacre in the next."

Of course – Sprinter Sacre, the Frankel of the jumps scene, the sure thing made flesh. The six-year-old's exhilarating translation of towering expectation into overwhelming superiority in the Arkle Chase provided Henderson with his first winner of the week, a winner endowed with a significance that went beyond the mere satisfaction of big-race success.

Why? We'll get to that, but first it's necessary to appreciate the overarching importance of the Cheltenham Festival where Henderson is concerned. The great four-day meeting is important to all, certainly, but for Henderson it informs his whole season. For 11 months of the year his thoughts turn often to the festival, for the 12th month he can think of nothing else.

"It gets a bit wild," he says. "Not just festival week, which I get through pretty much on adrenaline alone, but the entire month leading up to it. I turn into a bit of a Cadbury's Fruit & Nut case – there's a lot of responsibility and I know there are things that will go wrong, there always are."

Henderson's jovial description of himself is spot on. The Racing Post's pre-festival visit to the yard a couple of years ago provided an opportunity to view this particular example of grace under extreme pressure at first hand. It merits revisiting, purely for the purposes of illumination.

This is what the run-up to Cheltenham can do to a trainer. If Henderson were in a Tom & Jerry cartoon there'd be a thermometer suspended over his head and the mercury would be rising redly all the way to the top.

"Fraught," he says, when asked about the closing stages of the festival build-up, one word better than a thousand pictures. Does he try to get away from the yard for an hour or two each day, unwind the valve and ease the pressure? "I don't want to spend any time away from the yard at all," he says. "I want to be there where I can see everything that's going on, keep a close watch on everything.

"It's all about keeping your eyes and ears open for anything that might occur. And the fingers crossed."

HENDERSON'S past and present is bound up inextricably with the Cheltenham Festival. His father Johnny saved the racecourse from the threat of development in his role with the Jockey Club in the mid-1960s, while Henderson learned his trainer's craft at the knee of Fred Winter, whose festival pedigree was faultless. For Henderson, Cheltenham past is just as important as Cheltenham present, which is why the victory of Sprinter Sacre had a resonance all of its own.

It was Henderson's 40th festival win, equalling the record of the legendary Fulke Walwyn, and during a week when Henderson broke records left, right and centre this one meant a great deal to him.

"It wasn't something I was particularly pursuing, because how could you do that?" he says. "Was it a relief to equal Fulke's record? No, not really – it was more than that, it felt almost surreal. Look, Fulke Walwyn was a legend when I was still a schoolboy. I had a picture of Mill House on my bedroom wall where every other normal teenager would have had pictures of pretty girls. So doing

anything that could be compared to him, beating records set by people like him, is very special. I felt a bit humbled."

And then he tries to sidestep the issue by saying that with an extra day and many more races there are many more chances to win races at the festival; true, certainly, but that does little to diminish his achievement.

With an equal share of the record in the bag on day one, outright ownership seemed imminent. On the Wednesday morning, in anticipation of the one winner he needed to go out on his own at the head of the standings, in recognition of both past and present, Henderson put on an old tweed suit that had belonged to his father. It must have felt as though it was going to be a special day; it turned out to be special beyond imagining.

"It was one of those great, silly days," he says. "At the time you don't stop to think about it, you just keep cracking on, going from one race to another. In the second race Simonsig did what we'd hoped he'd do, reasonably straightforward, and in the next Bobs Worth was spectacular. He's a charming, uncomplicated horse, you can't help but like him, but oh, he'd been giving me nightmares since Christmas."

We are back to the Cadbury's Fruit & Nut. In Bobs Worth, Henderson had a horse who loved Cheltenham, who had won at the festival the previous year, who was a natural contender for the RSA Chase. His preparation serves as a salutary lesson for all those who think horses train themselves, shedding light on the potholes that pockmark the road to glory.

"He wasn't on the radar at all. In mid-January I thought he had no chance whatsoever of getting to Cheltenham," Henderson says. "He just looked dreadful. He had a wind operation after

Continues page 98

Worth the wait
Henderson's patience with Bobs Worth (left) paid off

running at Kempton over Christmas – Barry [Geraghty] wasn't happy with his breathing – and it's a straightforward operation, horses have it all the time.

"But it knocked him sideways, nearly knocked him over. We just had to leave him alone and hope he'd find his way back. In the end I had to get a run into him, and he ran well in the Reynoldstown, but then the question was how well he would come back from that race.

"He just got there. In the last week he started to bloom, and his coat was right for the first time in months on the Wednesday morning."

Then Finian's Rainbow ran the race of his life to win the Champion Chase. Henderson, watching from his usual spot on a manhole cover on the lawn in front of the grandstands – "I watched See You Then win the Champion Hurdle from there and I've made a point of standing there ever since" – was having the sort of afternoon that makes up for all the sleepless nights and restless work mornings.

No-one had ever trained more than three winners in a single afternoon at the Cheltenham Festival. It was time for Henderson to break another record.

"Une Artiste!" he says with a twinkling grin. "That goes to show what can happen when everything's going right. She was 40-1 – you couldn't put her with the others before the race but she did it beautifully."

There were few celebrations at the course. Henderson was keen to get home for evening stables and to check on his runners for the following day. Celebrations would follow, but all in good time.

"I have to be there every night," he says. "Because you never know what's going to greet you in the morning. I go round every night and all is well but it can all be different come the morning. There's a lot of pressure, pressure we place upon ourselves. The number of times I've had to phone an owner with bad news, that their horse has gone wrong . . . "

And here, amid the tales of glory, Henderson's thoughts still turn to the ones that got away, as if to reinforce the point he made about the number of things that can go wrong, do go wrong. He has won five Champion Hurdles and at Christmas nursed bright hopes of a sixth, only for the wheels to come off that particular wagon.

"It was an absolute catastrophe on the Champion Hurdle front. At one stage I had three top-rank contenders, but both Grandouet and Spirit Son were injured and Binocular was only fourth at Cheltenham.

"And don't forget Long Run, who was

favourite for the Gold Cup but finished third. He had a hard race at Haydock when Kauto Star walloped him and I don't think he ever really got over that. He never really showed his best all season, was never the horse he was the year he won the Gold Cup."

But then we come back to the magnificent seven, to Thursday's winner Riverside Theatre and thus to Bellvano, the last and most emotional winner of the week. Henderson makes a point of staging a strong challenge in the race named after his father, the Johnny Henderson Grand Annual Chase, and had six contenders in the final race of the meeting.

"Dad's race is the culmination of a long, stressful, emotional week," he says. "It's a race I always want to win. And it looked for all the world as if Tanks For That was going to win it for us, and then up came this thing in JP's colours and I was shouting, 'What's it bloody doing? Don't go and do that!'

"JP had several in the race and of course they all had different caps, and it wasn't until halfway up the run-in that I realised it was one of mine. Before the race I told Paul [Carberry] how to ride him – I said 'ride him with balls of steel', and of course that's the kind of race he's best at. Winning Dad's race was just the perfect way to end a wonderful week."

There was a big party afterwards, of course, and while neglecting to elaborate on any gory details Henderson does pay tribute to all at Seven Barrows, pointing out that while he holds the licence and steers the ship it's the team behind him that does all the hard work.

However, hard work and a record seven winners at a single Cheltenham Festival weren't enough to wrest the trainers' title from Paul Nicholls, although the outcome of the title race is one of the few things that Henderson isn't worried about at the sharp end of the season.

"No, it isn't an important thing, certainly not the be-all and end-all," he says. "It would be nice if it happened, but it's more important to me that I have good horses and they run well.

"I was champion years ago and it would be quite rare, I suppose, to regain the title after so many years – it might happen and it might not. I have a lot more to keep me awake at night without worrying about that."

That 'lot more' encompasses what is probably the most talented bunch of horses around at the moment, certainly the best bunch that Henderson has had in his yard since he took out a

licence in 1978. Here again he looks back before looking forward, the heroes of the past validating the stature of the current crop.

"I'd have to say this is my best lot of horses yet and the great thing about them is that the majority are young horses," he says. "I was with Fred Winter when he had that extraordinary team, a team of legends – Bula, Pendil, Lanzarote, Midnight Court – and I'm very lucky to have the horses I've got now.

"Take Sprinter Sacre. There's been this terrific aura about him all the way through, he's got everything you could look for in a chaser, great jumping ability, a high cruising speed – and he knows he's good, he's a terrible show-off. Watching him run frightens me half to death."

Henderson reckons Sprinter Sacre to be a "two-miler through and through", is entertaining thoughts of the King George for Finian's Rainbow, points to the likes of Captain Conan and Darlan as the next wave coming through, praises the strength of last season's bumper horses with a nod to Tistory, a half-brother to Punchestowns. And then, quickly paying his dues to fate, he adds the caveat we'd expect of a man for whom four days in March are career-defining as well as life-affirming.

"The future looks bright, but of course they all have to stay sound and we know how problematic that can be. There's a long way to go to next March, but we have a lot to look forward to."

Thanks to the Magnificent Seven – and there should be no stumbling over any of the names by now: Sprinter Sacre, Finian's Rainbow, Riverside Theatre, Bobs Worth, Simonsig, Bellvano, Une Artiste – there's a lot to look back on as well.

Flying high Finian's Rainbow takes the Champion Chase to give Henderson his fourth winner of the week

THE WINTER PROTECTION

✚ TWYDIL® ✚

AVAILABLE THROUGH YOUR VETERINARY SURGEON

IN UK CALL NOW (01379) 852885

TWYDIL® MUCOPROTECT

Complementary feedingstuff containing notably vitamin C, prebiotics, *Ginseng panax*, *Glycyrrhiza glabra* and *Hydrastis canadensis* which helps support the natural defences of the body.
Particularly indicated in the event of sudden cold, red mucosa, fatigue or lack of energy.

* *Withdrawal time before competition: 48 hours.*
* *Declared content guaranteed until expiry date.*

Used by most of the successful professionals in the world.

**HEAD OFFICE
PAVESCO AG**
CH-4010 Basel, Switzerland
Tel. (41)(61)272 23 72
Fax (41)(61)272 23 88

PAVESCO U.K. LTD.
116, High Road
Needham, Harleston, Norfolk IP20 9LG
Tel. (01379) 85 28 85
Fax (01379) 85 41 78

PAVESCO EQUINE HEALTH USA, LTD
321 N, 22nd Street
St.Louis, MO 63166, USA
Tel. (314) 421 0300
Fax (314) 421 3332

e-mail: info@twydil.com

WORLD

Big Buck's extended his winning sequence in another perfect season

Words by **Tom Kerr**

IF THERE was going to be a year when Big Buck's was vulnerable at Cheltenham, this was it. A year when Paul Nicholls's Ditcheat stable was under a cloud going into the festival and came out the other side with only two winners, one of them from the satellite yard in Dorset.

That Big Buck's was the only winner from the main yard was no surprise to the team at Ditcheat. Not only is he utterly

FOR THE RECORD

Big Buck's equalled Sir Ken's world record of 16 consecutive jumps wins (and broke it at Aintree)

He was the first to win the World Hurdle four times (previously held the record of three wins with Inglis Drever)

brilliant, he is also ultra-reliable and took his achievements to new heights at Cheltenham.

"He won at Cheltenham when I don't think he was quite at his best," Nicholls says. "Tactically Cheltenham was a little different this year. He was in front a lot of the way and he does idle in front.

"But you know the last part of the race is his strongest part. As Ruby says, he goes to sleep and races behind the bridle and you think you might be in trouble. Then you press the button and he's away."

CLASS

Remarkably, for the third time in four years his winning distance in the World Hurdle was a length and three-quarters, but as usual it didn't reflect his superiority. His RPRs in the 2011-12 season were lower than his peak performances (173 for the World Hurdle, 5lb below his best) but still there was no hurdler who could beat him.

Big Buck's was in position to equal Sir Ken's jumps record of 16 consecutive wins on the biggest stage at Cheltenham because Nicholls put an extra race into his schedule – five for the season, instead of the usual four.

"He's a bit laid back and takes plenty of work at home, and it was a long time from the Long Walk at Ascot to the World Hurdle," Nicholls says. "It's easy to get complacent at home. We just wanted to put in an extra race to maintain that fitness and it worked. We may have to do the same this season."

Having eclipsed Sir Ken with his 17th straight win at Aintree, a run dating back to New Year's Day 2009, the next target for Big Buck's is the overall British record (Flat or jumps) of 21 consecutive wins by Meteor between 1786 and 1788.

"All horses get beat some time," Nicholls says, "but we're going to focus on getting him right. It's pressure but he's just better than the rest, his aptitude for racing is very good, he's still very athletic and while he's like that he's going to be very hard to beat.

"To win 17 on the trot reflects well on the team, the horse, on everyone, but it's a new challenge with him now."

Fab four Big Buck's returns after his historic fourth win in the World Hurdle

FOR THE RECORD

Sprinter Sacre's Arkle was the first time ever that the best performance at the Cheltenham Festival was recorded in a novice chase

Words by **Steve Mason**

Force of nature

Sprinter Sacre was the most exciting chasing recruit in years and he achieved something no novice had ever done before

WHEN Sprinter Sacre left Peddlers Cross trailing in his wake at Kempton's Christmas meeting, some wondered whether it was a fluke. By the end of the season, after five wins by a total of 66 lengths in an unbeaten novice campaign, it was clear that he is just a freak.

Like all champions, Sprinter Sacre saved his best for the big occasion. He put up the performance of the Cheltenham Festival with his dazzling exhibition in the Racing Post Arkle Chase, bettering the Racing Post Ratings achieved by Big Buck's, Synchronised and the rest. Most significantly of all, his RPR of 176 for his seven-length win over Cue Card edged him in front of stablemate Finian's Rainbow (175) as the season's leading two-mile chaser.

It was the first time the festival's best performance had been achieved by a novice and, to put his Arkle figure into perspective, only Master Minded (186) and Moscow Flyer (182) have earned bigger winning RPRs in two-mile chases at the festival. Azertyuiop (179), Kauto Star (179) and Well Chief (179) are the only others to boast two-mile marks in excess of 176.

In terms of Racing Post Ratings a figure of 170 is a benchmark of excellence that only genuine championship contenders can achieve and just a handful of novices have posted such a lofty figure in the past two decades. While he could not quite eclipse Gloria Victis, whose mark of 177 makes him the best novice chaser in the history of RPRs, Sprinter Sacre compiled a string of top-class performances unmatched in terms of consistent high quality.

The fact that he was in the 170s on three occasions is a testament to his freakish ability. Along with his 176 in the Arkle, he recorded an RPR of 172 in open class when he beat French Opera, another stablemate, by six lengths in the Game Spirit Chase at Newbury and 170 when he rounded off his season with victory in the Grade 1 Maghull Novices' Chase at Aintree.

With so much achieved by the age of six, Sprinter Sacre's best is surely yet to come and it will be surprising if he doesn't go on to dominate the division and join the elite group of 180+ performers.

Keep on rolling

Quevega cemented her status as the queen of Cheltenham with another dominant performance in the Mares' Hurdle

Words by **Nick Pulford**

A CHANGE may be as good as a rest but with Quevega there is plenty of rest and very little change. In each of the past three years she has turned up only at Cheltenham and Punchestown in the spring, won at both festivals and promptly been put away for another ten months.

In 2012 she did it again, winning her fourth Mares' Hurdle at odds of 4-7 by four lengths from Kentford Grey Lady and following up in the World Series Hurdle at Punchestown. She has achieved the same double for three seasons in a row and has not been defeated since May 2009; at Cheltenham, she is simply unstoppable with a

100 per cent record from four visits.

The super mare's careful handling by Willie Mullins has turned her into a record breaker and, despite some calls for her to take on Big Buck's, the trainer will not be swayed. The aim in 2013 is to return for the Mares' Hurdle in a bid to equal Golden Miller's five wins at the festival.

"I don't think we'll change anything with Quevega," Mullins says. "I've said that if Big Buck's can get an entry into the Mares' Hurdle we'll take him on. Or if he wants to come to Punchestown we'll take him on there."

The bald form of Quevega's latest win at Punchestown – by five and a half lengths from Voler La Vedette, who had run Big Buck's to a length and three-quarters – was impressive but

misleading: her best RPR of 159 is a long way behind the 178 of Big Buck's.

Ratings hardly matter to Mullins and her owners, the Hammer and Trowel boys who also have Thousand Stars. Why, they ask, would you want to go looking for ways to get beaten when you have such a winning machine?

"You can't help but get a buzz from her," Mullins says. "It's always great to win at Cheltenham and then Punchestown was epic. Both camps – us and Voler La Vedette – went there on the crest of a wave. It was a great race, great for racing, a lot of people enjoyed it and it was great to watch.

"There are very few horses you can set your watch to, but she's one of them. She's a once-in-a-lifetime horse, I think, an exceptional mare."

CHELTENHAM
in pictures

1 Barry Geraghty celebrates after his dramatic Queen Mother Champion Chase triumph on Finian's Rainbow

2 Nicky Henderson enjoys a pint of the black stuff

3 Bellvano (centre) on his way to victory in the Grand Annual, giving Henderson his seventh winner of the festival

4 Colman Sweeney returns in trumph on Foxhunter winner Salsify, trained by his father Rodger and owned by his mother Joan

5 The huge field races away from the stands in the Coral Cup, won by Son Of Flicka

6 Salut Flo on his way to victory in the Byrne Group Plate

7 Teaforthree, a first festival winner for trainer Rebecca Curtis, leads the way in the National Hunt Chase

8 David Bridgwater shows his joy at The Giant Bolster's second place in the Gold Cup

9 Brindisi Breeze and Campbell Gillies score an impressive win in the Albert Bartlett Novices' Hurdle

10 Davy Russell and Sir Des Champs after their Jewson Novices' Chase success

11 Neptune Novices' Hurdle winner Simonsig, the first leg of Nicky Henderson's four-timer on the Wednesday

12 Champagne Fever, trained by Willie Mullins and ridden by his son Patrick, scores an all-the-way success in the Champion Bumper

MAJOR PLAYER

Willie Mullins enjoyed another spectacular season with a sixth trainers' title and 13 Grade 1 winners. Now he has his sights set on jump racing's ultimate prize

Words by **Jonathan Mullin**

WHEN it comes to jump racing in Ireland, this small County Carlow farm is like Willy Wonka's Chocolate Factory, a dreamland of talent. Somewhere, with the rain sheeting down on a day summer borrowed from his miserable brother winter, is the boss.

As he approaches, he takes a quizzical look at the recently arrived visitor, a quick glance at his watch, a sharp look at the emptying skies above and says: "I thought we were doing this over the phone?" No, I say, my impression was that it was to be a face-to-face encounter? "Well, then, you'd better come in."

Then the Mullins hospitality clicks in. By the time we're climbing the stepped arch into the kitchen, the champion trainer has the kettle singing, boiling water poured and is busy pressing a teabag against the wall of the mug. "Milk?"

Outside, in the rain, is an expanding training yard at the height of its powers. While there's no sense of complacency –

quite the opposite actually – it would be foolish not to expect some pride. "I think we're getting more quality," he consents eventually. "I thought last season the quantity of the quality was fantastic and I hope we can have more of the same this season."

Yet another barnstorming campaign in 2011-12 saw Mullins claim a fifth consecutive trainers' championship – and sixth in all – with more than three times the prize-money of his nearest challenger, Noel Meade. Scarcely a Sunday went by without Mullins tipping his hat to welcome another big-race winner. In all, there were 13 Grade 1 jumps winners and, for good measure, he won two races at Royal Ascot in the summer with Simenon. When the figures are put to him, he looks up quickly. "Had we that many? You sure? I'd have thought five or six!"

The competition is fierce just to get to the big races, even to put the horses on the track in the first place. It takes money and judgement – the people with the dough to buy the horses identified by
Continues page 108

CLAN ROYAL *The Mullins family has enjoyed notable success in the past year*

Willie Mullins
'The Untouchable' was crowned Ireland's champion jumps trainer for the sixth time. He won three races at the Cheltenham Festival, ten at Punchestown and the Grande Course de Haies at Auteuil with Thousand Stars

Tom Mullins
Willie's brother won the County Hurdle at Cheltenham and the Grade 1 Champion Novice Hurdle at Punchestown with Alderwood. In August he furthered his growing reputation for big handicap winners when Bob Lingo landed the Galway Plate for owner JP McManus

Patrick Mullins
Willie's son became champion amateur in Ireland for the fifth time and secured a champion bumper double on Champagne Fever when winning against the pros at Cheltenham and following up at Punchestown. He also won over Cheltenham's cross-country fences last season aboard Uncle Junior

Emmet Mullins
Willie's nephew (and son of George) had seven winners last season, including high-profile successes on Golden Silver in the Hilly Way and Sir Des Champs in the Greenmount Park at Limerick

Danny Mullins
Willie's nephew (and son of Tony) rode winners in both Ireland and Britain last season, including Dorset Square at Cheltenham's Open meeting for his uncle Willie. In September he won the Kerry National at Listowel on the Eric McNamara-trained Faltering Fullback

Fiona Mullins
Willie's niece (and daughter of George) landed her first success as a jockey when winning on First Friday for trainer Paul Hennessy at Tipperary in August

Mullins and his team as potential stars. "We're lucky to have the clients who can afford to buy that type of horse," he says. "It's a very competitive market at the top end of the jumping stock. You're trying to get horses before the sales and have them bought before the opposition gets them. It keeps you on your toes all right. There are only so many wealthy people for so few good horses and as a trainer it's vital you can compete. And of course they don't all work out."

Sometimes they do work out, but for other trainers. Brindisi Breeze, who beat Mullins' Boston Bob into second place in the Albert Bartlett Novices' Hurdle at Cheltenham, was one that got away. "We had been looking at the winner and left him behind us. Pat Doyle had recommended him to me and all I could do after the race was text him and say 'you were right.' You can't buy them all."

Boston Bob was one of the select bunch brought to the yard by Graham Wylie, who had to look for new trainers after Howard Johnson was disqualified. The injection of quality can be measured by the fact that one of the lowest-rated of the new arrivals, Felix Yonger, went on to be runner-up to Simonsig in the Neptune Novices' Hurdle at Cheltenham.

"The call came from out of the blue and I'm delighted it has worked out so well," Mullins says. "Felix Yonger probably came with no reputation from England but he ran a cracker at Cheltenham. My brother Tony, who sold them the horse, always held him in high regard and when the seven horses arrived he was the best athlete off the lorry. I thought there was something there."

Boston Bob was more fancied at Cheltenham and Mullins feels he didn't spark on the day. It's a sign of how far the stable has come in recent years that Boston Bob and Hurricane Fly, who finished third in his defence of the Champion Hurdle crown, were regarded as festival 'flops'. Even so, Mullins had three winners, including the mighty mare Quevega.

"We had a couple of disappointments, but then other horses won," he says. "If someone told you the week before Cheltenham you would have three winners, you'd take that. It's not easy having to travel and to take such a big team. The logistics are tough at that time of year and, with so many horses going over, everything is stretched.

"Every year we say we'll take fewer horses. But then you end up with a 33-1 winner over there and if you had brought a smaller team he might have been the one left at home. You have to take the horses you feel have a chance. What we've done in the last few years that we didn't do before is to take handicappers.

"We've been forced into it a bit. We have taken handicappers that there simply aren't races for in Ireland and it has paid off. It's definitely not a plan, it's just the case that these are the horses we have and if I don't take them to Cheltenham there are no races for them in Ireland until Punchestown. You have to take them and take your chance."

Cheltenham winners are all special but when family are involved – when the blood runs thick – those moments are too precious to be forgotten. The kitchen walls are decorated not with the countless Grade 1 winners but with smaller framed photographs of Mullins' son Patrick and his generation of cousins. They document Patrick's journey from pony club days to a second Champion Bumper success at this year's festival on Champagne Fever. Behind him were Barry Geraghty on New Year's Eve and Ruby

Sweet success
Champagne Fever gave Mullins special moments at Cheltenham and Punchestown with his son Patrick on board

Walsh on Pique Sous, the other Mullins runner.

"It was very special, you know, watching him come around the bend with Ruby and Barry, one each side of him. I didn't know whether he'd be swamped. When you come round the turn in those Grade 1 races, it separates the good from the bad. That's why we ran Champagne Fever in the race – to find out."

The day started in frustrating fashion. In the four-mile National Hunt Chase, Mullins went with two live chances, Allee Garde and Soll, and the worst of luck conspired: Allee Garde fell and brought down his stablemate. The previous day, Mullins had lost Scotsirish in the Cross Country Chase.

"I thought 'Lord Jesus, is this going to be our Cheltenham?' Day two couldn't have started any worse but it improved as it went along. These things happen and it's amazing what one winner can do. Champagne Fever was sweet, it was great having bought him, to see that vindicated."

The galloping grey with the peculiar head carriage went on to complete a Punchestown double on the same day Hurricane Fly won his second successive Rabobank Champion Hurdle. That stretched the Hurricane's winning run in Ireland to two and a half years, but his journey through the latest season was a rocky one. He didn't reappear until the Irish Champion Hurdle in late January and, although he won decisively at Leopardstown, he was beaten in the big one.

"I don't know what happened at Cheltenham," Mullins says. "He might not have had enough match practice before heading there. I thought his performance at Leopardstown was fantastic but sometimes when you're going for the big

Continues page 110

competitions you need match practice. Anyhow, it didn't go right on the day and that's racing. I thought his run at Leopardstown was exceptional. If I could get him to run like that all of the time . . ."

Hurricane Fly's absence before Christmas put the yard under suffocating scrutiny and, while Mullins doesn't accept he found the attention uncomfortable, it was a tense time. "We had setbacks early in the season and I wasn't happy with him," he admits. "When you're training a horse like him you're trying to train him to get him right. When you're not happy people are always guessing things. I was going to bring him out when I was ready and I didn't want to say any more except I wasn't happy with him. That probably upset people, or it could have generated more gossip and rumour. That's racing and it's the nature of it. It's funny, because we have so many horses nobody wants to know anything about."

Thousand Stars – with form figures of 123423 after running in six Grade 1 races in five months – kept going after Hurricane Fly had finished his campaign, winning twice at Auteuil including the French Champion Hurdle for the second consecutive year.

"He's an extraordinary horse," Mullins says. "I fired him at race after race and he kept coming up running. He runs his race all the time. To do what he did at the end of the season was something else because he was at every cockfight – Leopardstown, Punchestown, Aintree, Cheltenham, Fairyhouse and twice to Paris. He's made of iron."

The satisfaction is tinged with regret. "At the start of the season my target for him was the Aintree Hurdle, but we got sucked into this Big Buck's thing and I'm raging with myself that I took him to Cheltenham. He was beaten a neck at Aintree for the second year running and I know I left my Aintree race in Cheltenham. This season he'll definitely go back to France and I want to go back to Aintree for some unfinished business."

Among the younger brigade is a chaser who promises to fulfil one of Mullins' career ambitions by winning the Cheltenham Gold Cup. Sir Des Champs was unbeaten in five novice chases, landing the Jewson at Cheltenham and sauntering to a first Grade 1 victory at Punchestown.

"He looks like a Gold Cup horse," Mullins says. "What he has done so far is great and I hope he'll keep improving. I've felt all along that he's good. A lot of people thought he was iffy at Limerick at Christmas, but I felt differently. I didn't come home from Limerick thinking we had any worse a horse than we had going

there. He got into a lot of trouble at Leopardstown, got himself out of it and won – the sign of a good horse.

"And then he went to Cheltenham and did what he had to do. He answers the call every time and I'm hoping there's more to come. It's a big comfort knowing how he loves that hill."

Could Sir Des Champs be another Florida Pearl? "Oh, I think so, yes. He might not have Florida Pearl's speed but we think he has huge reserves of stamina."

Twelve years ago Florida Pearl surged

Star turns (*clockwise from top*) Quevega wins her fourth Mares' Hurdle, Quel Esprit on his way to victory in the Hennessy at Leopardstown, Sir Des Champs at Cheltenham, Simenon lands the first of his two Royal Ascot successes, Hurricane Fly at Punchestown and Grade 1 scorer Marasonnien

to the front of the Cheltenham Gold Cup field with two fences to jump and looked set to fill a void in Mullins' bulging cv. But just as he filled his lungs for one final thrust, the needle flickered and then plunged to 'empty', coinciding as it did with a decisive run from Looks Like Trouble.

The trainer's confidence in Sir Des Champs – at times only scarcely below the surface – hints that if a Mullins horse leads at the second-last next March, the outcome will be very different.

PUNCHESTOWN
in pictures

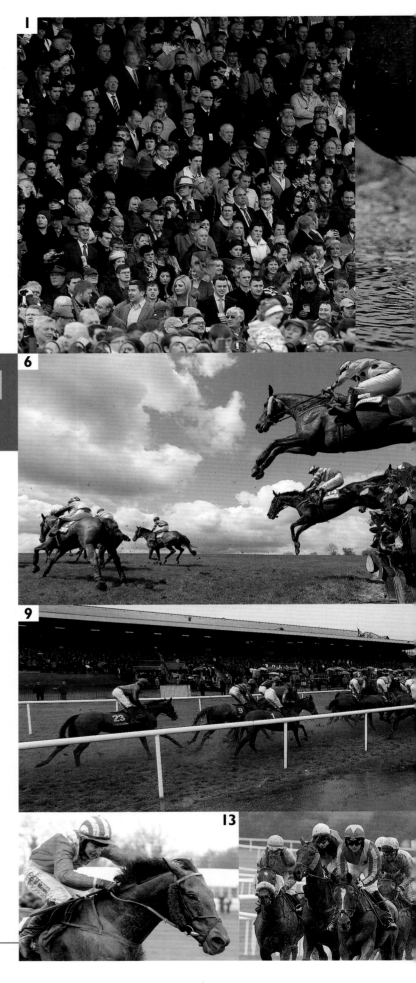

1 The five-day meeting attracts a total attendance of 91,500, down two per cent on the previous year

2 Rain hits the track on the Wednesday, causing the cancellation of both chases on the card

3 Lucky William takes the Ryanair Novice Chase for trainer Tom Cooper and jockey Barry Geraghty

4 Quevega after completing a hat-trick in the World Series Hurdle

5 Irish champion jockey Davy Russell puts on a brave face on wet Wednesday

6 The sky is brighter for the Irish Field Chase, won by Outlaw Pete, on the final day

7 A leap off Ruby's Double in the La Touche Cup

8 A fire-eater provides some entertainment away from the track

9 The field in the Martinstown Opportunity Series Final, won by Shamiran, on the Wednesday

10 Unknown Rebel flies high in the Champion Four Year Old Hurdle

11 Barry Geraghty with the Punchestown Gold Cup after his victory on China Rock

12 Champagne Fever completes a Cheltenham-Punchestown double by taking the Champion Bumper

13 Ian McCarthy pushes Shamiran to victory

14 Another view of the action in the Martinstown Opportunity Series Final

15 Runners in the La Touche Cup go through Joe's Water Splash

THE BIGGER PICTURE

Transcend, one of three Japanese raiders in the Dubai World Cup, walks towards the rising sun at Meydan the day before the big race. He finished last of the 13 runners
EDWARD WHITAKER (RACINGPOST.COM/PHOTOS)

THE ANNUAL 20

Our pick of the names and faces to watch in 2013 starts with five horses we can't wait to see in the big races

SPRINTER SACRE

'The Dark Aeroplane', as he was dubbed by Nicky Henderson, flew so high in his novice season that anything lower now will be a huge disappointment. But what we expect is more, much more.

Sprinter Sacre is an old-fashioned chaser, all size and scope, and he has been trained in the old-fashioned way. Henderson, in fact, was so excited about Sprinter Sacre's chasing potential that he wanted to put him away as a five-year-old and not send him for the 2011 Supreme Novices' Hurdle, in which he was third behind Al Ferof.

He hasn't been defeated since and took to fences so well there is more than a suspicion that he would have beaten the seniors in the 2012 Queen Mother Champion Chase. Henderson – who won that race anyway with Finian's Rainbow – instead kept him on the novice road that led to easy victories in the Arkle at Cheltenham and the Maghull at Aintree.

Henderson's patient work should receive its full reward in this second season over fences and Sprinter Sacre's Racing Post Rating is expected to be in the 180s before too long. By the time the 2013 Champion Chase rolls around, he could be fast approaching greatness.

Fasten your seatbelts.

SIR DES CHAMPS

"He's so lazy, it's unbelievable. It's hard to know how good he is, or might be, because he is that lazy." Davy Russell's summary of Sir Des Champs, at the end of a perfect five-race novice season, was as tantalising as his mount had been impressive in festival victories at Cheltenham and Punchestown.

The Willie Mullins-trained six-year-old is a dual winner already at the Cheltenham Festival, having landed the Martin Pipe Conditional Jockeys' Handicap Hurdle in his first season before following up in the Jewson Novices' Chase in 2012, and

that bodes well for the planned assault on the Cheltenham Gold Cup.

There was no hint of laziness in his Cheltenham hurdles success after a tremendous battle with Son Of Flicka, who also returned for a festival victory in 2012, and maybe he just needs a fight to bring out the best in him. A final-fence blunder at Punchestown perhaps stemmed from it all being too easy for him.

With Sir Des Champs kept away from the other top novices in his first season over fences, we don't know for sure whether he can take the next step up in class, but it's going to be fun finding out.

VIZTORIA

It is almost second nature to treat Irish-trained horses as mudlovers because they invariably race on soft ground and that seemed to be the bookmaker reaction after Viztoria had won her first two starts as a juvenile.

The first came for Adrian McGuinness by seven and a half lengths in a maiden and she then thrashed a bunch of 90-plus-rated fillies by the same margin in a Listed race for Eddie Lynam. Yes, the ground was bad and her victims may have been badly rated, but you have to mark every one of them down as having run well below par to stop Viztoria being one of the best two-year-old fillies around.

She had reportedly won a schooling race on Polytrack before her debut and her change of stable was accompanied by a message to Lynam that "she is a bit special". If she was trained by Aidan O'Brien she would surely have traded at around 3-1 for the 1,000 Guineas after her Listed win, rather than the 20-1 that was available.

Lynam is adamant she is not a sprinter and if it comes up soft for the Guineas, as it did in 2012, there will be few better able to handle the ground than Viztoria.

DAWN APPROACH

Jim Bolger was in no doubt. "He's capable of ruling the roost," the trainer said after Dawn Approach had given him a fifth Dewhurst Stakes in seven years. "My previous four Dewhurst winners were pretty smart but this one is right up there with them." Considering that group included the 2008 Derby winner New Approach, the sire of Dawn Approach, it was high praise.

Others were not quite as convinced by Dawn Approach's Dewhurst, the sixth win of a perfect juvenile campaign. He appeared to struggle to get past his pacemaker Leitir Mor at first, before lengthening clear once he found his stride up the hill.

Bolger will continue to train Dawn Approach even though Godolphin bought a controlling 51 per cent interest in the colt shortly after his Coventry Stakes win at Royal Ascot.

In 2008, Bolger won the Derby, Irish Champion and Champion Stakes with New Approach for Princess Haya of Jordan, Sheikh Mohammed's wife. Something similar would do nicely.

We won't know who's right about Dawn Approach until he returns to Newmarket for his planned assault on the 2,000 Guineas but therein lies the fascination of the opening Classics: we might just have a superstar in our midst.

'Her victims may have been badly rated but you have to mark every one as having run well below par to stop Viztoria being one of the best two-year-old fillies'

SIMONSIG

Before the Champion Point-to-Point Bumper at Fairyhouse in April 2011, Michael O'Leary vowed to offer €100,000 for the winner and he was as good as his word after Simonsig's impressive 13-length success. The problem was that Ronnie Bartlett, the grey's owner, was in no mood to sell: "Do you want to put another zero on that?" he asked.

Bartlett held on to Simonsig and now has an even hotter property on his hands. Switched from Ian Ferguson to Nicky Henderson to start his hurdling career, the grey went from strength to strength in

the 2011-12 season and wound up with impressive victories at the Cheltenham and Aintree festivals.

He was a two-and-a-half-miler as a novice hurdler but Henderson believes the Arkle will be ideal over fences. He could stay over hurdles, in which case the Champion Hurdle would be the target. Either way, two miles will be his trip this season.

His powerful display in the Neptune at Cheltenham suggests he will be difficult to stop when he rolls down the hill at the festival. For Bartlett, and for the rest of us, the prospect of what he might achieve is priceless.

RONAN WHELAN

Tony McCoy, Mick Kinane and Paul Carberry are just some of the graduates from the Jim Bolger academy and the master trainer of horses and jockeys has unearthed another gem in Whelan.

A graduate of the pony racing circuit, where he rode 95 winners and claimed the jockeys' title in 2008, Whelan was quickly snapped up by Bolger. "To work for someone like that, with all his experience, has been a brilliant learning curve," says the 19-year-old from County Kildare.

There are quite a few treats attached to working at Coolcullen, such as riding out Dawn Approach every morning. "I've been riding him since he started his work. I knew he was good, very good."

The leading Irish apprentice looks pretty good too and outside trainers have been quick to recognise his talent. He struck up valuable partnerships with Pat Shanahan – his Listowel success on Romininthbeglomin was one of four victories for the rookie trainer – and Paul Deegan, with Fromajacktoaking racking up a hat-trick in nurseries.

Those outside rides could be the key to success for Whelan once he steps on to the big stage as a fully fledged professional. He looks made for it.

MICHAEL JM MURPHY

Ebullient, fast-talking and a demon in the saddle, Murphy was a young man in a hurry in 2012. He found rides hard to come by after graduating from the Irish racing academy, so he got on the phone to Buckinghamshire trainer Alan Jarvis and got himself a job as stable apprentice. He arrived in March, won on his first ride in June and didn't look back, with another 26 winners over the next four months at a strike-rate of 20 per cent.

Murphy, 19, does not hail from a racing background – his dad is a farmer and his mum works in a supermarket – and he fell into riding through his youth club. But he knows the value of hard work and has a talent to match.

He has made them proud – and a little richer – back home in Wexford, where the local bookmaker put up a sign saying: 'No more bets taken on Michael Murphy's rides'. As Jarvis reported: "His brothers, sisters, uncles and aunts have cleaned the bookies out."

With his claim well intact for 2013, Murphy is set for another big year.

MARTIN HARLEY

Some champion apprentices have too much, too young but there is a long history of the British title winner going on to further glory in the senior ranks, as shown by the examples of Frankie Dettori, Seb Sanders, Paul Hanagan, Ryan Moore, Tom Queally and William Buick among others.

Martin Harley, the 2011 champion, looks likely to join them after an outstanding first full season without his claim. The highlight was his first Classic victory on Samitar in the Irish 1,000 Guineas, when he showed many of the attributes that have made him a rising star: judgement of pace to sit on the heels of the leaders, confidence to wait on the rails for a gap to appear and strength in the finish to see off the challenge of runner-up Ishvana. And it was even more impressive because it was his first ride on Samitar as well as his first in a Classic.

Harley, 23, from County Donegal, spent four years with master tutor Jim Bolger before joining Mick Channon for the 2011 season. Some of the better rides in the stable were denied him at first but, having doubly proved himself with the apprentice title and a Classic victory, the doors are wide open now.

CLARE BALDING

Few emerged from 2012 with as much credit as Clare Balding and she has another big year ahead as she takes the lead role on Channel 4's revamped and exclusive terrestrial coverage of horseracing.

With diligence and no little talent, Balding, 41, has developed into one of the best sports broadcasters of the age and she won universal acclaim for her poolside coverage of the Olympic swimming and her anchor role on the Paralympics.

Her on-the-hoof interview with the emotional father of gold medallist swimmer Chad Le Clos was one of the broadcasting highlights of the Olympics and she was equally at home across a variety of sports, from her whispered reports on Tiger Woods at the Open golf for Radio 5 Live to reeling off the names of every player as they emerged from the tunnel for rugby league's Challenge Cup final.

The skills learned and honed at the BBC will bring a fresh focus to Channel 4's coverage – even if one commentator noted that "sometimes Clare seems to be not so much engaging the camera as grabbing it with both hands, pinning it to the wall and letting it have it".

Racing is lucky she has not outgrown the sport she grew up with.

CHARLIE LONGSDON

In six seasons since launching his training career at the age of 31, Nicky Henderson's former assistant has made sure and steady progress.

Having laid solid foundations from modest beginnings – ten horses when he started in 2006 – Longsdon, now 37, is on the up. Having had around 20 winners for three consecutive seasons, he jumped to 44 in 2010-11 and again to 69 in the latest season, when he landed his biggest success with Paintball in the Imperial Cup.

Just as impressive is his strike-rate (20 per cent and 19 per cent in the last two seasons) and level-stake profit (£110.50 to a £1 stake over the past two seasons), which suggests he has been a well-kept secret from most punters.

The Oxfordshire trainer is aiming to take another step forward with his ever-expanding string in the 2012-13 season and, if he does that, he is likely to break into the top ten for the first time. The icing on the cake would be a big festival winner and surely that is only a matter of time.

'He sent out 69 winners in the latest season and just as impressive was his strike-rate and level-stake profit'

CHARLIE HILLS

For years we were used to seeing the Hills family name in the upper reaches of the Flat trainers' table, preceded by the initials B.W. More of the same was expected when Barrington William, the patriarch, passed on the baton to his fourth son, Charlie, in August 2011 but the transition has not been quite as smooth as expected.

In 2010, Barry's last full season, he finished ninth in the table but Charlie barely made it into the top 25 in 2012. His strike-rate was one of the lowest among that group.

It may be harsh to judge any first-season trainer too strictly, yet Hills, 34, does have the advantage of one of the best yards in Britain and some of the most powerful owners.

There were some bright spots that suggested he might do better in 2013. His strike-rate was higher with two-year-olds and from that group he finally got a first Group winner on the board when Just The Judge took the Group 2 Rockfel Stakes on Newmarket's Future Champions day.

The second full season for the new master of Faringdon Place will tell us a lot more.

SIR MICHAEL STOUTE

Stoute, 67, is becoming the racing equivalent of Liverpool Football Club – on top for so long but no longer capable of a place in the champions' league.

Seventh place in the trainers' table in 2011 seemed a blip, considering the ten championships that had gone before, but now he has slipped even further down the table. He had more winners in 2012 than the year before and his strike-rate was impressive, but his prize-money total was not even a third of his earnings when he last took the title in 2009.

In 2010, when he was runner-up to Richard Hannon, Stoute was still top dog in Newmarket but that tag has passed to John Gosden for two years running.

Most alarmingly, Stoute's flow of Group winners has reduced to a trickle in the past couple of years and his best performers have been Sea Moon and Carlton House – admirable colts but not a patch on his old champions. One or two of his juveniles look promising, but they do not cause the stir they once did.

Something needs to happen – and quickly.

LONG RUN

He was the second-best chaser in Britain and Ireland in the 2011-12 season, but second-best simply wasn't good enough after his exploits of the previous campaign. Greatness had beckoned after his victories in the King George VI Chase and the Cheltenham Gold Cup as a six-year-old; instead, stagnation set in. "One can't deny last season was a bit of an anti-climax," trainer Nicky Henderson admitted at his open day in September.

If Long Run's defeats by a revitalised Kauto Star in the Betfair Chase at Haydock and the King George at Kempton were forgivable, on the basis that neither course is ideal for him, his limp effort in the Gold Cup was much less so.

On official ratings Long Run had at least a stone in hand on all of his Gold Cup opponents bar Kauto Star and he was 1.5 in running after his biggest rival was pulled up early in the race. When push came to shove, however, he could not match the determination of Synchronised and The Giant Bolster up the hill. A question mark hangs over him now.

THE FOUR-YEAR-OLDS OF 2013

The Classic crop of 2012 wasn't much cop, was it? It's a rhetorical question, of course: a matter of fact rather than a matter for debate. From Camelot down, they were the most disappointing bunch of three-year-olds in years.

They had a hard act to follow, given the exploits of the Frankel-led generation of 2011, but pretty much all they did was follow. As Frankel and his contemporaries swept through the summer like a firestorm,

the three-year-olds were burned time after time. In 2011 the July Cup, King George, Sussex Stakes and Arc were among the major races won by three-year-olds, but in 2012 they all fell to the Frankel generation again and the three-year-olds struggled.

For Camelot and his contemporaries, 2013 will be a year of reckoning. But, with several top older horses kept in training at five and an emerging Classic crop headed by Dawn Approach, the four-year-olds could find themselves between a rock and a hard place.

PAUL HANAGAN AND SILVESTRE DE SOUSA

When they left the north for lucrative jobs in Newmarket, having finished first and second in the 2011 Flat jockeys' championship, both would have expected a drop in their number of winners.

That duly came to pass in 2012, but without the compensation of a marked upgrade to better-quality winners for their new employers.

Hanagan, having taken over as No.1 rider for Sheikh Hamdan Al Maktoum, won his first British

Group 1 in 2012 but it was for his old boss, Richard Fahey, on July Cup victor Mayson. His biggest success for the sheikh was in the Tattersalls Millions on Ghurair.

De Sousa had to make do with the scraps off the Godolphin table, with Mickael Barzalona and Frankie Dettori on the big winners. His biggest supporter remained Mark Johnston, who provided more winners than the main Godolphin trainers combined.

Both jockeys will hope for more in 2013.

LORD WINDERMERE

Described as a slow learner by trainer Jim Culloty, this six-year-old didn't hit the point-to-point circuit and nor did he run at the big festivals as a novice hurdler. He has been saved for a chasing career, pure and simple.

Lord Windermere did not begin his racing career until November 2011 and he had a tough first lesson with a fall at the fourth hurdle. Yet he was back to win a maiden hurdle at Thurles only a fortnight later and, four weeks after that, he stepped up to win a Listed hurdle at Punchestown. Perhaps not such a slow learner, after all.

He was then pitched into Grade 1 company, finishing fourth to Benefficient in the Deloitte Novice Hurdle, before an easy win in a Naas novice hurdle. A big run was expected on his final outing, at Fairyhouse, but he was a well-beaten eighth. It was his only disappointing effort of a promising first season.

Culloty believes Lord Windermere is crying out for two and a half miles and, most importantly, that "fences should be a formality for him".

The trainer has bided his time and this budding chaser should be worth the wait.

ROYAL GUARDSMAN

Colin Tizzard's bumper runners have been given more respect in the betting market since Cue Card's 40-1 success in the 2010 Champion Bumper and Royal Guardsman was sent off 6-1 second favourite for the 2012 edition at Cheltenham.

The five-year-old finished only tenth but was probably the hard-luck story of the race, having lost his place when hitting trouble at the top of the hill.

He had won two of his three bumper starts before Cheltenham, having reportedly outperformed Cue Card on the gallops prior to his winning debut at Fontwell in April 2011. He disappointed on his reappearance at Aintree six months later but Tizzard's horses weren't firing at the time and he bounced back to win one of the better bumpers of the season at Ascot in February.

He is reported to have schooled well and, despite the Cheltenham disappointment, it would be no surprise to see him back at the festival in 2013 as a leading contender for one of the top novice hurdles.

LIBER NAUTICUS

Sir Michael Stoute's filly announced herself as a bright prospect for middle distances in 2013 and quite possibly a live candidate for the Oaks with a debut victory in September.

An Azamour filly from the family of Breeders' Cup Turf, King George and St Leger winner Conduit, Liber Nauticus made a striking first impression in a mile maiden at Goodwood, where Stoute introduced his Derby winners North Light and Workforce.

Well supported in the market, she looked green in the early stages and was in danger of being boxed in, with five fillies in front of her as they passed the two-furlong marker. However, when Kieren Fallon got after her as the false rail ended, she quickened well to make up four lengths on the leaders and win going away.

By maiden standards the form was solid and the time was close to the juvenile record. She plainly made a big impression on Fallon, who always felt confident of victory despite the ground he had to make up.

Provided she winters well, she looks one of the best hopes for a revival of Stoute's fortunes in the Classics and we can expect to see her in one of the Oaks trials, perhaps even the Musidora.

FERGAL O'BRIEN

He's got the right name to make a success of training and he's got the right pedigree too – 19 years as assistant to Nigel Twiston-Davies and, before that, three years with the late Tim Forster.

O'Brien, 40, who was a successful point-to-point trainer alongside his job with Twiston-Davies, is in his second season with a full licence at Cilldara Stud, Gloucestershire, where his landlord is leading jump jockey Timmy Murphy. He has built a solid reputation in jumping circles and his first winner, Horsham Lad in October 2011, was owned by William and Angela Rucker of State Of Play fame. Raymond Anderson Green and Lord Vestey are other well-known owners who have supported O'Brien.

At the other end of the spectrum, he trains Gud Day for the 'People's Horse' free ownership scheme run by Racing For Change for the Twitter community and he has already won with the young grey. O'Brien is going to have a lot of followers on Twitter and a strong start to his second season suggests punters will soon be following him too.

And the name? Well, he's no relation to a famous racing O'Brien. His father was a bus driver in Limerick.

'O'Brien is going to have a lot of followers on Twitter and a strong start to his second season suggests punters will soon be following him too'

RELAX

The Venetia Williams-trained chaser may not be quite festival class, but he's with the right trainer to make the most of the generous official rating of 125 on which he started the 2012-13 season.

The French import took time to come to hand for Williams but made great strides in the spring of 2012 with three wins and two seconds from five runs in the space of two months. It would have been four wins if he hadn't lost the ability to jump in the latter stages of a race at Chepstow and his only other defeat in that period came at Bangor when he was trying to give a stone to Kauto Relko, who subsequently went up 10lb in the official ratings.

Relax, who acts on good ground but is probably better on soft, has the potential to develop into a 145+ chaser in his second season in Britain.

Celebrity Race Clubs

RACING VIP STYLE

Want to be part of the most exciting new race club in horse racing?
Want to meet your favourite celebrities and footballers?
Want to party VIP style?

Well, Celebrity Race Clubs is for YOU!

From as little as £10 per month

HOW IT WORKS

The Club has linked up with Jamie Laing from Made In Chelsea;
CAN Associates, who manage Peter Andre and Amy Childs;
Sunderland Football Club and Everton Football Club!
Each group have a racehorse ready to run under their name and colours!
Everytime a horse runs, we PARTY!

Visit celebrityraceclubs.com to join NOW!

THE
BIGGER
PICTURE

Wrotham Heath flashes past the Derby day
revellers at Epsom on his way to victory in
the Diamond Jubilee Handicap. With the
Queen in attendance, Epsom was at the
heart of the Diamond Jubilee celebrations
and drew a crowd of 130,000 on Derby day
EDWARD WHITAKER (RACINGPOST.COM/PHOTOS)

SHINING LIGHT

A tribute to Lord Oaksey, a founding father of the Injured Jockeys Fund and celebrated journalist, broadcaster and amateur jockey, who died in September aged 83

Words by **Alastair Down**

AFTER a long struggle one of the great hearts lies still at last. There comes a time when you urge those you love to go. They have had more than enough and you wish for them a final and irrevocable peace in some quieter pasture, hard-earned and richly deserved.

So it must have been for those closest to John Oaksey as the last hours were logged of his wonderful life. But although you have prepared yourself for the inevitable and know full well it is coming, there is still a fierce, painful pang of shock at the finality of the end.

Those who loved John without reservation – and whom he loved in return – suddenly find the harbour lights of their life have been extinguished. But those same, bright lights were an enduring guide to more than family and friends because in every nook and cranny of these islands there are folk whose lives have been enriched, enlivened and uplifted by the diminutive powerhouse and force for good that was Oaksey.

And although he was born to privilege it was often in the humblest of abodes that his light shone. Hundreds upon hundreds of beneficiaries of the Injured Jockeys Fund were given back their lives, dignity and sense of purpose because of one man's vision and volcanic compassion.

Racing has always sown seeds of glory but the downside of the wonder is a sad harvest of men with shot nerves and shattered bodies, the punch-drunk and the paralysed.

But until John's Damascene moment in the early 1960s we did little more than wring our hands over the crushed and crocked. Yet he seized the burning brand and lit a fire that has illuminated many dark places of the soul with a tireless and practical kindness that no other sport has ever matched.

Many others have been involved in the IJF but its first steps were powered by the heartbeat of one man. Every great cause needs its prophet and the voice crying in the wilderness for injured jockeys was Oaksey. The ongoing health and vigour of racing's pre-eminent charity remains his crowning glory.

Oaksey was ever a man of action. His father, Geoffrey, was a lawyer of huge distinction and the principal British judge at the Nuremberg trials. Indeed, when Oaksey was 16 he spent part of one summer at that most pivotal weighing of the scales of justice, where his father was president of all the judges.

But despite having had a Group 1 education at Eton, Oxford and Yale, John decided against following the expected path into the law. Instead of becoming "my learned friend" he became, through deed in saddle, erudition of pen and exercise of humanity, perhaps the finest friend racing had during his incarnation.

And, by God, he was some amateur jockey in an age when there were some cracking fellow Corinthians about and when the pros would do everything in their power to make their afternoons a misery before buying them a drink, or 12, in the evening.

The triumphs were many, including his extraordinary victory in the 1958 Hennessy on Taxidermist when the race was run at

'He became, through deed in saddle, erudition of pen and exercise of humanity, perhaps the finest friend racing had during his incarnation'

Hands on Oaksey turns the first sod as building starts in 2007 on the rehabilitation centre in Lambourn that now bears his name

Cheltenham. All of us have seen the world change in seconds up that most famous of racing's hills, but never so spectacularly or unbelievably as by the run conjured out of Taxidermist, who came from no place visible to stuff his rivals good, proper and comprehensive.

And in 1963, riding Carrickbeg in the Grand National, he was touched off close home by Pat Buckley and Ayala. Pausing but momentarily to rue the narrowness of his flirtation with jumping folklore he weighed in and then made his way over the Ormskirk Road to file his copy for the Telegraph.

In the years that followed he would entertain friends – and at after-dinner speeches the well-oiled and well-heeled – with the story of being stopped by a passer-by one evening in Piccadilly, who said: "I know you! You're the bugger who got tired before his 'orse."

John had a very long incarnation writing as Marlborough in the Telegraph but the fact that his prose was light years ahead of his prowess as a judge meant that not all his readers were appreciative of his efforts.

One much-valued letter read: "Dear Bastard, You couldn't tip more shit if they gave you a bloody wheelbarrow. What's more, with that awful toffee-nosed accent of yours, you make it sound like all the bleedin' losers went to Eton!"

But if Oaksey was an ordinary tipster, please believe me that he was a

Pioneer The Injured Jockeys Fund is Oaksey's greatest legacy. He was a driving force behind the founding of the charity in 1964 following the paralysing falls suffered by two leading jump jockeys, Tim Brookshaw and Paddy Farrell. In its 2012 annual report the IJF said it had given support to more than 400 beneficiaries in the past financial year and paid out almost £700,000 in grants to injured jockeys. Oaksey served as chairman of the IJF for 20 years (1982-2002) and then as president until his death. His name is immortalised in Oaksey House, the IJF's care and rehabilitation home in Lambourn

"For setting up the Injured Jockeys Fund all jockeys are grateful to him and it's fitting that Oaksey House carries his name" – Frankie Dettori

Jockey Oaksey enjoyed great success in a 20-year career as an amateur jump jockey, winning the Whitbread Gold Cup and Hennessy Gold Cup on Taxidermist in 1958, the Kim Muir twice (Jimmy Scot in 1966 and Black Baize in 1971), the National Hunt Chase (Sabaria in 1959), the Foxhunter at Cheltenham (Bullock's Horn in 1973) and the Fox Hunters' at Aintree twice (Subaltern in 1966 and Bullock's Horn in 1973). He was champion amateur twice (1957-58 and 1970-71). His most memorable ride came in defeat, when he was caught close home on Carrickbeg in the 1963 Grand National and beaten three-quarters of a length by Ayala

"He did not have any natural riding ability, it was pure application, but he did become most successful" – Sir Peter O'Sullevan

Journalist Oaksey was one of the foremost racing writers, notably for the Daily Telegraph, Sunday Telegraph and Horse & Hound. His evocative reports of Mandarin's amazing win in the 1962 Grand Steeple-Chase de Paris at Auteuil and Carrickbeg's National defeat are widely regarded as pinnacles of racing journalism. He wrote a number of books, including his 2003 autobiography Mince Pie for Starters

"There has been nothing like [his writing] before or since. It was elegant, informed, clear, humorous, forceful and unbelievably evocative" – Brough Scott

Broadcaster Having joined ITV as paddock commentator and interviewer in 1969, Oaksey was a core member of the ITV Seven team and later Channel 4 Racing. He once did a bungee jump live on air in aid of the IJF and on another occasion triggered the newspaper headline 'His Lordship Turns The Air Blue' when, believing his microphone to be switched off, he exclaimed, "Bugger! Dammit!" on air when his fancy for a race was beaten by a short head

"He was a great racing broadcaster and writer who was kind, considerate and had great integrity" – Clare Balding

sublime writer, whom the angels had indeed dipped in something special at birth. When I was ten and receiving a wonderful education at an institution for the cosseted, I recall picking a book off the library shelf entitled I Was There – a collection of the best pieces penned by the Telegraph's sports writers.

It is as if I held the book now that I remember it, cellophane-bound and heavy with promise. Alone in that small room I opened it up, looked for the bit about racing that had to be there somewhere. And it was then that I read the article by John Lawrence, as he then was, that is beyond any doubt the reason I write this piece.

Without any licence or exaggeration I can recall to this second the way in which the shivers ran up my spine as John took the reader through that spellbinding afternoon when a bitless Mandarin and a heroic Fred Winter won the Grand Steeple-Chase de Paris.

It was in those moments, when John grabbed me by the scruff of my neck and hurled me across the Channel and plonked me down in the Bois de Boulogne at Auteuil, that I suddenly grasped a truth – that it was possible to take people anywhere they wanted to go courtesy of the power of words driven by genuine passion. Those minutes spent reading John's words and feeling them rip through my mind and emotions drew my path in life.

Eventually, with a touch of luck and a following wind, you meet your heroes. Needless to say 99 per cent of them are a disappointment. But Oaksey was the one per cent, an unvarnished joy.

I see him now in his many roles.

Hard-charging and implacable amateur jockey, a writer never frightened of sheer emotion, founder of an institution, and a broadcaster with the insight of having done the job himself. But when I think of him now I also see him in later years, standing in the bitter cold of his 70s alongside his beloved Chicky selling IJF Christmas cards in some frozen corner of a shires outpost with the dedication of a man with a fraction of his mileage. A dedication born of nothing else but love.

And now he is dead. And if that passing is some form of sweet relief to him and those who loved him then I am glad he is gone – the hunter home from the hill at last.

I remember last November, after his home-bred Carruthers won the Hennessy, being embarrassed at sitting in the press room at Newbury unable to contain my tears at the fact he was not there. But I am not ashamed of my tears, nor do I see them as a weakness, because 46 years ago as I read John's loving account of Mandarin's deeds I saw in a blinding flash that jump racing is all about emotion and the power of man and horse to both shake and shape your core.

So farewell to you John Oaksey. And thank you from the countless hearts and souls of the many of us who believe that, with your passing, the ranks of jump racing's immortals have been augmented by someone utterly special. And as is the way with immortals, Oaks, you will live forever as long as there are folk who think that jumping a fence flat out on a winter's afternoon is a blessed piece of devilment forever worth the doing. And may that prove to be always.

First published in the Racing Post on September 6

THE
BIGGER
PICTURE

A spectacular view of the Kent National at Folkestone on the extra day in the leap year, February 29. The race was won by Upham Atom, who gave owner-trainer Kate Buckett her biggest success under rules
EDWARD WHITAKER (RACINGPOST.COM/PHOTOS)

final furlong
stories of the year – from the serious to the quirky

Silver lining
Cook lifts the clouds at joyful Olympics

A dark year had a brighter side for Tina Cook at the London Olympics, where she played a vital role in the GB three-day eventing team and provided racing with its closest link to the Games.

Equestrianism was one of the surprise hits of London 2012 and the first of 16 medals for Team GB at the Olympics and Paralympics was the silver won by the three-day eventers: Cook, Mary King, Zara Phillips, William Fox-Pitt and Nicola Wilson.

Cook, 42, was at the centre of it all on her grand campaigner Miners Frolic. In the dressage they had to perform in a thunderstorm, before the cross-country Cook's nerve was tested by a lengthy wait and, finally, she was the rider on whom everything rested in the show jumping. A double clear secured silver for the team.

She failed to add an individual medal to go with the team and individual bronzes she won with Miners Frolic at the 2008 Olympics, but that disappointment was washed away by pride and joy.

"For a horse to compete at two Olympics is pretty unusual and to have three medals to his name even more so – I'm not sure any horse has done that before," she says. "He was amazing all the way through. In the show jumping it was important to stay focused and not to think about the medals, because then you can transmit the wrong vibe to the horse. He went brilliantly."

Getting there had been far from easy. Josh Gifford, Cook's father and the famed trainer of 1981 Grand National hero Aldaniti, died at the age of 70 in February, piling personal sadness on to an already difficult struggle to make the Olympics team. Miners Frolic had been close to death the previous summer with colitis and he faced a race against time to make the qualifying standard. On top of that, Cook's marriage broke down.

"The whole year has been very bad for me personally, it's been a difficult year for the family and, with the horse being incredibly ill, the Olympics was pushed to one side for a long time," she says. "But at the same time it kept me motivated to carry on. I am incredibly proud of what we achieved."

Best in show Cook celebrates on Miners Frolic at the end of their decisive clear round in the show jumping at Greenwich

Having been far from the main action at the Beijing Olympics, when the equestrian events were held in Hong Kong, Cook revelled in the special atmosphere of London 2012. The team stayed in the athletes' village and after her event she attended the closing ceremony and the London victory parade. "Meeting other athletes and being part of the buzz was an experience I'll never forget," she says. "Even after the Games people were so enthusiastic."

Cook, assistant trainer to her brother Nick at the family yard in Findon, West Sussex, was not the only member of the equestrian team with links to racing. Nick Skelton, father of Paul Nicholls' assistant trainer Dan Skelton, won gold in the team show jumping and Yogi Breisner, the Lambourn-based jumps guru, was performance manager for the British eventing team.

"The Games showed the public that equestrian sport is for people from all walks of life, it's not just for the wealthy," Cook says. "If you're prepared to work hard, you can succeed in this sport."
Words by Nick Pulford

Dvinsky runs into record books

WHEN Dvinsky made his debut as a raw two-year-old on August 20, 2003, it's a fair bet owner Michael Tabor wasn't dreaming of the day when his €200,000 purchase would become the best-known old-aged pensioner in British racing.

Having been set the six-furlong Convivial Maiden Stakes at York's Ebor meeting as his first test, the son of Stravinsky was plainly expected to be more of a bottle rocket than a slow-burning Roman candle and when he won on his second start at Goodwood he looked ready to light up the sky.

Nine years, six owners, eight trainers and 45 jockeys down the line, however, at Wolverhampton on September 21, he ran for the 218th time, thereby setting a modern-day British record that may also be an all-time record and a world record to boot, for all we know.

One thing is for certain, the prolific bay has grabbed the attention of a racing public that loves a trier almost as much as it loves a winner. Not that Dvinsky hasn't troubled the judge in his time; 19 wins testify to the fact that he has always been a potent force in his grade; it's just that his grade quickly became established as well down the pecking order.

Having soon proved himself no superstar, he left Gerard Butler's Academy for the Hopefully Gifted and passed through the hands of Tony Carroll, Declan Carroll, Roy Bowring and Mark Allen before joining Paul Howling in the heady surrounds of some rented boxes at Sir Henry Cecil's Warren Place yard and donning the colours of entrepreneur Richard Berenson for a knockdown price of £6,000.

Barring a spell when

Howling took a year out of the game in 2011, horse and trainer were destined to be together for the duration. Outright ownership was taken over by part-owner David Hardaker, who has been rewarded with three more wins and enough runs to earn Dvinsky a little place in the history books.

Howling has never managed to restore the heroic horse to his 90-rated peak or even begin to approach the ambitions once held for him, and the economics of the sport mean he has been a costly hobby down the years, but the blinkered, front-running beast with a mind of his own and a lingering zest for racing has repaid in full every penny ever paid for him (even if Michael Tabor might not agree).

Sometimes success can be measured in more than money.

Words by Peter Thomas

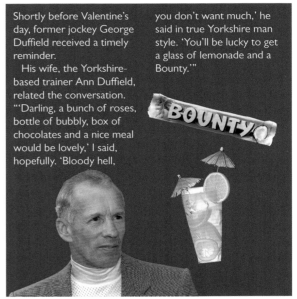

Shortly before Valentine's day, former jockey George Duffield received a timely reminder.

His wife, the Yorkshire-based trainer Ann Duffield, related the conversation. "'Darling, a bunch of roses, bottle of bubbly, box of chocolates and a nice meal would be lovely,' I said, hopefully. 'Bloody hell, you don't want much,' he said in true Yorkshire man style. 'You'll be lucky to get a glass of lemonade and a Bounty.'"

'What is a national broadcasting corporation for if it isn't to broadcast national events like the Derby?'
Sir Peter O'Sullevan on the loss of the BBC's racing coverage

The Annual Awards 2012

Our pick of the best of the year

Horse of the Year (Flat)
Frankel

We thought about this long and hard – in fact, we had sleepless nights worrying if we'd made the right choice – but in the end the vote went to the world's best horse, probably the best most of us will ever see. It was a close-run thing, though – about as close as the Queen Anne Stakes.

Horse of the Year (Jumps)
Big Buck's

He's an idle, stroppy cry-baby – according to the people who know him best at Paul Nicholls' yard – but he does have his good points. Like class, pace, power, an iron constitution and an incredible winning spirit. Simply the best.

Ride of the Year (Flat)
Josh Baudains on Rusty Rocket

"Golly Josh!" was the Racing Post headline after the inexperienced 7lb claimer won rodeo-style on Rusty Rocket

at Catterick in August. The colt tripped and hit the rail, causing Baudains to lose an iron before the home bend. No matter, he just kicked out his other foot and carried on regardless. "It was interesting," he said, and pretty impressive considering it was only the 14th win of his career.

Ride of the Year (Jumps)
Tony McCoy on Synchronised

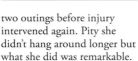

He pushed, he shoved, he kicked, he fought, he never gave up, he won – it's a common description of McCoy (left) rides down the years and the only difference this time was it came in the Cheltenham Gold Cup. Synchronised, so sadly taken a month later, was all heart too. What a combination.

Race of the Year (Flat)
Diamond Jubilee Stakes

It wasn't quite what we expected but it was still a

thriller as 'brain fade' entered the lexicon of British racing thanks to Luke Nolen's dramatic easing-up of Black Caviar. We could think of other ways of describing Luke's lapse but he won, so let's leave it at that. Oh, but if he hadn't . . .

Race of the Year (Jumps)
Ryanair Chase (right)

Three in a line going to the last, still nothing between them with 100 yards to go, and in-running punters couldn't call it. Albertas Run hit a low of 1.13 and Medermit 2.04, but in the end the somewhat reluctant Riverside Theatre produced a show-stopping performance to win a thriller. "He was beaten everywhere," said winning jockey Barry Geraghty – yes, everywhere except where it mattered.

Comeback of the Year
Snow Fairy

The little mare with the big heart likes nothing better than giving Ed Dunlop and his team palpitations and then carrying on her Group 1-winning ways as if nothing had ever happened. She was at it again in 2012, coming back from a serious tendon injury to win Group 1s on her only

two outings before injury intervened again. Pity she didn't hang around longer but what she did was remarkable.

Unluckiest horse
Danedream

Swamp fever, eh? Even when you haven't got it yourself, it's still enough to leave you feeling sick. Five days before the Arc came the news that a case of equine infectious anaemia (popularly known as swamp fever) had been discovered near Danedream's stables in Cologne and she would not be allowed to travel to Paris to defend her title. How unlucky is that? Very.

Most improved horse
Hunt Ball

Young trainer has young

chaser rated 69 and thinks, "I know, let's see if we can turn him into a Cheltenham Festival winner and a Grade 1 contender by the end of the season." Couldn't happen, surely, but it did. And for added entertainment value, there was his madcap owner Anthony Knott.

Disappointment of the Year
Long Run

He was the best thing since sliced bread (or possibly since a young Kauto Star) but now we're not so sure. Having found the old Kauto Star too good for him a couple of times, the biggest disappointment came when we found out he wasn't up to it in the Gold Cup even with his big rival out of the way.

Finish of the Year

This has got to be a Photoshop creation, right? Wrong, it's the finish of an otherwise unremarkable seven-furlong Class 4 handicap at Ayr on May 30. The winner, Ginger Jack, is in the centre and the distances between the first five were a short head, head, short head and short head. Yes, we know, the Grand National finish wasn't bad either.

THE **Alternative Awards**

The Andrew Mitchell award for outstanding work in the field of snobbery
Ascot and its orange dot team

The royal racecourse managed to orchestrate its own version of 'Plebgate' in January by sticking orange labels on racegoers who did not conform to the new dress code.

The Jeffrey Bernard sore head in the morning award
Jean-Charles Briens

Cheltenham decided to make the French photographer feel at home during the festival by holding its own little version of the French revolution with Wishfull Thinking replacing the guillotine as he catapulted through the rail in the Champion Chase. Monsieur Briens suffered a broken nose but his head stayed intact. C'est la vie!

The Lester Piggott award for legendary acts on returning to the saddle
Mick Kinane

Having steered Sea The Stars to victory in the Arc, Kinane hung up his saddle and retired into apparent obscurity. But now Kinane has transformed himself into a Superman-type figure. By day he is a retired small-time farmer but when the time comes he is a super jockey returning to the course to beat the bookies and win Legends races – something

The Mickael Barzalona special merit award for causing a scene whenever possible
Anthony Knott

We all thought Knott had been consigned to the history books after his impromptu early celebration when winning for the one and only time as a jockey in 2008. But Knott was back – with a vengeance. First he leaped aboard Hunt Ball as his star novice was coming back into the winner's enclosure and then told the world to 'do' the bookies before Hunt Ball won at Cheltenham, an event that led the dairy farmer to declare "bugger the cows!". Oh yes, and he sparked a security alert when piloting a helicopter back from Aintree. Life's never dull when Knott is around.

he did in spectacular style at Aintree and Doncaster.

The 'that was even more of a certainty than Frankel' award for inevitability
The BBC

You knew the game was up for racing on the channel when James Sherwood was dropped from the Royal Ascot fashion coverage. And so the props cupboard at Broadcasting House – or that new place in Salford – will store Willie Carson's box and John Parrott's top hat on the off chance horses return to the national broadcaster one day. Don't hold your breath.

The Kevin Keegan golden microphone for best rant in an interview
David Bridgwater

In a bristly interview after The Giant Bolster had finished second in the Cheltenham Gold Cup, seeking to get across how good his horse is, Bridgwater said: "When the handicapper

gave us a mark of 145, I said f*** 145 we should be 175." Reminded he was on live television, he replied: "I don't care where I am, he's a good horse." He is believed to have added off camera that he would "luv it if The Giant Bolster won the Gold Cup next year, luv it".

The Clive Brittain award for racecourse dancing
Sheikh Mohammed

Brittain's funky chicken strut set the standard but this year the prestigious title is presented to Sheikh Mohammed for his fist-in-the-air jiggle performed to a captivated audience after Monterosso's Dubai World Cup win in March. It would appear 'dad dancing' is a worldwide phenomenon.

The Clive Brittain award for eternal optimism
Punchestown

Why was there ever any doubt about this year's festival? Torrential rain, flooded course, high winds – we can't see what the concerns might have been . . .

The Dick Francis commemorative bookmark for creating a real-life racing thriller
Charlie Brooks

Picture the scene: public school-educated former trainer returns after years away hoping to make a few bob selling horses only to be caught up in one of the biggest 'Gates' of them all. Yes, it could be lifted from a Francis novel but is instead the life and times of Charlie Brooks, recipient of this notable award. Good to have you back, Charlie.

DONALD MCCAIN achieved a notable double this year not at Cheltenham or Aintree but in the big staying handicaps on the Flat that are fast becoming his forte.

Having won the 2011 Chester Cup and the 2010 Northumberland Plate with Overturn, McCain sent out Ile De Re to win both races in 2012 – a double last achieved in 1974 by Attivo, who was owned by legendary BBC commentator Sir Peter O'Sullevan.

McCain had the one-two at Chester, with Ile De Re beating Overturn, and seven weeks later, off an 8lb higher mark, Ile De Re revelled in the heavy ground at Newcastle to win again.

To be fair, not all the credit was due to McCain as Ile De Re had been transferred to him from Ian Williams' yard just three weeks before Chester.

"Ian was the first person to come over and say well done," McCain said. "A lot of the credit must go to him. Ian is a good mate and these things are never easy, but he made it very smooth."

FROM Ascot to Cheltenham via Chantilly, the Gamble family from West Sussex have declared their love of racing in an unusual way.

Julian and Christine Gamble are regulars at their local track, Fontwell, but they looked a little further afield for inspiration when naming their six children: Alden Ascot, Sophia Tralee, Isobelle Ayr, Cicely Naas, Juliette Chantilly and Eleanor Cheltenham.

"We enjoy a day at the races so much that we decided to make the sport a more permanent fixture in our household by naming the children after various racecourses," Christine said.

Long and winding road

Royal Diamond takes an unusual route to Classic glory

WHERE was the first place you could have seen a Classic winner in 2012? The unlikely answer is Fakenham on January 1, just 13 hours into the new year. The horse in question, Royal Diamond, didn't even win – he was beaten 32 lengths into third in a maiden hurdle – but eight months later he landed a thrilling Irish St Leger to give trainer Tommy Carmody and jockey Niall McCullagh their first Classic winner.

His journey to the Curragh was circuitous to say the least. In October 2009, Andrew Tinkler forked out 400,000 guineas for the then three-year-old after four wins in staying handicaps for Sir Mark Prescott. He went first to Michael Dods in Durham and then to Jonjo O'Neill's Jackdaws Castle stable, but he could not recapture that form.

His display at Fakenham on New Year's Day confirmed suspicions that Royal Diamond wasn't going to make a hurdler, at least not a good one. But there was one last resort that hadn't been explored. Back at the Curragh, Carmody had decided to rejoin the training ranks at the age of 55. This time he had moved to Johnny Murtagh's Curragh base and they had struck up a good rapport. Maybe they could rekindle Royal Diamond's enthusiasm.

The retrieval mission began at Dundalk in mid-March. Running off 85 in a mile-and-a-half handicap, Royal Diamond gave Carmody a smidgen of hope by finishing third of seven behind Keep It Cool, beaten just under two lengths.

Perhaps all was not lost. Royal Diamond went to Leopardstown the following month for another handicap, this time over a mile and three-quarters. Sent off at 14-1 in the 16-runner event, he was given an aggressive ride by Murtagh, who kicked on at halfway and gradually increased the tempo. Entering the final furlong, Royal Diamond was clear and he wasn't coming back to the pack. The winning margin of four and three-quarter lengths didn't flatter him. It was a performance that prompted Tinkler to proclaim: "That is the horse we thought we bought and I'm delighted he's done that."

The next step on the road to recovery was the Paddy Power Premier Handicap on Irish 1,000 Guineas day at the Curragh. This was much tougher, especially with a 12lb rise for his Leopardstown success. Murtagh fired Royal Diamond to the front again. This time he was caught, but only just. A narrow defeat by Midnight Soprano was nothing to be ashamed of. Paul Deegan's magnificent mare went on to lower the colours of top stayer Saddler's Rock and Grade 1-winning hurdler Unaccompanied in a Listed Leopardstown contest.

Carmody was certainly doing something right. Third place behind Alhellal in the Magners Ulster Derby a month later was a bit of a damp squib but a two-month break in preparation for the Ebor at York in late August was just what the doctor ordered. A refreshed Royal Diamond engaged in a thrilling tussle with Willing Foe inside the final furlong and, while Frankie Dettori and Godolphin spoiled their party, it was only temporary heartbreak.

Some questioned

whether Royal Diamond deserved his place in the line-up for the Group 1 Irish St Leger. He was rated 14lb inferior to favourite Fame And Glory, but his silver-haired 43-year-old jockey wasn't worried about the step up in class. "I remember looking up at the prices on the board as I came out of the weighing room and seeing he was 16-1," McCullagh recalls. "I knew he wasn't a 16-1 shot. I had ridden him in a few bits of work earlier that week and he was flying."

He wasn't wrong. As the race developed, it became apparent Fame And Glory was starting to get tired, the fancied Hartani was struggling and British raider Aiken was having the kitchen sink, a couple of pots and a

saucepan thrown at him by Jimmy Fortune.

McCullagh was starting to get a real tune out of Royal Diamond and, as in the Ebor, they were in the thick of things when it mattered most. But Massiyn was battling hard on his inside and Brown Panther was gathering a head of steam down the outside.

Surely Carmody and McCullagh wouldn't be agonisingly denied again. Would they? Brown Panther had it. No, it was Massiyn's race. Then Aiken came again. The four flashed past the winning post almost in line. Those in the stands weren't sure; nor were punters on the exchanges. But McCullagh knew he had won, even if he didn't want to admit it.

"I knew I was up but

I didn't want to start celebrating. I've seen that go wrong a few times before and I didn't want to be the latest one to get caught. But I did, I knew. I can't even describe the feeling. To win a Group 1 and an Irish Classic after spending so many years trying was just surreal. It's a moment I'll cherish and never forget. The next morning Christy Roche rang me and told me I should soak it up and really enjoy it and that's what I did. It was very special."

So how could a failed hurdler suddenly transform into a Classic king? "He got a bad fall at Huntingdon last year and I think that knocked the stuffing out of him for a while," McCullagh explains. "He got a break when he came to the Curragh and he just blossomed and kept improving. It's a great set-up. With Tommy and Johnny working together, they do a tremendous job. It's a tightly knit unit and the horses get really well looked after. I think that helped Royal Diamond. He was treated so well and he seemed to blossom in his surroundings. We knew he was in top shape before the Irish Leger."

Some journey, some race, some result.

Words by David Jennings

Classic moment
Niall McCullagh returns in triumph on Royal Diamond after the Irish St Leger

Rebel yell (but so nearly hell)

ONE celebration led to another when Rebel Fitz landed the Galway Hurdle in August, but only after a few moments of panic in a finish that was much closer than it should have been.

Davy Russell, believing he had the race won on Rebel Fitz, started waving his whip to the crowd before the winning post. But he had failed to notice the fast-finishing Cause Of Causes, ridden by Davy Condon, and in the end he only just squeezed home by a head.

Michael Winters, who trains Rebel Fitz in Kanturk, County Cork, feared the worst. "I thought everyone with me had gone mad cheering Rebel Fitz as the winner," he said. "I was convinced the other horse had caught him."

Confirmation of the result sparked wild scenes in the winner's enclosure as Winters rose up from the ground on the shoulders of what appeared to be the whole of Kanturk roaring: "Ole, ole, ole, ole. Ole. Ole."

Rebel Fitz is held in high regard by Winters – "when he won his first bumper he reminded me of Master Minded" – and amid the celebrations owner Brian Sweetnam's father Jerry said: "In the vicinity and all around the locality, everybody knows Rebel Fitz. Whether it's at mass in the church or in the shop they talk about the Rebel when he's out. You can see how popular he is from the carry-on in here."

Russell, meanwhile, was contrite as he relived his 'Black Caviar moment'.

"I deserve a kick up the arse," he said. "I was watching the big screen and thought I was clear. I shouldn't have done it and I can promise you it will never happen again."

Tony McCoy *Synchronised, Cheltenham Gold Cup*
It's all about jumping in the Gold Cup unless you have McCoy on your side. A never-say-die attitude can be just as important

Tom Cannon *Inthejungle, Plumpton, April 27*
Inthejungle pitched badly on landing at the fourth-last, leaving Cannon hanging on to his neck. The rider hauled himself back on board, coolly slipped into his irons and went on to victory

Daryl Jacob *Neptune Collonges, Grand National*
Creep, creep and creep some more. That's just what Jacob did to nose out Sunnyhillboy in the closest National finish

Barry Geraghty *Riverside Theatre, Ryanair Chase*
One doesn't like Cheltenham and the other loves it – luckily for all connected with Riverside Theatre, Geraghty wasn't prepared to let his mount give in

Campbell Gillies *(above) Brindisi Breeze, Albert Bartlett Novices' Hurdle*
Gillies kicked on down the Cheltenham hill while keeping enough up his sleeve to record a great success made all the more poignant by future events

Ruby Walsh *(below) Aerial, Newbury, March 3*
He was sixth two out, fourth at the last, then it looked as if he was getting up, then it didn't. Finally, in one last desperate lunge, Walsh got home by a short head

Proud day Ginger McCain's widow Beryl, son Donald and daughter Joanne at the unveiling

GINGER McCAIN became one of the few horseracing figures to be honoured with a sculpture when a bust of the legendary Grand National-winning trainer was unveiled at Aintree's big meeting in April.

The rarity of the accolade is clear in a database of Britain's sporting statues, which details 120 around the UK. Almost half of those are from the world of football and McCain, who died in September 2011, is only the fourth horseracing personality to be honoured.

He joins Lester Piggott and Frankie Dettori, who are celebrated at Haydock and Ascot respectively, and the late Lord Oaksey, whose statue stands at the jockeys' rehabilitation centre named in his honour in Lambourn.

Many great horses are, of course, remembered with statues, including McCain's three-time National winner Red Rum, who stands nearby his old master at Aintree.

At the unveiling of the McCain bronze, which was sculpted by Nigel Boonham, the trainer's widow Beryl joked: "It's lovely – now you can all go and tell him what you think of him."

Her son Donald said: "It's a great reminder of what he achieved here and there could be no better tribute. Publicly he would say it's a lot of fuss about nothing, but privately he'd be thrilled. It would have meant the world to him."

'The flag man looked a bit windy and he should, perhaps, be given an incontinence pad and a better pair of trainers' Flat trainer Mark Johnston, who was at the final fence for the Queen Mother Champion Chase, gives an eyewitness report on the controversial bypassing

Flying the flag

Turner's US Grade 1 win leads women's movement

A LATE change of mind gave Paul Hancock his biggest win in ten years as an owner when King's Warrior landed the John Smith's Cup at York in July.

The five-year-old had disappointed in his two runs before York and was due to go to the sales on the eve of the race before trainer Peter Chapple-Hyam prompted a rethink.

Hancock said: "Peter phoned me up on Tuesday [four days before the race] and said, 'We can't sell him. He's working too well, he's jumping out of his skin.' If the trainer says that, it's the sort of call you want to receive."

King's Warrior lined up as a 33-1 shot for the £150,000 race but won decisively by four and a half lengths. "This is definitely my biggest win," Hancock said. "Peter's a great trainer. If he's got the right horse, he'll always win the right races."

And, he might have added, Chapple-Hyam had made the right call too.

A FELINE intruder came within a whisker of catastrophe in an eye-popping incident at Maisons-Laffitte in April.

With the five runners in the Listed Prix de Suresnes inside the final furlong, a ginger cat sped across the track just in front of leading pair Sir Jade and Mustaheel.

The cat made it to the stands rail in the nick of time but with only eight of its nine lives still intact.

FROM Jessica Ennis to Hannah Cockcroft, Katherine Grainger to Sophie Christiansen, Nicola Adams to Katie Taylor, it was a golden summer for sportswomen. All of them, and many more, became household names in a year when women's sport took centre stage.

In racing, too, there are growing signs of a seismic shift in the way women are viewed in the sport as they start to push back age-old boundaries. Hayley Turner is the flagbearer, having added a US Grade 1 win in 2012 to her two Group 1 victories of the previous year, and a growing army is marching in step with her. Official recognition came with a women's Flat jockeys' championship and an all-female team in the Shergar Cup – both new in 2012.

Turner's triumph on I'm A Dreamer in the Grade 1 Beverly D Stakes at Arlington in August came in similar circumstances to her maiden Group 1 success on Dream Ahead in the 2011 July Cup. She got a late call-up for Dream Ahead from David Simcock when William Buick was unavailable and the same trainer turned to her again in Chicago when Ryan Moore opted to stay in Britain rather than take the ride.

She had won on I'm A Dreamer before and this time she got first run on local hope Marketing Mix before holding on by a head in a driving finish. The places went to top US-based jockey Julien Leparoux and Buick – and therein lies a major difference between racing and other sports: on the racetrack women have to compete on level terms with the men.

Turner's achievements were singled out for special attention in May when she was named Sportswoman of the Year, ahead of Ennis

American dream Hayley Turner scores a landmark victory in the Beverly D on I'm A Dreamer

and Rebecca Adlington, in Glamour magazine's Women of the Year awards. While Julie Krone is regarded as the mould-breaker in the US, Turner believes success for female jockeys means much more on this side of the Atlantic.

"You can't take away what Julie Krone, Chantal Sutherland and Emma-Jayne Wilson have achieved, but I do think that riding in North America is easier," she says. "I don't think they're as strong, because in America it's all about keeping a horse balanced. An American jockey will ride at the same track for three months against the same riders and horses. Coming to Ascot and racing over two miles on soft ground is a different experience. If there is a flaw in anyone's riding it will show up in the UK."

Turner was not the only

landmark achiever in 2012. Over jumps, northern-based conditional Lucy Alexander last season set a British women's record of 38 winners – almost double the previous record held by Lorna Vincent for 23 years – and Katie Walsh had the best-ever placing by a female jockey in the Grand National when she finished third on Seabass.

The days are long gone when women set their sights merely on getting round in the National; Walsh was there to win on 8-1 joint-favourite Seabass and she did not give way until the Elbow. At Aintree the day before the National, Rachael Green had a career-high when she won the Listed mares' bumper.

Ferdy Murphy, who has helped guide Alexander's career, is one of many good judges who rate the 21-year-old highly. "She's positive, has plenty of ability,

a good racing brain and is making into a good rider," the trainer says. Further recognition of Alexander's growing profile – and the marketablity of female jockeys – came with a sponsorship deal with Markel Insurance, whose other two racing clients are Buick and Sam Thomas.

The Flat apprentices, led by Amy Ryan, have made a positive impact too. Richard Hughes is among those impressed by their work ethic. "There's no doubt in my mind that, as a group, girl apprentices work harder than boys," he said in his Racing Post column. "They graft, they ride out and give everything 100 per cent effort and commitment."

In 2012, in racing as in many other sports, woman's work had its reward.

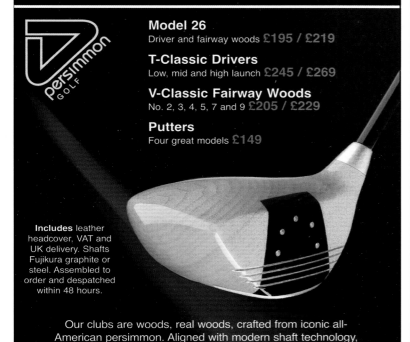

Fast learner

Lee makes impressive switch to Flat

GOODWOOD and Aintree, the Stewards' Cup and the Grand National, Hawkeyethenoo and Amberleigh House – polar opposites that have one thing in common: Graham Lee.

It took the Galway-born jockey almost ten minutes to ride his way into Aintree folklore when Amberleigh House conquered the National fences and 38 rivals back in 2004. In stark contrast, Hawkeyethenoo and Lee needed little more than one minute and ten seconds to rocket to victory in one of Flat racing's most prestigious sprint handicaps in August.

While the 36-year-old would have us believe there's little difference between riding in a four-and-a-half-mile chase and a six-furlong sprint, his seamless transition from jump racing to the Flat in 2012 was little short of miraculous.

It was while lying stricken on the turf following another sickening fall at Southwell in February – before he'd even learned he had dislocated his right hip – that Lee decided enough was enough. While many jump jockeys are heavier and taller than their Flat counterparts, Lee's the opposite, almost a ready-made Flat jockey. To make the 9st 11lb required to ride in jump races, he would punish himself in the gym, trying to bulk up and put on weight as opposed to shedding pounds and ounces like so many of his colleagues. A spell on the sidelines meant the weight concealed in Lee's muscular frame would be lost and the depressing thought of trying to start from scratch was enough to prompt a career change. Rarely can

The long and short of it Lee, a Grand National winner in 2004 with Amberleigh House (inset), has enjoyed notable sprint success on the Flat, including at Chester on Jack Dexter (above)

such adversity have been the catalyst to immediate success but that was the story of Lee's season. He shone around the tight turns of Chester at the May meeting, notching two winners on his first visit to the idiosyncratic track. With the victories of Absinthe and Jack Dexter came belief that he could succeed on the Flat and, although he is not one to set targets, Lee was already averaging a winner from every five rides.

Jack Dexter's win came in a competitive six-furlong handicap and it's in the sprint division, so different to what Lee was accustomed to over jumps, where he has excelled. The same horse provided him with another notable success when bolting up in the Bronze Cup at Ayr in September, on the track where the jockey landed the Scottish Grand National on Grey Abbey in 2004. "I don't think it's a big deal," said

Lee, as he drew comparisons between the two codes. "Whether you're riding a horse over five furlongs or in the National, you have to let the horse breathe. You have to make decisions more quickly on the Flat but it's not hugely different."

Lee believes his transition was helped by the atrocious summer weather, which brought 'jumping ground' for much of the season. It was almost unraceable at Newcastle's Northumberland Plate meeting at the end of June but, with racing surviving, Lee reached another landmark as he unleashed Maarek with a race-winning burst in the Group 3 Chipchase Stakes – his first success at Group level.

Rides on good horses had dried up over jumps, which is one of the main reasons Lee decided to switch codes, but on the Flat he has been

in action at many of the bigger meetings. Another of Lee's Group performers was James Fanshawe's stayer High Jinx, who was runner-up in the Lonsdale and Doncaster Cups before another second place in the Group 1 Prix du Cadran on Arc day in October, and of course there was that Glorious Goodwood highlight on Hawkeyethenoo.

After only 31 winners in his injury-hit and curtailed final season over jumps, Lee more than doubled that total on the Flat and his prize-money more than trebled. Financial security and longevity in the saddle are two of the other benefits of his switch. "I'd love to think I could ride for another ten years. I want to be as successful as this game lets me be and as long as I'm providing for my wife and two kids it's happy days."

Happy days indeed.
Words by Lewis Porteous

HAS there ever been a more delighted owner than Christopher Ash after Sahrati's victory at Fontwell in June?

The gelding, despite recent form figures of 388707, was backed into 9-4 from a morning price of 20-1 and Ash told on-course reporters: "You can keep this concise, you'll only need two words, 'gamble landed'."

But it wasn't just about the money. "This is the greatest feeling, so much better than the money," Ash added. "To have a winner is just magic, my heart is going a million miles an hour."

RACING POST reader Kay Oxley, of Carlton Miniott, near Thirsk, sent in this photo of her creation for the annual village scarecrow festival, which had television characters as the theme.

Kay and her grandson Owen MacGregor opted for Frankie Dettori performing his flying dismount and John McCririck studying the form in the Racing Post, but they were beaten to first prize by Nora Batty and Compo from Last of the Summer Wine.

"I wonder how John feels about being pipped at the post by Nora with her wrinkly stockings and Compo and his smelly wellies?" said Kay.

'I can always rely on him to get me out of the s**t!' Robin Dickin puts his faith in his hurdler Thomas Crapper

Day trip pays off for Webber

PAUL WEBBER joined the British hordes heading to Spain in the summer but, rather than the tourist hotspots of Benidorm and Marbella, his destination was the Basque city of San Sebastian with his dual-purpose grey Australia Day.

It was time well spent because the Oxfordshire trainer returned with a victory and valuable prize-money at a time when opportunities for Australia Day were almost non-existent at home. By contrast, San Sebastian offered good prize-money and was perfect for the nine-year-old – sharp and right-handed with fast ground.

"He was on a mark of 85 on the Flat here, which is not easy for him to win off, and there was nothing for him over hurdles until the end of September and no chase for him until the end of October," Webber says. "I was aware of San Sebastian because Jean-Claude Rouget [the French champion trainer] has been a pal of mine for a long time and I thought it was worth a shot."

Having boarded for a couple of days at Rouget's Pau

yard in south-west France, Australia Day crossed the border for the Premio Copa de Oro de San Sebastian – a mile-and-a-half conditions race on turf – on August 15. He was the first British-trained runner at the track since 1998 but luck was against him, as his saddle slipped and he finished third.

Three weeks later he was back for the Gran Premio de San Sebastian, this time over a mile and three-quarters. Sent off at 4-5, he won by four and three-quarter lengths under Oscar Urbina. It was the second-most valuable of his ten career victories and made him the first British horse to win at San Sebastian since the Queen's Enharmonic in 1993.

"He won €26,000 and the trip cost us €6,000," Webber says. "If you can tell me where else an 85-rated horse can win that sort of money at that time of year, you're a cleverer man than me. We've got to look for these opportunities where we can."

A case, perhaps, of the maths being more important than the history.

A THREE-WAY dead-heat for third place was called at Newmarket in June after the track was hit by a power cut.

"The power went and all I had to go on was a freeze-frame from Racing UK," explained Dave Smith, the judge. "I could pick the winner and the second, but three horses were in a line for third spot and I thought the best policy was to give a triple dead-heat."

THE MOBOT, the trademark celebration of double Olympic champion Mo Farah, is one of the enduring images of 2012. And the inspiration came from none other than Clare Balding on a May edition of Sky's sports show A League Of Their Own.

Farah was another of the guests and James Corden, the host, suggested he needed a unique way of marking Olympic victory.

Balding came up with the solution. "I think you should do the 'M' from YMCA, the M for Mo," she said, demonstrating the pose to illustrate her point.

"I'll definitely do it, I'll give it a go," Farah said. Corden then added the finishing touch by giving the move its name.

The rest, as they say, is history.

QUESTIONS were asked after Forced Kin made his debut in a bumper at Thurles in February – say the name quickly and you'll see why.

"The BHA and Weatherbys did query how the name was allowed and the owners explained it came from the dam's side," said Horse Racing Ireland registrations supervisor Vicky McWey. "His dam's name is Force Divine, so it does make

sense to call him Forced Kin. The BHA accepted this explanation."

Patrick Whelan, one of Forced Kin's owners, admitted: "We were surprised it went through to be honest, but when it's written down it probably doesn't look so bad."

RACING folk are a superstitious bunch and perhaps a few jitters were in order when Michelangelo's

connections were handed the St Leger trophy following his victory in the Cocked Hat Stakes at Goodwood in May – four months before the final Classic.

It was a promotional ploy by Goodwood and Ladbrokes, the Leger sponsor, and the track's managing director Adam Waterworth said: "Everyone knows the Cocked Hat is the best St Leger trial, so we thought

we'd save time and hand them the trophy now."

He had a point because Michelangelo's owner Bjorn Nielsen and trainer John Gosden had done the Cocked Hat-St Leger double in 2011 with Masked Marvel, but as it turned out Michelangelo was only third at Doncaster behind Encke and Camelot.

TIM EASTERBY had two winners of the same race at

Pontefract in April when stablemates Deauville Flyer and Mirrored dead-heated in a mile-and-a-quarter handicap.

Both horses were making their seasonal debut and Easterby seemed surprised that either had won, never mind both. "I thought they might both need the run," he said. "I've had a few dead-heats before but never had two of mine doing it."

Dynamic duo
Casey and Flemenstar make headlines

TRAINER Jo Hughes said she wasn't surprised when Lights Of Broadway won at Taunton in January, but almost everyone else was.

The six-year-old, having her fifth outing, won at the mammoth odds of 200-1 in a mares' novice hurdle, with the minor places filled by 50-1 and 33-1 shots. The only longer-priced winner in British racing history was Equinoctial at 250-1 at Kelso in 1990 and Lights Of Broadway was just the fourth 200-1 winner in Britain since then.

Hughes said: "It's not a major surprise as she's been working well. I must admit I did not tell anyone to back her as she is going to need fences before we see the best of her."

One of the owners in Hughes's Lambourn yard did back Lights Of Broadway, scooping £2,400 with a £10 each-way bet, but only because she likes to follow jockey Mark Grant.

Pauline Nye, a retired army major from West Sussex, said: "I always have a bet when he's aboard. I watched the race on television and they could have heard me in the next town when I cheered her home."

Lights Of Broadway quickly reverted to type. Sent chasing on her next start, she finished third at 8-1 – the shortest odds of her career – unseated at 10-1 and was fourth of five at 9-1.

'I've just got the one horse, so he's the best and the worst' Banbury-based permit-holder Richard Harper after the victory of Chapel House at Hereford in April

What about the horse? Photographers crowd round Casey after Flemenstar's victory in the Powers Gold Cup at Fairyhouse

FLEMENSTAR is that rare type of young chaser who makes the blood rise with excitement – but RTE viewers in Ireland were surprised just how passionate he made Peter Casey on a cold January afternoon.

Interviewed live on air by Tracey Piggott after Flemenstar's breakthrough Grade 1 win in the Arkle Novice Chase at Leopardstown, the 70-something trainer told the nation just how he was going to celebrate the moment – "I'll have f***ing sex tonight and everything," he exclaimed.

Back home at his stables outside Stamullen on the Meath/Dublin border, the phone was soon ringing off the hook. Junie, Casey's wife of 50 years, had watched the race but not the post-race interview. It wasn't long before she found out what had been said. "Jesus, what did he say that for?" was her instant reaction.

After half a million YouTube views of the infamous interview, Casey is a household name. He appeared on the RTE chat programme The Saturday Night Show and was the centre of attention when Flemenstar landed a second Grade 1 win in the Powers Gold Cup at Fairyhouse in April. He gave the media what they wanted: "I'll be looking forward to celebrating with my wife in bed at midnight," he said.

Casey, who variously gives his age as "in the 70s", then 75, "or is it 77?", is loving the ride with Flemenstar. He wanted to be a jockey but was an only son and his father needed him to work on the land. Training came late to him – kindled by the interest of his three boys in pony racing – and he sees similarities in his unlikely fame with the rise to folk-hero status of Danoli and Tom Foley in the 1990s.

Unlike his trainer, who instigates laughter whenever he appears in front of a microphone, Flemenstar has done all his talking on the track.

Finishing second to Bog Warrior on his chasing debut at Navan was the stepping stone to a stunning 2011-12 season that yielded five wins on the bounce under regular jockey Andrew Lynch and prompted bookmakers to make him as short as 8-1 for the 2013 Cheltenham Gold Cup. The last three of his wins – with a Grade 3 at Naas sandwiched between the two Grade 1s – all merited a Racing Post Rating of 164, although the highlight for Casey was the 19-length Leopardstown success that propelled both horse and trainer into the national spotlight.

"That day in Leopardstown was just something else," he says. "I just couldn't believe how far he won by. I was in shock. My son Francis had told me he was getting better and better but I never thought he was going to be as good as he turned out to be.

"The whole thing with Tracey was great too. We got great publicity from that. I was down on holidays in Wicklow during the summer and some fella came up to me and said: 'Is Tracey on her way, Peter?' Sure, we knock great banter out if it."

Casey hopes Flemenstar will have developed into a genuine Gold Cup contender by next March and he has no hesitation when asked what makes his stable star so special. "It's his jumping. That's what Andrew and everyone else tells me. He's just so good over his fences. He reminds some people of Arkle the way he gets from one side to another."

And if he does go on to win the Gold Cup? "I won't sleep for a month," Casey says. Perhaps it's best not to ask him why.

Words by David Jennings

OWN1.CO.UK
SET YOUR HEART RACING!

OWNING A RACEHORSE IS THE ULTIMATE THRILL.

Watch with pride and anticipation as your horse is paraded before the off, feel the exhilaration as it gallops down the home straight, and – maybe, just maybe – savour the adulation and jubilation as it is led into the Winner's Enclosure.

Now a new website, www.Own1.co.uk shows you how to realise your dream.

The site takes you through the four steps to becoming an owner, each with its own fascination and fun.

There's advice on:

– Finding a horse to suit your pocket through the different kinds of ownership

– What to look for in a future winner

– Picking your trainer

– Choosing your horse's name and its colours

Own1.co.uk takes you through each step and highlights some owners' experiences.

LOVE the RACES

Inspiration lives on

The lasting legacy of Campbell Gillies

H E is gone but he is in no way forgotten. Go to Arlary House Stables, home to the most powerful string of jumpers in Scotland, and you might even think Campbell Gillies is still with us.

You would be wrong, for it is not Campbell you see but a young man who as a 16-year-old in June came chock full of excitement and ambition to work at the same racing yard as his famous cousin. Later that month he was grieving for him, ripped apart emotionally but fuelled to the brim with a desire to carry on the good work of his lost relative.

Hamish McNeill looks like Gillies, almost eerily so, and he rides on the saddle that once belonged to Gillies, but Gillies he is not. He is his own man, setting out on a racing life with an added motivation that few of us could ever understand.

"I was given Campbell's saddle and I've been riding out on it," McNeill says. "It's not the most comfortable. He must have had a bony arse but I'm getting used to it."

Lucinda Russell, her partner Peter Scudamore and the rest of the Arlary House team are also getting used to having Hamish. It will take them far longer to get used to not having Campbell but horses do not permit long periods of mourning. However broken your heart has been left, the horses need riding, feeding, grooming and mucking out. That first morning in June when news sank in of Gillies' death, Russell and her team had to carry on as normal on a day that veered as far from the norm as it is possible to get.

How quickly despair followed joy remains hard to comprehend. What happened in March is still in the recent past yet what took place thereafter has made it seem

Big-stage talent Gillies wins the Albert Bartlett Novices' Hurdle on Brindisi Breeze, just three months before his tragic death

like a lifetime ago. Aboard Brindisi Breeze, a bold front-runner owned by Sandy Seymour, Gillies enjoyed the finest moment of a career that was rapidly on the rise. The campaign would end with the ever-cheerful jockey having posted a best-ever total of 38 winners, but the biggest of them by far – for Gillies, the horse, his owner and trainer — was undoubtedly the Cheltenham Festival's Albert Bartlett Novices' Hurdle, in which the six-year-old embryonic chaser held off hot favourite Boston Bob.

Fate then had one of her cruellest twists in store. Two months later, Brindisi Breeze was no more – one of the three horses who won on the final day of the 2012 festival to perish soon after. Synchronised and Bellvano were followed by Russell's great hope, who jumped out of a paddock and was hit by a tanker. On an even

more tragic morning one month later, Russell was informed Gillies had died in a swimming pool accident while on holiday in Corfu. He would have celebrated his 22nd birthday the following day.

"That they've both gone so soon after Cheltenham is absolutely macabre," said Scudamore two days before Gillies' funeral. "It's horrible but at least Campbell had Brindisi, who allowed him to show on the sport's biggest stage what a very good jockey he had become."

The many hundreds of people, a collection of family, friends, colleagues and admirers, who attended the Edinburgh funeral, heard Russell's stable jockey, Peter Buchanan, attempt to define what it was that set his late deputy apart.

"He was someone you only had to meet once for ten minutes and you

thought you'd known him your whole life," he said. "It was the twinkle in his eye, the infectious smile and the unique personality of the wee man that had him standing head and shoulders above us all." Yet Buchanan stressed that Gillies was not just a fine person but also a fine jockey. "I know he was certainly nipping at my heels," he admitted. "In fact, he had my foot half off."

We will never know just how big a mark Gillies would have made on the sport. He has, however, left a lasting legacy. On September 3, £15,000 was raised for the Injured Jockeys Fund at a golf day staged in his honour and, on October 5, Hexham opened a brand new facility called The Campbell Gillies Lodge, providing excellent accommodation for stable staff. The venue was a fitting one for, according to his friends, Gillies' proudest

moment had come not at Cheltenham but Hexham, where in 2011 he was voted Britain's best-looking jockey by a discerning group of young ladies. He mentioned it once or twice in the days, weeks and months that followed.

And so at Hexham, as elsewhere, the name of Campbell Gillies lives on. His desire to succeed as a jockey continues through Hamish McNeill, who this winter will seek to make his mark in point-to-points before transferring to the professional sphere. "I hope I'm half as good as you were," McNeill wrote on Twitter soon after learning of his cousin's death. Half as good would be no mean achievement but there will be very many people hoping he can do even better than that.

Words by Lee Mottershead

Established 1942

Westerlands Stud

"There is something about the outside of a horse that is good for the inside of a man"

Sir Winston Churchill

"I have travelled the world, made a success in business, but nothing quite beats watching your own horse race."

David Jamison, Chairman

Dedicated to the care of all racehorses

from birth, to winning, to winning again, to breeding the future and to a lasting retirement

Specialising in boarding, foaling and sales preparation

Westerlands is located at the foot of the South Downs, 15 minutes from Goodwood; the ideal location for mares to nurture the future of racing bloodstock. Westerlands offers state of the art facilities, 62 boxes, isolation areas, a horse walker and lunge pit; within 300 acres of prime, nutrient-enriched grazing. Our paddocks are well secured and range from nursery to all-weather areas.

Westerlands Stud was founded in 1942 by breeding expert and pioneer of 'quality over a pretty face', Florence Nagle. Florence came 2nd in the Derby in 1937 with her self-trained horse Sandsprite which went on to stand as a popular stallion. We are a family business and plan to continue this success story. Our strength is our belief in and history of good breeding and we pride ourselves in the high level of hands on care our team provides.

Graffham, Petworth, West Sussex GU28 0QJ
Tel: +44 (0)1798 867 644

www.westerlands.com

Quiz of 2012

It was a memorable year – or was it?

HAVE you heard the one about Willy Beamin? Crazy name, crazy horse. "Unbelievable, unbelievable," said owner James Riccio after the three-year-old had landed a fairly remarkable victory at Saratoga in August.

Sent off an 11-1 shot, the gelding came with a wet sail to win the Grade 1 King's Bishop Stakes by half a length. What was especially noteworthy about this triumph was that it came in a $500,000 contest over seven furlongs – just three days after Willy Beamin had won a minor stakes race restricted to state-breds over a mile and a furlong.

Riccio had claimed Willy Beamin for just $25,000 in a race at Aqueduct on March 23 before sending him to Rick Dutrow, still in business in New York under a stay of proceedings despite incurring a ten-year ban for repeated medication violations.

The King's Bishop was Willy Beamin's fifth win on the bounce for Dutrow. "I was just looking maybe to win an allowance race for New York-breds," Riccio said. "But he started getting good, good, good." You can say that again.

And the name? Evidently it's slang for an advanced state of inebriation, as in "I was steamin', willy beamin'. Or a 'Willie Beamin' is a boastful soul with a big tip for themselves. Oh, and Willie Beamen is Jamie Foxx's character in Any Given Sunday. So now you know.

Notable firsts

1. Which jockey had his first Group 1 winner in Britain when Mayson landed the July Cup?
2. Which trainer had his first major Classic winner with Samitar in the Irish 1,000 Guineas?
3. Which filly gave Francois Doumen his first British Group 1 when she won the Sun Chariot Stakes?
4. Who rode his first Grade 1 winner when 50-1 shot Benefficient landed the Deloitte Novice Hurdle at Leopardstown?
5. Which Yorkshire trainer had a first Royal Ascot winner with Prince Of Johanne?

They share a name

6. Cheltenham Festival winner and 1968 film musical starring Fred Astaire
7. Royal Ascot winner and 18th century cabinet maker
8. British Classic-placed colt and great Renaissance artist
9. British Classic winner and comet named after astronomer
10. Royal Ascot dual winner and creator of fictional detective Jules Maigret

Identify the winners with a regal name

11. Irish St Leger
12. Ribblesdale
13. 1,000 Guineas
14. Royal Hunt Cup
15. Cheveley Park

PICTURE QUESTION Name these super greys who won big races in 2012

Big prices

16. At 40-1 in the Fred Winter Juvenile Handicap Hurdle, which horse was the longest-priced winner at the Cheltenham Festival?
17. Which Oliver McKiernan-trained chaser was the 50-1 winner of the Grade 1 Betfred Bowl at Aintree?
18. Who trained 33-1 Wokingham winner Dandy Boy?
19. Which 50-1 shot was runner-up to Synchronised in the Cheltenham Gold Cup?
20. Name the 25-1 winner of the French Derby.

Beaten favourites

21. Name the 8-1 joint favourites in the Grand National.
22. Which stablemate of the winner was 13-8 favourite in the 1,000 Guineas?
23. Who started 6-5 favourite in the RSA Chase?
24. Which John Gosden-trained filly was 11-4 favourite in the Oaks?
25. When the Aidan O'Brien-trained Windsor Palace won the Group 3 Mooresbridge Stakes at the Curragh in May, which stablemate was runner-up as 2-5 favourite?

What links . . . ?

26. Champion Hurdle winner; Irish St Leger winner; Nunthorpe Stakes runner-up
27. Aintree Hurdle winner; Champion Bumper winner; Cheltenham Gold Cup fourth
28. Dante Stakes winner; Triumph Hurdle winner; Supreme Novices' Hurdle winner
29. 2,000 Guineas runner-up; Rebecca Curtis-trained Cheltenham Festival winner; French Champion Hurdle winner
30. Craven Stakes winner; Ayr Gold Cup winner; RSA Chase runner-up

Answers page 168

THE whip rules were revised again in 2012 but that did not end the rumblings of discontent.

Ambrose Turnbull, owner of Pokfulham, was so frustrated by his six-year-old's defeat in a controversial finish at Hamilton in June that he immediately contacted the Racing Post to complain.

The winning jockey, David Allan on La Bacouetteuse, was given a four-day ban for using his whip 11 times and Turnbull believed it was unfair he kept the race at the expense of Pokfulham and Danny Tudhope, who had ridden within the rules and lost by only a nose.

"Allan rightly got a ban for hitting his horse, which surely made the difference of a nose," Turnbull said. "When is this sort of blatant infringement going to result in a demotion of the winner, especially when the winning margin is so close?

"One jockey rides to the rules and the other breaks them, yet the rule breaker is the winner. Surely this cannot how the rules were meant to be administered?"

Always winning (at Aintree)

ALWAYS WAINING'S form figures since the start of 2010 are 8P1**0067**04**1**8**44**0**9**1 – not an impressive sequence overall, but the crucial numbers are the five in bold. Those are his runs at Aintree, the magical place where he comes alive every spring.

The amazing story of the Peter Bowen-trained chaser reached new heights in April when he claimed his third consecutive Topham Chase over the daunting National fences, a feat never achieved before and which earned comparison with the Grand National exploits of Red Rum.

Always Waining's owner Peter Douglas, a businessman from Uttoxeter, always travels to Aintree more in hope than expectation. "It would be ridiculous to say we were going there thinking he was going to win," he says. "Every time we've gone there, he's been out of form and yet he's always come up trumps."

Bowen has some idea what makes the difference at Aintree. "He loves jumping those fences and he makes ground jumping them," he says. "Over park fences he might jump a bit too big and lose ground that way, but he jumps the National fences so well he finds it easier to stay in the race. He loves the place. The minute he gets off the lorry you can tell he's up for it. At any other track he doesn't want to know."

The aim for 2013 is the

Aintree magic
Always Waining in the Topham

National itself and victory there really would put his name alongside Red Rum as an Aintree great. Douglas, however, may not be there to see it. This summer he suffered a tragic loss when his daughter Lisa, a 38-year-old mother of two, died in a house fire. Going racing without her is difficult to contemplate.

"Lisa was the biggest Always Waining fan in the world," he says. "She was such an avid racegoer and it's spoiled all that for us. At the moment it's too raw for us to go to the races. Uttoxeter's our local course and we've got a box there, but we can't go back. The little horse deserves

his chance in the National, but whether we'll be there to watch him is another matter."

Douglas would like a permanent mark of Always Waining's achievement – a trophy or a race named in his honour – but, again, his daughter's death has put any plans on hold.

Maybe, like the Brazil football team after their third World Cup triumph in 1970, Douglas could keep the trophy. Now there's a thought. "When we took the trophy back the first year we thought that's the last we'll see of that. This time I won't even bother taking it back, I'll just keep it."
Words by Nick Pulford

6 OF THE BEST
Small wonders

Countrywide Flame
He's "only 15.1 hands and a fingerprint" according to trainer John Quinn, but he stood tall to win the Triumph Hurdle at Cheltenham and came mighty close in the Cesarewitch too

Danedream
What she lacks in size, she makes up for in heart as she showed by coming out on top in a tremendous fight with Nathaniel for the King George

Borderlescott (below)
"He was small, but he could walk. If they can walk, they can run," was trainer Robin Bastiman's view of Borderlescott when he bought him as a yearling. The dual Group 1 winner was still going strong in 2012 at the age of ten, winning the Listed Beverley Bullet

Sunnyhillboy
This "good little 'un" was beaten in the Grand National, but he was so brave. Oh, and he won the Kim Muir at the Cheltenham Festival

Always Waining
'Mini Red Rum' you could call him after his amazing hat-trick in the Topham Chase over the National fences

Efistorm
He turned 11 in 2012 but won five times, at five different tracks, and has now scored at least once in each of the past seven seasons. After almost 140 races, he shows no sign of stopping. "He loves racing and he loves life," said trainer Joseph Tuite. And we love him

---

THOMAS GALLIGAN, a former builder's labourer from Newcastle, won almost £400,000 on the Scoop6 in June for a £2 stake but missed a shot at the £250,000 bonus because he failed to register in time.

It was the first time in the 13-year history of the Scoop6 that a winner had not come forward in time to play for the following week's bonus. Confusion arose because Galligan's selection in the

first race was a non-runner and he didn't realise that, under Scoop6 rules, his stake had been transferred automatically to the favourite, which won. His other five horses also won, leaving him as the sole winner of the £394,487 prize.

Betfred knew the bet had been placed in a shop in the Benwell area of Newcastle but were unable to identify the punter. The winner was not tracked down until the

following Saturday evening when his daughter Amber, who had placed the bet, returned to the shop to put on another bet.

"I was at the counter when the assistant told me they'd been looking for me and I knew he wasn't joking as he was so deadly serious," she said. "When he first told me the bet had won I thought it was the place part and might have been a few hundred pounds, not hundreds of

thousands of pounds. I couldn't believe what he was telling me."

Galligan, 53, who suffers from arthritis, said: "I don't bet during the week but I do the Scoop6 when I can afford it on a Saturday. I thought my first horse had got beat and then I watched as the next five won. I never realised I was the winner as I thought I was out in leg one."

The father-of-four added: "Amber is my angel – she and

all my kids and grandkids mean the world to me. I've had years of pain with arthritis in my legs and Amber pops down the shop to place my Saturday bet.

"Our first priority with the win will be to buy a bigger place to live and I also want to take them on the holiday of a lifetime. We don't really do holidays as we have just enough to get by, and I can't remember the last time we went on one – if ever."

Golden Ball

From Class 5 to Grade 1 in one remarkable season

MEN and women have been trying to turn base metal into gold for millennia. In the 2011-12 jumps season Keiran Burke perfected the alchemist's art in the shape of a seven-year-old gelding called Hunt Ball, who started off as scrap metal and ended up as gold standard.

When a novice Hunt Ball went to Folkestone for his first outing of 2011-12, he was rated 68 but actually ran off 69 in the Class 5 race because he was a pound out of the handicap. Eight runs later he was rated 157, following victory at the Cheltenham Festival and a hugely meritorious third place in Grade 1 company at Aintree. He therefore improved by 89lb, by more than six stone in the space of five months, a transformation unparalleled in recent times.

"We thought he was good, but we didn't realise he was that good," says Burke, his first season with a training licence illuminated by this firecracker of a horse. "We had an idea, because before that first start in November we took him for a racecourse gallop with Holmwood Legend, who had won

the Byrne Group Plate at the festival and was rated 149. Hunt Ball worked all over him, no contest – we half-knew then that we had something."

That little knowledge proved dangerous to the bookies when Hunt Ball won at Folkestone – Burke's almost coy admission that "we backed him a little bit" almost certainly understating the case. Having touched 11-4, Hunt Ball was returned a well-supported 6-4 favourite.

Burke, 26, who has few horses and fewer facilities at his tiny Somerset yard (all fast work is done by boxing his horses to Richard Barber's all-weather gallop a few miles away), had ridden Hunt Ball during his jockey days and found him on the weak side, a shell of a horse with the scope to strengthen up as he matured.

"That's been the key to him," Burke says. "We had him 100 per cent for his first start because he was rated 68, there was no point doing otherwise because we just wanted to get a win out of him. After that he just got stronger, a blend of mental strength and physical

strength. He learned to race, and because he was getting stronger he took his races so well.

"He doesn't need much downtime after a race, I just throw him out in a field and the next day he's charging around like a lunatic, bucking and kicking."

After that Folkestone victory Hunt Ball won at Fontwell off a mark of 75, then returned to strike again at Folkestone (85) before getting stuck in the mud at Plumpton (102). "The ground was bottomless and we shouldn't have run him – he prefers genuinely good ground," Burke says.

Normal – abnormal? – service was resumed with two wins at Wincanton (108 and 117) before a virtuoso

performance at Kempton (127) gave Burke and endearingly eccentric owner Anthony Knott licence to dream big dreams.

"To be honest I fancied him more at Kempton than I had at Folkestone," Burke says. "The field was mostly old handicappers who had reached their limitations, whereas my horse was nowhere near his. He'd been improving so much I went there with a lot of confidence."

Knott had designs on the Gold Cup before settling for the easier festival option of the Pulteney Land Investments Novices' Handicap Chase, a race with a long title that Hunt Ball made short work of, bounding home by eight lengths off a mark of 142 in the hands of Nick Scholfield. By then the horse had developed a public following, attracted by his feelgood story.

Then Hunt Ball stepped up in trip and class for the Betfair Bowl at Aintree and finished a bare neck behind Gold Cup fourth Burton Port, both behind 50-1 winner Follow The Plan. The result was almost of

secondary importance; Hunt Ball had proved he belonged in the big league.

"He improved again at Aintree, it was quite incredible," Burke says. "And, you know, it might have been a race too many for him after a busy season. Obviously we have the Gold Cup in our minds now, although off a mark of 157 he still needs to find another stone to be a genuine contender. He's done really well over the summer, though, he looks bigger and stronger."

After nine races in 2011-12, Hunt Ball is likely to have just four in 2012-13 and one might be the King George. "It could be just his sort of race, the easy three miles round Kempton will suit him perfectly," Burke says. "It's all very exciting."

And then a note of wistfulness enters Burke's voice. "I wish he was starting off on a mark of 69 again." Alchemy doesn't work like that, but it truly was a golden year.

Words by Steve Dennis

'The day he mounted another horse out at exercise and knocked the rider off was the day I thought "that's enough". It wouldn't have been quite so bad, but the horse he was trying to mount was a gelding' Trainer John Holt explains *why Old Newton Cup winner Number Theory had to be gelded*

The other Triple Crown

America's version finds itself mired in controversy

THE racing year 2012 had a tale of two Triple Crowns. In Britain, a patient that had been ailing, if not completely dead, for several decades was revived by the drama of Camelot's near-miss at Doncaster.

On the other side of the Atlantic, their Triple Crown is a different beast. Forget the Breeders' Cup: the Kentucky Derby is the only time the sport truly attracts the attention of the wider public. Apart from when the Triple Crown is on the line at Belmont Park five weeks later, that is, as looked to be the case after I'll Have Another followed up his victory at Churchill Downs on the first Saturday in May with more of the same in the Preakness Stakes.

Hopes were high that a notorious 34-year drought would be ended by this cheaply bought colt and his little-known Mexican jockey, the Classic rookie Mario Gutierrez, who seemingly provided all the basics for a feelgood story that would revitalise a beleaguered sport.

Except that instead of sprinkling the gold dust of positive PR, I'll Have Another's journey down the Triple Crown trail was accompanied by publicity that cast racing in an almost wholly negative light.

It didn't help that the Doug O'Neill-trained colt never had the chance to capture the holy grail after he was scratched on the eve of the Belmont Stakes with a minor tendon injury. It was quite an anticlimax given that two nights earlier the Empire State Building had been lit up in the purple, green and white colours of owner Paul Reddam.

Yet to some extent the damage had been done even before the no-show. Racing

Strike two I'll Have Another (left) on his way to victory in the Preakness, before injury denied him a shot at the final leg

---

ROCKY ROAD *The story of the US Triple Crown*

KENTUCKY DERBY A startling race framed by a frantic pace set by Mike Smith on the Bob Baffert-trained favourite Bodemeister, who went so fast that not even the sprinter Trinniberg could get in front of him. The majority of Bodemeister's rivals were in trouble half a mile out and he was four lengths clear as they entered the stretch. If he had won, it would have been one of the most amazing displays in the race's rich history, but he didn't. I'll Have Another, a 15-1 chance trained by Doug O'Neill, had been towards the head of the chasing pack throughout and ran on strongly to catch Bodemeister 100 yards out and win going away by a length and a half under Mario Gutierrez.

PREAKNESS STAKES Not far off a carbon copy of Churchill Downs, with Bodemeister again favoured to turn the tables given the lack of front-end rivals and the fact that the Preakness is half a furlong shorter than the Kentucky Derby. Although Mike Smith was able to set more sensible fractions this time,

the result was the same as I'll Have Another ran on well under pressure to claim his second Classic by a neck.

BELMONT STAKES *(left)* I'll Have Another's Triple Crown bid was dramatically derailed the day before the final leg when he was retired owing to a minor tendon problem. With Bodemeister also absent, two new faces dominated the closing stages of a Belmont thriller as Union Rags, for so long burdened with a huge reputation, came good with a determined victory for trainer Michael Matz, driven up the rail by John Velazquez to beat front-running Paynter – the third runner-up of the series for the Bodemeister team of Bob Baffert and Mike Smith.

---

in America has been under the microscope for some time over those intertwined push-button topics of equine welfare and drug abuse. With that in mind, the US racing community could have done without O'Neill, a trainer with a history of medication violations, being the man in pole position to give the sport a much-needed fillip.

In an unfortunate piece of timing, a belated inquiry into O'Neill's latest brush with authority – a positive test dating back to August 2010 – took place slap, bang

in the middle of the Triple Crown, thereby adding fuel to a rancorous public debate fostered by a series of New York Times exposes that highlighted the incidence of catastrophic breakdowns on US tracks, in both the quarter horse and thoroughbred worlds.

The Times also put O'Neill under the microscope. "Derby victory brings more scrutiny for trainer, his troubling methods," read its headline, claiming that O'Neill had "more than a dozen violations for giving his

horses improper drugs" over 14 years and in four states.

The allegations and implications could hardly have come at a worse time for a sport in decline as the US racing community faces schism, notably with regard to the anti-bleeding agent Furosemide, better known as Lasix, its former trade name.

It didn't help that none of the Triple Crown principals were still racing by the autumn after Belmont winner Union Rags and Bodemeister, runner-up in both the Kentucky Derby

and Preakness, joined I'll Have Another in being retired through injury. Not the best publicity.

It isn't just O'Neill who is facing the difficult questions, it is the whole of US racing. "We had the black cloud before he won the Derby," said legendary trainer D. Wayne Lukas. "Now it's just gotten darker."

Fortunately, that never happened when Camelot went to Doncaster. Even though, like all the Americans since Affirmed, he got beat.
Words by Nicholas Godfrey

Lion king

National glory for Gibney's small stable

LION NA BEARNAI, translated into English, reads 'fill in the gaps' and that's exactly what the Irish Grand National winner did for trainer Tom Gibney and jockey Andrew Thornton, who enjoyed the biggest day of their careers at Fairyhouse on Easter Monday.

"I was really struggling to justify what I was doing. The horses simply weren't paying the bills," admits Gibney, who was five years into his training career and had only five horses in his small yard in Kells, County Meath. Lion Na Bearnai, the first horse he bought, for a syndicate that included old school friends, was his first runner in the Irish Grand National.

"He has taken the thing to a new level," Gibney says. "I have ten horses in training now. I've got three new owners and things are starting to look up. The whole thing was just fantastic. For me it was a dream come true to win the Irish National and everything went perfectly to plan."

Nor have the past five years been easy for Thornton since he decided to have a second try as a professional jockey after quitting briefly to ride in pony races. The 3lb claimer more than doubled his prize-money for the season with his National success, having given Lion Na Bearnai "a copybook ride" according to Gibney.

Lion Na Bearnai's starting price of 33-1 may have suggested his National success was a shock but it wasn't for the trainer. This was a plan put in place

Lion's roar The celebrations start for jockey Andrew Thornton and winning connections as Lion Na Bearnai comes home in front

almost 18 months previously after the gelding finished second to Droim Toll in the Porterstown Handicap Chase at Fairyhouse.

"The Irish National was the only thing on my mind from New Year's Day the previous year," Gibney says. "He was second in the Porterstown and I knew he had the look of a National horse, so I geared everything towards making him into one."

Not that everything went quite as Gibney planned. "I ran him in the Grade 2 at Navan in mid-February in the

hope he would show up well enough and we could come back a few weeks later for a handicap chase at the track.

"I never thought he would win the Grade 2, but he did and he went up enough for winning that to allow us to get into the National. The rest, as they say, is history.

"Everything went like clockwork. Even in the race itself, it couldn't have gone better. He loved the big, galloping track, jumped for fun and won really well in the end."

Gibney's new long-term plan is geared to Aintree. "The Irish National has been the best trial for the English National in recent years and that's very much on our agenda now.

"But I'm not going to run him over hurdles or anything like that. I'm keen to let him have a shot at a couple of the big handicaps and then, come next April, hopefully he'll be all set for Aintree. He could be the type that really takes to those fences as he jumps so well."

Words by David Jennings

WHEN Paddy Mangan stumbled to safety seconds after Acapulco had sent him crashing to the Leopardstown turf last Christmas, he knew something was up.

His worst fears were confirmed when an MRI scan revealed damage to a cruciate ligament. It's an injury that has kept many a Premier League star out for a whole season, but it couldn't stop the young Irish conditional chasing his dream.

"When the scan revealed it was my cruciate, I had a pretty tough decision to make," Mangan says. "It was sore but I knew I had a big chance of winning the conditionals' title. I didn't want to let anything stop me. That's why I put the operation off until the summer when things would be a bit quieter."

Mangan soldiered on and fought his way through the pain barrier. Was it worth it? "Definitely," he replies emphatically. "It was a great season and I got to ride some top horses."

Best of all, he was crowned champion conditional. With 27 winners, the 22-year-old edged out Eddie O'Connell by one to claim the title. Few begrudged him shading the photo-finish given the lengths he went to in pursuing his goal.

After having the knee op on May 25, Mangan returned to the saddle four months later for the Listowel Harvest Festival and looked none the worse for his absence as he steered Fair Dilemma to victory in the beginners' chase on his first day back.

From one dilemma to another, Mangan had not done too badly.

'The most expensive day for the industry ever – and that includes Dettori day' Ladbrokes' view sums up British bookmaker reaction to the Budget, which targeted betting-shop gaming machines and offshore operators

Superhuman Jorge Ricardo (left) and Russell Baze meet at the Shergar Cup in 2008

Ricardinho back in front

WITH little obvious fanfare, one of the most astonishing records on the racing books was broken in May 2012 when Brazilian legend Jorge Ricardo rode the 11,596th winner of his career.

After three years spent chasing his long-term rival Russell Baze, the Buenos Aires-based jockey reclaimed the all-time record for career victories when he guided the two-year-old Winning Prize to victory in the Group 1 Gran Criterium at San Isidro in Buenos Aires on May 26.

Perhaps the lack of trumpets is easily explained since both 'Ricardinho' and his northern Californian-based counterpart Baze have a habit of making the miraculous seem mundane.

Ricardo, 51, and Baze, 54, have been involved in a ding-dong battle – albeit separated by the length of two continents – for more than half a decade.

It was Baze who became the winningmost rider of all time on December 1, 2006, when he rode his 9,531st winner to surpass a mark established seven years earlier by Panamanian legend Laffit Pincay. To put this into context, the British record still stands at Sir Gordon Richards' mark of 4,870.

Baze had overtaken Ricardo only a few months before and, when Pincay's record was broken, the South American rider was just 27 behind. Four weeks later, Ricardo emulated Baze in surpassing Pincay's mark.

Ricardo, who won 26 titles in Rio de Janeiro before moving to Argentina in 2006, became the first jockey in the world to reach 10,000 wins in January 2008, but Baze beat him to 11,000, which he reached in August 2010.

The lead flip-flopped several times in the following months until Ricardo established a decent gap – only to forfeit his advantage when he was forced to spend six months on the sidelines to fight cancer in 2009.

Ricardo benefits from riding on cards featuring as many as 20 races, while Baze has spent the vast majority of his career away from the bright lights at tracks like Golden Gate Fields and Bay Meadows.

What they share are the superhuman levels of consistency, durability and self-discipline that enable them to ride to a high standard, day in, day out, over several decades. The numbers boggle the mind: both have topped the annual 400 mark several times, with Ricardo's personal best of 477 in Rio de Janeiro in 1992-93 outshining the 448 achieved by Baze in 1995.

By the way, they have met just once, when they both rode in the 2008 Shergar Cup at Ascot. Ironically, neither rode a single winner. Which is not something you are likely to see very often.
Words by Nicholas Godfrey

Danedream
The only filly to win both the Arc and King George, earner of £3.2 million, bought for just €9,000. An all-round fairytale, except for that nightmarish ban on travelling to the Arc

Body And Soul
Tim Easterby's juvenile filly won £122,000 in the Super Sprint at Newbury and, after narrowly missing out on another big sales race at York, landed £125,000 for her victory in the Two-Year-Old Trophy at Redcar. Total earnings of £285,956 in six runs: not bad for a £7,500 yearling

Lion Na Bearnai
The first horse Thomas Gibney bought when he started training was Lion Na Bearnai for €8,800. Five and a half years later, the now ten-year-old won 16 times that amount (€141,000) in the Irish Grand National

Gordon Lord Byron
Snapped up for €2,000 as a foal by owner Morgan Calahan's daughter Jessica, Gordon Lord Byron took his earnings to €350,000 with his Group 1 victory in the Prix de la Foret on Arc day. Who cares that it cost €100,000 to supplement him for the Foret? He's still a quarter of a million euros up

Kian's Delight (below)
Almost anyone could have bought this horse when he went to the sales as a three-year-old in October 2011, having won twice in nine starts on the Flat. It took just one bid of £1,000 to buy him but within a year he had won five times over hurdles for Peter Bowen, earning almost £40,000. "Why he only made a thousand I'll never know," said Bowen

Sendmylovetorose
A Group 3 victory by the Andrew Oliver-trained filly on her second start was a pretty good return on the £5,000 she cost as a yearling; winning the Group 2 Cherry Hinton on her third start was even better

AFTER spending the winter paddling in the shallow waters of Dundalk's lowest-grade handicaps and dropping to a rating of just 50, Bubbly Bellini seemed likely to sink rather than swim over the summer.

But he came back a different horse after a three-month break and from there on he was in the fast lane. In four magnificent months, Bubbly Bellini collected five wins under Ian Brennan, including a brace of premier handicaps, and went up a staggering 44lb in the ratings. That left trainer Adrian McGuinness thinking of stakes races rather than Dundalk dates.

"It's just been incredible," he says. "And the best thing of all is that Ian doesn't think he's stopped improving yet. He thinks there's more to come. If there is, I'd like to think he could be a Listed or Group horse next year."

How did McGuinness put the fizz into Bubbly Bellini? "I'm putting it down to the break we gave him in March," he says. "He just wasn't firing for us at all over the winter at Dundalk. He might have had a virus or something. But we gave him a full month off in March and it did him the world of good. He had the sun on his back and he turned inside out. It was a big help having Ian in the yard too as he rode him out every day and got to know him so well.

"To win one premier handicap in a year is hard enough, but to win two is just incredible. He's such a super servant to the yard and we love him to bits."

Hot streak Inis Meain, ridden by Chris Hayes, wins the Guinness Handicap at the Galway festival in August to continue his rapid rise

Handicap good thing

No stopping Inis Meain as he flies up the ratings

EXPLOITING a lenient Flat mark with a hurdler isn't as simple as it sounds. Face Value couldn't take advantage of a 65lb difference at Down Royal in September, while 130-rated hurdler Earls Quarter failed to land a blow in the big amateur handicap during Galway week despite being 53lb lower on the Flat. It's a familiar tale of woe that has left many punters with burnt fingers.

Some suspected Inis Meain didn't even deserve his lofty hurdle rating of 117 at the end of the last jumps season,

which probably explains why he was sent off at odds of 7-2 in a 47-65 Flat handicap at Killarney in July off the lowest mark possible.

Those who did subscribe to the theory that he was thrown in were rewarded, however, as promising apprentice Ronan Whelan had a bigger job pulling up than getting him going. The winning distance was four and three-quarter lengths. It was visually impressive and left trainer Denis Hogan with little option but to get him out again as quickly as possible.

Three days later he turned up at Leopardstown. With

just a mandatory 5lb penalty, Inis Meain looked like Usain Bolt lobbing alongside a cluster of Jan Molbys. Joe Doyle did the steering and he justified 2-5 favouritism with the minimum of fuss.

This was a horse going places and only the handicapper could stop him. He did his best by slapping a 23lb rise on him and it appeared to work when Inis Meain could finish only second to Call Me Bubbles in a competitive mile-and-a-half handicap during Galway week. The following evening Inis Meain lined up for what looked a better race. Chris

Hayes sent him straight to the front and he galloped a high-quality field into submission, winning by seven lengths.

Another 13lb was shovelled on to him. Once again the handicapper seemed to have him in his grasp as Inis Meain was reeled in close home by Diplomat at Killarney off a mark of 83.

Despite the defeat, the handicapper had another go. This time an extra 4lb was applied. A competitive nine-furlong handicap at Listowel in September was next on the agenda and Inis Meain, backed into 4-1 joint-

favourite after being available at double those odds, did what he does best. He made all, had everything else in trouble turning for home and allowed Hayes the luxury of easing him down for the final furlong.

That win put Inis Meain up to a rating of 100 and on the verge of Listed class. "This horse could genuinely be anything. I don't know how far he can go," Hayes said.

It's all a far cry from the 47-rated performer who started the season. And he can jump a hurdle too. Exciting times ahead.

'She seldom referred to me as Michael. "Silly boy" was her usual form of address, uttered in the same voice as Captain Mainwaring when speaking to Private Pike in Dad's Army. Pike was a "stupid boy" and I was a "silly boy"' Michael Dickinson on life with mother Monica

Life-changing bet

Murphy takes up training in US after winning a million

SHORTLY before Christmas 2011, Conor Murphy had two dreams. One thing led to another and six months later both had turned to reality as Murphy, former second head groom to Nicky Henderson but by now a millionaire, set out on his own training career.

From Seven Barrows in Lambourn – a place he knew so well after two stints at Henderson's yard spanning six years – Murphy departed for equally familiar surroundings in the United States. Having previously worked for Niall O'Callaghan at the Skylight training centre in Kentucky, Murphy set up camp there himself and in October had his first runner as a trainer when Dimension competed in an allowance race at Keeneland.

Going into training wasn't quite the gamble it might have been, because of the wager Murphy had landed at the Cheltenham Festival. In December he had placed a £50 accumulator on five Henderson-trained Cheltenham prospects – Sprinter Sacre, Simonsig, Bobs Worth, Riverside Theatre and Finian's Rainbow, the Champion Chase contender he had looked after from a young age. As unlikely as it seemed at the time, all five won at the festival to land him bet365's maximum £1 million payout on the accumulator.

"I placed the bet the week before Christmas," says Murphy, 28, originally from Ballineen, County Cork. "I've always had an accumulator at the big meetings and I just felt those five were our best chances going to Cheltenham. But you never expect to have five winners."

Sprinter Sacre landed the first leg in the Arkle on the opening day of the festival and a wonderful Wednesday

for the Henderson stable – with four winners, including Simonsig, Bobs Worth and Finian's Rainbow – put the million within touching distance for Murphy. It took him a while to notice, however, as his attention was fixed on Finian's Rainbow, the apple of his eye.

"Without question Finian's winning the Champion Chase was the greatest moment of my career and I doubt I'll ever top it," he says. "Having believed in the horse for so long, it was great to see him go and do it. When he won I was on such a high I forgot about the bet. Someone mentioned Riverside Theatre to me later that night and then it clicked with me I had this five-horse accumulator going."

The celebrations went on long into Wednesday night and recovering from an almighty hangover – rather than hedging the bet – was Murphy's only concern as

the clock ticked round to Riverside Theatre's run in the Ryanair Chase on the Thursday.

"You think it's too good to come true and it wouldn't have happened if it wasn't for Barry Geraghty. It was the greatest ride I've ever seen anyone give a horse. It was an unbelievable race to watch because he looked beat everywhere bar the line."

Around the same time he placed the bet, Murphy had made another decision – one he was determined to see through, no matter how difficult the journey. "As much as I enjoyed working at Nicky Henderson's, I felt before Christmas I needed to do my own thing. I'd saved money to put into the business and, although I was going to be trying to make ends meet, I was determined to do it. Winning that bet couldn't have come at a better time. It gave me a bit of breathing space."

His departure was a blow to Henderson, who had earmarked him as the replacement for his long-serving head groom Corky Browne. "I must remember to padlock the front gates to make sure he stays with us," Henderson remarked after Murphy's big win.

It was Browne who had encouraged Murphy to return from the US for a second stint at Seven Barrows and the young pupil has nothing but thanks for his education. "I've been with a great trainer in Nicky Henderson and I've learned more off Corky in the past five or six years than I've learned off anyone else in my entire life," he says.

Murphy's plan is to build up gradually, starting off by breaking and pre-training other people's horses and building a reputation that will lead eventually to full-time training. "I've got a good few yearlings in already, but

if I was solely training I'd be struggling to get a lot of horses," he says. "In an ideal world, I'd have started in England or Ireland but the prize-money is just not good enough for people starting out. Having been here before is an advantage. It's a small centre, only three trainers, and it's a beautiful environment for training horses."

The biggest investment Murphy made with his windfall was Dimension, bought from James Fanshawe after a seven-furlong handicap win at York and a creditable eighth in the Royal Hunt Cup. He runs in the company name chosen by Murphy for his new venture – Riverside Bloodstock. "I'm sure you'll know where I got the name from," he says.

A constant reminder of the fifth Cheltenham winner that changed everything for Murphy.

Words by Nick Pulford

MURPHY'S DREAM ACCA

Sprinter Sacre
(Arkle) **6-1**

Simonsig
(Neptune) **12-1**

Bobs Worth
(RSA) **6-1**

Finian's Rainbow
(Champion Chase) **8-1**

Riverside Theatre
(Ryanair) **10-1**

Stake £50

The accumulator would have returned more than £3 million but Murphy's payout was limited to bet365's maximum of £1 million

'I know I've been on the cold list for a long time but that's just statistics. For instance, if you asked Snow White she would say six of the seven dwarves aren't happy' Jon Scargill, scoring at Yarmouth after 599 days without a winner

Golden oldie Marked Man leads the field in a staying handicap chase at Towcester in March

MARKED MAN was the grandaddy of them all as he raced on at the ripe old age of 16, making him the oldest horse to run in Britain or Ireland in 2012.

Richard Lee's remarkable chaser, whose name comes from his blotchy complexion, took his career starts past 80 in his 11th consecutive season of racing. He has never had a break of longer than six months.

Marked Man's career started inauspiciously when he was a five-year-old, with five defeats in Ireland by a total of more than 300 lengths, but he has been a stalwart of Lee's stable since moving there in 2006. He has won races at nine courses, over distances from two miles to three and a quarter miles, although Lee said it had taken him eight years to work out the gelding's trip.

Five of Marked Man's 11 wins have come since his age hit double figures and the most important factor, according to Lee, is that he remains young at heart.

"He thinks he's six," Lee said. "His enthusiasm is absolutely amazing. He has lived in a five-star hotel all his life and enjoys a wonderful life. I've no idea what he'll do when he's retired."

6 OF THE BEST
Rising stars

Nicole Nordblad
The 17-year-old Swede can't drive and has to rely on lifts to get the races, but she sure can ride. A 14 per cent strike-rate and a healthy level-stake profit make her an apprentice worth watching

Lucy Alexander (below)
The 21-year-old daughter of trainer Nick Alexander dropped out of university to pursue her dream of race-riding and graduated with honours when she claimed the British record for jumps winners by a female rider in a single season

Darren Egan
After a couple of false starts back home in Ireland, the 20-year-old joined Ron Harris on a three-month trial in November 2011 and ended up as one of the top apprentices. He aims to keep his claim well into 2013 and another good season beckons

Jack Quinlan
The 20-year-old was born into racing – his uncle is Mick Quinlan and his dad is Noel Quinlan, Mick's assistant trainer – and the talent nurtured from an early age shone through as he formed a strong partnership with John Ferguson

Anthony Honeyball
Few, if any, can beat the Dorset trainer for strike-rate and profit to a level stake and his target of a third consecutive seasonal-best in 2012-13 looks realistic

David O'Meara
The Yorkshire-based Irishman is a master at improving horses and is climbing fast, having trebled his number of winners since his first season in 2010. A second Great St Wilfrid with Pepper Lane, the Portland with Doc Hay and Group 2s with Penitent and Blue Bajan were all testament to his skill

WHAT'S IN A NAME?
Embarrassingly, with two of the biggest stars of 2012, it was an extra letter.

Racing's biggest TV audience of the year saw the first gaffe as BBC cameras zoomed in on Neptune Collonges' name being added to the Grand National honours board. The only problem was he had become 'Neptunes' with an extra s.

The misspelling curse struck again the following month and this time it was none other than Frankel who fell victim.

You might have thought being the world's best racehorse would bring a certain familiarity but apparently not, as he was transformed into 'Franklel' on the giant name board that accompanied him into the parade ring before his reappearance in the Lockinge.

City slicker

Doyle takes his chance in the big time

DUBAI WORLD CUP night at Meydan is a perfect place to announce yourself on the big stage and that's exactly what James Doyle did on March 31. Riding in his first Group 1, the 24-year-old dismissed any pre-race nerves to partner Cityscape to a first prize of almost £2 million in the Dubai Duty Free. It was the launch pad to a second consecutive seasonal-best back in Britain and a place in the championship top ten for the first time.

Doyle was a Meydan expert by World Cup night, after a few weeks in Dubai turned into months of sustained success. Originally he had joined Dhruba Selvaratnam as cover until William Buick arrived to take over as stable jockey, but things went so well that Doyle stayed on and took his chances even with Buick around. He ended the winter fourth in the Emirates jockeys' table.

Back at home, opportunity knocked again in more unfortunate circumstances. Steve Drowne, stable jockey for Roger Charlton, suffered a blackout at home in March and Doyle stepped up to strengthen a link with the Beckhampton trainer that had developed the previous year.

"It's never nice, is it, but what can you do? You have to take a chance when it presents itself," Doyle said, when asked about the way the job came about. "Steve is a gentleman, he's been a great help to me. We talk about

Free and easy
Doyle puts his Meydan experience to good use with a comfortable win on Cityscape in the Dubai Duty Free

the horses and he tells me anything I should know."

It didn't take Doyle long to double his Group-race haul back on home soil as he partnered Al Kazeem to victory in the Group 2 Jockey Club Stakes. Just 40 minutes later he rode in a first Classic aboard Top Offer in the 2,000 Guineas before rushing to Heathrow to board a flight to Hong Kong to partner Cityscape in the Champions Mile at Sha Tin.

Despite neither horse running to form, it marked a remarkable reversal from the Doyle of two years earlier, when he was struggling to make the jump from star apprentice to the senior ranks. As a 5ft 10in teenager, he had concerns about how long a career in the saddle might last and as a result he rode out his claim quicker than most, having come close to landing the apprentice title in 2006.

But no claim meant a lack of decent rides and his total of winners plummeted from 73 in 2006 to less than 30 in 2009 and 2010. He started to eye a different path, even booking himself on to a plumbing course, but with hard work and a little luck he has turned his career around.

Another star for Doyle in 2012 was Bated Breath, narrowly beaten into second in the King's Stand Stakes at Royal Ascot and third in

the Haydock Sprint Cup, while the next generation for Charlton and Doyle is led by Dundonnell, who gave the jockey more Group-race success in the Acomb Stakes at York.

Given the alternative career he considered, it may be unkind to say he plumbed the depths. But he reached new heights in 2012 – and that made the success all the sweeter.

Words by Lewis Porteous

'I think it's very proper gentlemen show their respect to the main participants, namely the horses, and their sensibilities would be disturbed by brown shoes with morning suits' Sir Peter O'Sullevan on changes to Ascot's Royal Enclosure dress code

'I kept thinking of AP McCoy. He would have finished with a broken leg, so I couldn't be a wuss' Lisa Delany, manager of the Jockeys Employment and Training Scheme, on her determination to finish the London Marathon after both her knees gave out at 21 miles. She did finish, in 4hr 37min 15sec

New world order

Barzalona shines in Godolphin blue

MONTEROSSO'S victory in the 2012 running of the Dubai World Cup was notable for a number of reasons – not least that it was the first time in six years Godolphin had landed the world's richest race.

Indeed, not merely content with claiming the $6 million contest, Sheikh Mohammed's team enjoyed a one-two as Capponi finished three lengths behind his stablemate to complete a hometown victory that was sorely needed.

Maybe that's why Mickael Barzalona celebrated like he'd just won the Derby again, standing up in his stirrups as they crossed the line. Or perhaps he was just calculating his percentage. Either way, it was a perfect way to start his role as a retained rider for Sheikh Mohammed's operation.

While Monterosso was Godolphin's sixth winner in 17 World Cups, he was their first since Electrocutionist in 2006. That horse represented the old firm of Frankie Dettori and trainer Saeed Bin Suroor; both this year's principals were saddled by Godolphin's new man Mahmood Al Zarooni, with Barzalona and Ahmed Ajtebi doing the riding honours. A changing of the guard was in the air.

Perhaps Mark Johnston deserved as many plaudits as anybody else given that Monterosso had started out in the Maktoum nursery section of his Godolphin base. Sheikh Mohammed was well aware of the trainer's efforts, saying: "It is a very special night and I'm very, very pleased. Mark Johnston did a good job with this horse." And with the runner-up, he might well have added.

Dubai World Cup night once again exemplified the Dubai Carnival as a whole in providing a mix of the good, the bad and the indifferent – plus, of course, the richly endowed.

Criticism of the all-weather surface at magnificent Meydan continued after another shock result in the World Cup. Upsets will happen – they are part of what we call the glorious uncertainty – but in three years of the Dubai World Cup at Meydan, not one horse sent off at a single-figure starting price with British bookmakers has made the first three.

Previous experience appears more significant than form on any other surface, no matter that horses jetting in from the United States, Japan and Europe may have stones in hand on official figures. For a race with world championship pretensions, that cannot be right.

At the time of writing Monterosso and Capponi, both five-year-olds, have between them run only once since, Monterosso beating just one horse home behind Nathaniel in the Eclipse. Such a post-race record doesn't help the World Cup's tarnished credibility since it went to Tapeta. Perhaps they'll come good again at the 2013 carnival.

On a more positive note, World Cup night also featured a lavishly rewarded victory on turf for the Roger Charlton-trained Cityscape in the Dubai Duty Free under the trainer's new stable jockey James Doyle, the grand old gelding Cirrus Des Aigles held off St Nicholas Abbey to take the Dubai Sheema Classic, Kieren Fallon did the steering on Bahraini-trained Krypton Factor as he floored Rocket Man in the Golden Shaheen and Australian mare Ortensia gave a taste of things to come in the Al Quoz Sprint.

Much of this action, though, was overshadowed by the Group 3 Dubai Gold Cup, officially won by Godolphin's Opinion Poll. A new addition to World Cup night, this two-mile event was scheduled as the second race on the card, only to be stopped at halfway in sickening circumstances when Fox Hunt broke a leg in front of the Meydan stands.

Controversially, the race was re-run at the end of the card almost five hours later. Bronze Cannon broke a leg, Grand Vent was pulled up injured, Japanese-trained Makani Bisty came to a virtual standstill after making the running and Mikhail Glinka was eased right down. It was a sorry spectacle that took the gloss off what had gone before. With hindsight, the science that's seldom wrong, it is hard to escape the conclusion the race should never have taken place.

Words by Nicholas Godfrey

Stone Of Folca a world-beater

STONE OF FOLCA set a five-furlong world record of 53.69sec at Epsom on Derby day, beating by 0.01sec the time of Spark Chief over the same course 29 years earlier.

Incredibly, the John Best-trained four-year-old achieved the feat on his return from a nine-month break and from an unfavourable draw. He was sent off a 50-1 outsider in a field of 20 and his flying victory under Luke Morris was only the second of his career on his 13th start.

"To be honest, I didn't think we could do it from stall two – if he had been drawn high we would have had a punt on the big price," Best said. "I told Luke to let him jump and edge across as much as he could. It's unbelievable."

Stone Of Folca has always been difficult to handle, even after being gelded, and Best added: "He's a nightmare at the races and, while gelding has obviously helped, he was still an

absolute handful going to the start."

Coming back, with a following wind, was a breeze and he won the Investec Specialist Bank Dash by half a length from the high-drawn Desert Law.

The winning time was short of the hand-timed 53.6sec reputedly recorded by Indigenous when scoring under Lester Piggott at the Derby meeting in 1960. Epsom has always recognised that as the record but John

Randall, the Racing Post's historian, disputes that view.

"Times taken by hand, with a stopwatch calibrated merely to one-fifth of a second, were bogus; they flattered the winner because watch-holders were slow to react to the start but anticipated the finish," he wrote in the Racing Post. "There is little doubt that, if films of their two races could be superimposed, Stone Of Folca would beat Indigenous. He is the real record-holder."

Blink and you'll miss it Stone Of Folca sets a five-furlong world record of 53.69sec at Epsom on Derby day

---

'Merigo is beginning to get up . . .'

AS the 2012 Scottish Grand National builds to a crescendo, so too does Channel 4 commentator Simon Holt. "They race towards the final fence, Auroras Encore and Ryan Mania on the nearside, Merigo and Timmy Murphy on the far side. And Auroras Encore is running on stoutly here, he leads by a length."

Just then, Holt's voice – pitch-perfect, as always – begins to rise in rhythm with the battle unfolding before him: "Merigo is coming back on the far side, the Scottish chasing hero. Merigo is beginning to get up. Auroras Encore nearside . . . Merigo

wins again. Merigo wins his second Scottish Grand National."

Seven days after the closest Grand National finish in history, the Scottish National had also gone down to the wire and, once again, it was the gritty late finisher who had got up close home to claim victory. They don't come much tougher than Merigo, winner of the Scottish National in 2010, runner-up in 2011 and winner again in 2012.

"He hates getting beat in a piece of work, never mind a race," says Andrew Parker, who trains the 11-year-old at Ecclefechan, Dumfriesshire,

about 50 miles from Ayr as the crow flies. "He's won three times by half a length or less. He won the Eider in a close finish, he won his race before the Scottish National by a neck and then he beat Auroras Encore by a head."

Ayr, where Merigo has won five times and never been out of the first three in eight runs, holds the key. "What he likes is two straight lines to get into a good rhythm," Parker says. "He hates going up and down hills, it completely wrecks his rhythm. He's got one gear and when he gets into it he'll go in that gear all day. He'd run for eight miles."

Merigo might already be a

three-time Scottish National winner but for a narrow defeat in 2011, when he was forced to run from 12lb out of the handicap and beaten three-quarters of a length. "I felt cheated in that one," the trainer says. "I've watched it a few times and I feel gutted every time."

The chance for a hat-trick will come in 2013. "We'll do the same as we've done the last couple of years and we'll try to get him there again. It will be his swansong," Parker says. "He's got the most unbelievable stamina and he still retains that will to win, which not many horses do at the age of 11 rising 12."

QUIZ ANSWERS

1. Paul Hanagan
2. Mick Channon
3. Siyouma
4. Bryan Cooper
5. Tom Tate
6. Finian's Rainbow
7. Thomas Chippendale
8. Michelangelo
9. Encke
10. Simenon
11. Royal Diamond
12. Princess Highway
13. Homecoming Queen
14. Prince Of Johanne
15. Rosdhu Queen
16. Une Artiste
17. Follow The Plan
18. David Marnane
19. The Giant Bolster
20. Saonois
21. Seabass and Shakalakaboomboom
22. Maybe
23. Grands Crus
24. The Fugue
25. St Nicholas Abbey
26. Precious stones (Rock On Ruby, Royal Diamond, Spirit Quartz)
27. Alcoholic drinks (Oscar Whisky, Champagne Fever, Burton Port)
28. Fire (Bonfire, Countrywide Flame, Cinders And Ashes)
29. Numbers (French Fifteen, Teaforthree, Thousand Stars)
30. Army ranks (Trumpet Major, Captain Ramius, First Lieutenant)
A. Colour Vision
B. Simonsig
C. Neptune Collonges
D. Ile De Re
E. Thousand Stars

'She's some rider – she's got balls of steel'
Ferdy Murphy praises Lucy Alexander with a rather unfortunate turn of phrase

THE BIGGER PICTURE

The Parisian business district of La Defense forms the backdrop to the Prix de la Celle Saint-Cloud at Longchamp on May 13. The one-mile, three-furlong race for unraced three-year-old fillies was won by the Aga Khan's Ridasiyna, who graduated to the top level five months later when she won the Group 1 Prix de l'Opera on Arc day
EDWARD WHITAKER (RACINGPOST.COM/PHOTOS)

Older horse

FRANKEL

Trainer **Sir Henry Cecil**
Owner **Khalid Abdullah**

RACING POST RATINGS

Frankel	143
Cirrus Des Aigles	132
Excelebration	131
Nathaniel	127
Moonlight Cloud	127
So You Think	127

We would never have seen the best of Frankel if he had not stayed in training as a four-year-old.

He became the first horse to rate above 140 on RPRs, doing it not once but twice. On his reappearance in the Lockinge he matched the RPR of 139 he had achieved as a three-year-old and then he went on to record 143 in his Queen Anne romp and again on his first run over a mile and a quarter in the International at York.

Three-year-old colt

CAMELOT

Trainer **Aidan O'Brien**
Owners **Derrick Smith, Mrs John Magnier, Michael Tabor**

RACING POST RATINGS

Camelot	127
Pastorius	122
Encke	121
French Fifteen	120
Caspar Netscher	119
Saint Baudolino	119

Unbeaten in five races by the time he scored a third Classic success in the Irish Derby, Camelot seemed set to improve on the RPR of 127 he had earned for his five-length win in the Derby at Epsom but only disappointment followed. After his defeats in the St Leger and Arc, it seemed something of a hollow victory to be divisional leader among the worst bunch of three-year-olds in years – only four colts managed to reach 120 and they were continually put in their place by the far superior older generation.

Three-year-old filly

RIDASIYNA

Trainer **Mikel Delzangles**
Owner **HH The Aga Khan**

RACING POST RATINGS

Ridasiyna	121
Valyra	120
Beauty Parlour	119
Elusive Kate	118
Fallen For You	118
Great Heavens	118
Mince	118
The Fugue	118

The three-year-old fillies were hardly a vintage group but at least they did manage to win a handful of Group 1 races against their elders.

One of those was the Prix de l'Opera on Arc day, in which Ridasiyna completed her progress from debutante to Group 1 winner in the space of five months. Her rise helped to make up for the loss of the Aga Khan's French Oaks winner Valyra, who had been the divisional leader but was put down after fracturing a leg while exercising on the beach at Deauville.

Sprinter

MOONLIGHT CLOUD

Trainer **Freddy Head**
Owner **George Strawbridge**

RACING POST RATINGS

Moonlight Cloud	127
Black Caviar	122
Society Rock	122
Bated Breath	121
Mayson	121
Ortensia	121

No horse has come closer to beating Black Caviar than Moonlight Cloud, even if the head margin at the end of the Diamond Jubilee Stakes flattered her. The great Australian mare was nowhere near her best that day (her top RPR in Australia is 133) and nor, as it turned out, was Moonlight Cloud. Next time out, she beat subsequent Abbaye winner Wizz Kid by five lengths in the Prix Maurice de Gheest to earn a career-best RPR of 127. It was easily enough to put her top of a weak division.

Stayer

COLOUR VISION

Trainer **Saeed Bin Suroor**
Owner **Godolphin**

ENCKE

Trainer **Mahmood Al Zarooni**
Owner **Godolphin**

RACING POST RATINGS

Colour Vision	121
Encke	121
Camelot	120
Opinion Poll	119
Fox Hunt	118

Godolphin had the top two stayers in Ascot Gold Cup winner Colour Vision and St Leger scorer Encke. Colour Vision's best performance was not at Ascot – where he recorded an RPR of 118 – but on his previous start in the Sagaro Stakes at Kempton, where he beat 2011 Melbourne Cup runner-up Red Cadeaux by a length and a half. In foiling Camelot's Triple Crown bid at Doncaster, Encke improved his RPR from 115 to 121.

Two-year-old colt

DAWN APPROACH

Trainer **Jim Bolger**
Owner **Godolphin**

RACING POST RATINGS

Dawn Approach	123
Reckless Abandon	118
Moohaajim	118
Gale Force Ten	117
Olympic Glory	117

Having started his winning run in the first juvenile race of the year in Ireland, Dawn Approach was always at the head of the two-year-old division. He made it four out of four when taking the Coventry from subsequent Prix Jean-Luc Lagardere winner Olympic Glory and then, after a three-month break, came back to win the National at the Curragh and the Dewhurst at Newmarket. The RPR of 123 for his National success just shaded the 122 of his Dewhurst, with both runs putting him clear of the other juveniles.

Two-year-old filly

VIZTORIA

Trainer **Eddie Lynam**
Owner **Mrs K Lavery**

RACING POST RATINGS

Viztoria	113
Certify	112
Purr Along	111
Sky Lantern	111
What A Name	110

Nothing really stood out in this division, although there were signs of promise. Viztoria earned her RPR of 113 when she won a Listed contest at the Curragh in September by seven and a half lengths. The ground was heavy, as it had been when she won by an identical margin on her Naas debut in July.

Certify climbed the ladder from Group 3 to Group 2 and finally to Group 1 in the Fillies' Mile, with narrow victories over Purr Along and Sky Lantern along the way.

FLAT WINNERS 2012

BRITISH GROUP I WINNERS 2012

Race	Distance	Course	Month	Age	Winner	RPR	SP
2,000 Guineas	1m	NmkR	May	3	Camelot	122	15/8
1,000 Guineas	1m	NmkR	May	3	Homecoming Queen	117	25/1
Lockinge	1m	Newb	May	4+	Frankel	139	2/7
Oaks (F)	1m 4f	Epsm	Jun	3	Was	114	20/1
Coronation Cup	1m4f	Epsom	Jun	4+	St Nicholas Abbey	126	8/11
Derby	1m 4f	Epsm	Jun	3	Camelot	128	8/13
Queen Anne	1m	Ascot	Jun	4+	Frankel	142	1/10
King's Stand	5f	Ascot	Jun	3+	Little Bridge	124	12/1
St James's Palace	1m	Ascot	Jun	3	Most Improved	118	9/1
Prince Of Wales's	1m 2f	Ascot	Jun	4+	So You Think	127	4/5
Gold Cup	2m4f	Ascot	Jun	4+	Colour Vision	118	6/1
Coronation (F)	1m	Ascot	Jun	3	Fallen For You	118	12/1
Diamond Jubilee	6f	Ascot	Jun	3+	Black Caviar	122	1/6
Coral-Eclipse	1m2f	Sand	Jul	3+	Nathaniel	129	7/2
Falmouth (F&M)	1m	Nmkj	Jul	3+	Giofra	118	10/1
July Cup	6f	Nmkj	Jul	3+	Mayson	122	20/1
King George VI & Qn Elizabeth	1m4f	Ascot	Jul	3+	Danedream	124	9/1
Sussex	1m	Gdwd	Aug	3+	Frankel	138	1/20
Nassau (F&M)	1m2f	Gdwd	Aug	3+	The Fugue	118	11/4
International	1m2f	York	Aug	3+	Frankel	142	1/10
Darley Yorkshire Oaks (F&M)	1m4f	York	Aug	3+	Shareta	119	2/1
Nunthorpe	5f	York	Aug	2+	Ortensia	118	7/2
Sprint Cup	6f	Hayd	Sep	3+	Society Rock	122	10/1
St Leger	1m7f	Donc	Sep	3	Encke	121	25/1
Fillies' Mile	1m	NmkR	Sep	2	Certify	112	4/6
Cheveley Park (F)	6f	NmkR	Sep	2	Rosdhu Queen	108	4/1
Sun Chariot (F&M)	1m	NmkR	Sep	3+	Siyouma	119	12/1
Dewhurst	7f	NwmR	Oct	2	Dawn Approach	122	30/100
Middle Park Stakes	6f	NwmR	Oct	2	Reckless Abandon	118	9/4
Queen Elizabeth II	1m	Ascot	Oct	3+	Excelebration	131	10/11
Champion	1m 2f	Ascot	Oct	3+	Frankel	136	2/11

Mayson lands the July Cup

IRISH GROUP I WINNERS 2012

Race	Distance	Course	Month	Age	Winner	RPR	SP
Irish 2,000 Guineas	1m	Curr	May	3	Power	118	5/1
Irish 1,000 Guineas (F)	1m	Curr	May	3	Samitar	112	12/1
Gold Cup	1m3f	Curr	May	4+	So You Think	127	2/11
Irish Derby	1m4f	Curr	Jun	3	Camelot	121	1/5
Pretty Polly (F&M)	1m2f	Curr	Jul	3+	Izzi Top	118	6/4
Irish Oaks (Fillies)	1m4f	Curr	Jul	3	Great Heavens	118	5/4
Phoenix	6f	Curr	Aug	2	Pedro The Great	105	10/1
Matron	1m	Leop	Sep	3+	Chachamaidee	116	11/2
Irish Champion	1m2f	Leop	Sep	3+	Snow Fairy	126	15/8
Moyglare Stud (F)	7f	Curr	Sep	2	Sky Lantern	111	7/1
Vincent O'Brien National	7f	Curr	Sep	2	Dawn Approach	123	2/5
Irish St Leger	1m6f	Curr	Sep	3+	Royal Diamond	110	16/1

FRENCH GROUP I WINNERS 2012

Race	Distance	Course	Month	Age	Winner	RPR	SP
Prix Ganay	1m3f	Long	Apr	4+	Cirrus Des Aigles	130	8/13
Poule d'Essai des Poulains	1m	Long	May	3	Lucayan	115	33/1
Poule d'Essai des Pouliches (F)	1m	Long	May	3	Beauty Parlour	116	8/13
Prix Saint-Alary (F)	1m2f	Long	May	3	Sagawara	107	9/4
Prix D'Ispahan	1m1f	Long	May	4+	Golden Lilac	117	6/1
Prix Du Jockey Club	1m3f	Chant	Jun	3	Saonois	118	25/1
Prix De Diane Longines (F)	1m3f	Chant	Jun	3	Valyra	120	25/1
Grand Prix De Saint-Cloud	1m4f	St-Cl	Jun	4+	Meandre	122	8/1
Prix Jean Prat	1m	Chant	Jul	3	Aesop's Fables	117	12/1
Grand Prix De Paris	1m4f	Long	Jul	3	Imperial Monarch	118	6/5
Prix Rothschild (F&M)	1m	Deauv	Jul	3+	Elusive Kate	118	9/4
Prix Maurice De Gheest	7f	Deauv	Aug	3+	Moonlight Cloud	127	4/5
Prix Jacques Le Marois	1m	Deauv	Aug	3+	Excelebration	126	5/2
Prix Jean Romanet (F&M)	1m2f	Deauv	Aug	4+	Snow Fairy	119	4/1
Prix Morny	6f	Deauv	Aug	2	Reckless Abandon	115	6/4
Prix Vermeille (F&M)	1m4f	Long	Sep	3+	Shareta	114	7/2
Prix Du Moulin	1m	Long	Sep	3+	Moonlight Cloud	123	10/11
Arc de Triomphe	1m4f	Long	Oct	3+	Solemia	124	33/1
Jean-Luc Lagardere	7f	Long	Oct	2	Olympic Glory	117	6/4
Cadran	2m4f	Long	Oct	4+	Molly Malone	112	14/1
Opera	1m2f	Long	Oct	3+	Ridasiyna	121	12/1
Foret	7f	Long	Oct	3+	Gordon Lord Byron	121	5/2
Abbaye	5f	Long	Oct	2+	Wizz Kid	116	7/1
Marcel Boussac (F)	1m	Long	Oct	2	Silasol	107	10/1

Nathaniel winning the Eclipse

BRITISH HANDICAP WINNERS 2012

£k	Race	Dist	Crse	Month	Winner	OR	SP
£140	Ebor	1m6f	York	Aug	Willing Foe	101	12/1
£100	Cambridgeshire	1m1f	NmkR	Sep	Bronze Angel	95	9/1
£97	53rd John Smith's Cup	1m2f	York	Jul	King's Warrior	91	33/1
£97	Ladbrokes Mobile	1m4f	Ascot	Sep	Ahzeemah	95	11/1
£93	Challenge Cup	7f	Ascot	Oct	Skilful	105	6/1
£86	Northumberland Plate	2m	Newc	Jun	Ile De Re	101	5/2
£78	Betfred Mile	1m	Gdwd	Aug	Fulbright	102	7/1
£78	Wokingham	6f	Ascot	Jun	Dandy Boy	106	33/1
£78	Royal Hunt Cup	1m	Ascot	Jun	Prince Of Johanne	100	16/1
£75	Ayr Gold Cup	6f	Ayr	Sep	Captain Ramius	100	16/1
£62	Betfred "The Bonus King"	6f	NmkJ	Jul	Fulbright	96	10/1
£62	Lincoln	1m	Donc	Mar	Brae Hill	95	25/1
£62	Chester Cup	2m3f	Chest	May	Ile De Re	93	10/1
£62	Britannia	1m	Ascot	Jun	Fast Or Free	87	6/1
£62k	Stewards' Cup	6f	Gdwd	Aug	Hawkeyethenoo	103	9/1
£62k	Betfair Summer Double Leg1	7f	Ascot	Jul	Field Of Dream	99	25/1
£62k	Betfair Summer Double Leg2	7f	Gdwd	Aug	Imperial Guest	98	12/1
£62k	Betfred Mobile Sports	5f	Ascot	Jul	Barnet Fair	88	7/1
£62k	Old Newton Cup	1m4f	Hayd	Jul	Number Theory	92	8/1
£60k	Victoria Cup	7f	Ascot	May	Global Village	88	9/1
£52k	Bond Tyres Trophy	6f	York	Jun	Sholaan	87	10/1
£52k	Fly London Southend Airport	7f	Ascot	Sep	Don't Call Me	96	25/1
£47k	Betfair. Don't Settle For Less	1m	York	Aug	Trade Storm	98	12/1
£47k	Buckingham Palace	7f	Ascot	Jun	Eton Forever	103	14/1
£47k	"Dash"	5f	Epsom	Jun	Stone Of Folca	93	50/1
£44k	Melrose	1m6f	York	Aug	Guarantee	95	9/1
£44k	Great St Wilfrid	6f	Ripon	Aug	Pepper Lane	99	20/1
£44k	Dubai Duty Free	1m2f	Nbry	Sep	Hajras	96	13/2
£44k	Challenge	1m	Sand	Jul	Trade Commissioner	98	2/1
£44k	Duke Of Edinburgh	1m4f	Ascot	Jun	Camborne	97	11/2
£37k	Piper Heidsieck & Levy Board	1m2f	Sand	Sep	Labarinto	95	16/1
£37k	Portland	6f	Donc	Sep	Doc Hay	97	20/1
£37k	Silver Bowl	1m	Hayd	May	Gabrial	91	9/2
£34k	King George V	1m4f	Ascot	Jun	Fennell Bay	85	12/1
£34k	Ascot Stakes	2m4f	Ascot	Jun	Simenon	95	8/1
£99k	Cesarewitch	2m2f	NwmR	Oct	Aaim To Prosper	107	66/1
£47k	Coral Sprint	6f	York	Oct	Regal Parade	103	14/1
£32k	Future Stars Apprentice	7f	Ascot	Oct	Jack Dexter	93	11/2

Society Rock (black) wins the Sprint Cup

IRISH HANDICAP WINNERS 2012

£k	Race	Dist	Crse	Month	Winner	OR	SP
£58k	Topaz Mile	1m	Glwy	Jul	Vastonea	89	7/1
£48k	Irish Cambridgeshire	1m	Curr	Aug	Punch Your Weight	86	16/1
£43k	Sprint	6f	Curr	Jun	An Saighdiur	80	20/1
£42k	Rockingham	5f	Curr	Jul	Bubbly Bellini	81	11/2
£40k	September	7f	Leop	Sep	Lily's Angel	96	10/1
£35k	Derby Festival	1m4f	Curr	Jun	Ursa Major	98	11/4
£35k	Ladbrokes Mobile App Handicap	7f	Glwy	Aug	Pintura	98	5/1
£35k	Galway City	2m	Glwy	Jul	Midnight Music	82	11/1

MAJOR US GRADE 1 WINNERS 2012

Race	Dist	Crse	Month	Age	Winner	OR	SP
Kentucky Oaks (F)	1m1fD	CDwns	May	3	Believe You Can	118	138/10
Kentucky Derby	1m2fD	CDwns	May	3	I'll Have Another	125	153/10
Preakness	1m2fD	Pimli	May	3	I'll Have Another	126	16/5
Belmont	1m4fD	Blmnt	Jun	3	Union Rags	123	11/4
Hollywood Gold Cup Hcap	1m2fAW	HwdP	Jul	3+	Game On Dude	125	2/5
Man O' War	1m 3f	Blmnt	Jul	3+	Point Of Entry	113	59/20
American Oaks (F)	1m 2f	Hollyw	Jul	3	Lady Of Shamrock	105	6/4
Haskell Invitational	1m1fD	Monm	Jul	3	Paynter	123	Evens
Beverly D (F&M)	1m2f	Arling	Aug	3+	I'm A Dreamer	114	63/10
Arlington Million	1m2f	Arling	Aug	3+	Little Mike	119	39/10
Travers	1m2fD	Sarat	Aug	3	Alpha	120	12/5
(dead-heat)					Golden Ticket	120	34/1
Turf Classic	1m4f	Blmnt	Sep	3+	Point Of Entry	118	3/4
Jockey Club Gold Cup	1m2fD	Blmnt	Sep	3+	Flat Out	123	73/20

UAE GROUP 1 WINNERS 2012

Race	Dist	Crse	Month	Age	Winner	OR	SP
Al Maktoum Challenge	1m2fAW	Meyd	Mar	3+	Capponi	119	9/1
Jebel Hatta	1m1f	Meyd	Mar	3+	Master Of Hounds	115	16/1
Dubai Golden Shaheen	6f	Meyd	Mar	3+	Krypton Factor	123	13/2
Dubai Duty Free	1m1f	Meyd	Mar	3+	Cityscape	126	8/1
Dubai Sheema Classic	1m4f	Meyd	Mar	3+	Cirrus Des Aigles	125	11/4
Dubai World Cup	1m2fAW	Meyd	Mar	3+	Monterosso	126	20/1
Al Quoz Sprint	5f	Meyd	Mar	3+	Ortensia	115	6/1

GERMANY GROUP 1 WINNERS 2012

Race	Dist	Crse	Month	Age	Winner	OR	SP
Deutsches Derby	1m4f	Hamb	Jul	3	Pastorius	113	25/1
Grosser Preis Von Berlin	1m4f	Hopp	Jul	3+	Meandre	119	4/5
Bayerisches Zuchtrennen	1m2f	Munch	Jul	3+	Pastorius	122	3/1
Preis Der Diana (F)	1m3f	Duss	Aug	3	Salomina	110	12/5
Grosser Preis Von Bayern	1m4f	Munch	Aug	3+	Temida	113	135/10
Grosser Preis Von Baden	1m4f	B-Bdn	Sep	3+	Danedream	116	7/10
Preis Von Europa	1m4f	Colgn	Sep	3+	Girolamo	115	74/10

European results up and including October 20. Other results up to and including September 30

Izzi Top takes the Pretty Polly

FLAT JOCKEYS 2012

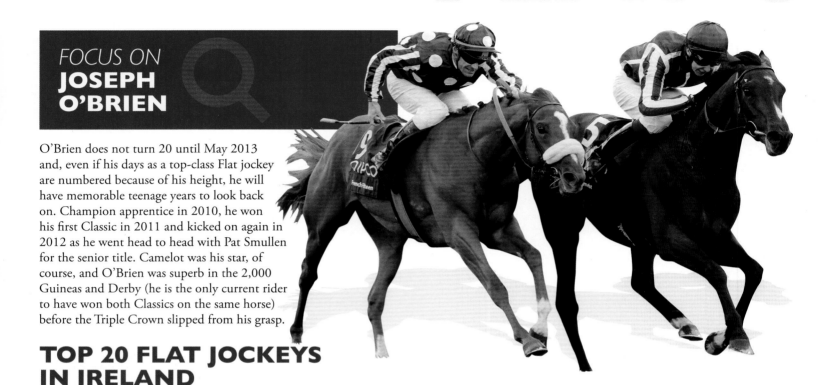

FOCUS ON JOSEPH O'BRIEN

O'Brien does not turn 20 until May 2013 and, even if his days as a top-class Flat jockey are numbered because of his height, he will have memorable teenage years to look back on. Champion apprentice in 2010, he won his first Classic in 2011 and kicked on again in 2012 as he went head to head with Pat Smullen for the senior title. Camelot was his star, of course, and O'Brien was superb in the 2,000 Guineas and Derby (he is the only current rider to have won both Classics on the same horse) before the Triple Crown slipped from his grasp.

TOP 20 FLAT JOCKEYS IN IRELAND

	Wins-rides	Strike rate	Win and place prize-money €
1 Joseph O'Brien	83-387	21%	2,660,674
2 Pat Smullen	78-538	14%	1,831,646
3 Wayne Lordan	61-402	15%	1,154,011
4 Shane Foley	55-463	12%	952,702
5 Chris Hayes	53-437	12%	1,016,192
6 Johnny Murtagh	44-237	19%	1,364,287
7 Fran Berry	41-329	12%	647,493
8 Kevin Manning	40-389	10%	1,221,850
9 Ronan Whelan	28-228	12%	381,329
Declan McDonogh	28-351	8%	586,684
11 Gary Carroll	25-319	8%	408,108
12 Niall McCullagh	23-290	8%	655,948
13 Ben Curtis	22-328	7%	291,285
14 Danny Grant	19-172	11%	215,622
Billy Lee	19-265	7%	366,173
16 Sam James	17-209	8%	228,492
Colm O'Donoghue	17-225	8%	466,533
18 Emmet McNamara	16-130	12%	209,287
Leigh Roche	16-179	9%	200,655
20 Conor Hoban	15-199	8%	202,322
Seamie Heffernan	15-292	5%	664,875

Covers period from March 25 (first day of championship) to October 15

TOP FIVE APPRENTICES IN IRELAND

	Wins-rides	Strike rate	Win and place prize-money €
1 Ronan Whelan	28-231	12%	381,329
2 Sam James	17-211	8%	228,992
3 Leigh Roche	16-183	9%	202,055
4 Conor Hoban	16-202	8%	211,673
5 Emmet McNamara	16-131	12%	209, 288

Up to and including October 18

FOCUS ON WILLIAM BUICK

While the merry-go-round of top jockeys swirled around him in 2012, Buick remained happily settled with John Gosden and their mutually beneficial partnership went from strength to strength, although for sheer coolness his best ride was surely the Nunthorpe win on the Australian mare Ortensia. With a string of big-race successes for Gosden, he passed his previous-best total of 106 winners before the end of September.

TOP 20 FLAT JOCKEYS IN BRITAIN

	Wins-rides	Strike rate	Win and place prize-money £
1 Richard Hughes	162-781	21%	2,041,767
2 William Buick	114-614	19%	3,143,040
3 Silvestre de Sousa	113-784	14%	1,060,048
4 Ryan Moore	104-553	19%	2,288,598
Paul Hanagan	104-667	16%	1,712,423
6 Joe Fanning	92-647	14%	795,867
7 Jim Crowley	91-568	16%	930,941
8 Kieren Fallon	79-574	14%	1,557,112
9 James Doyle	78-548	14%	853,137
10 Graham Lee	72-647	11%	665,395
11 Jamie Spencer	71-519	14%	1,005,940
12 Daniel Tudhope	70-442	16%	685,122
Tom Queally	70-538	13%	1,928,538
Luke Morris	70-768	9%	577,858
15 Neil Callan	68-572	12%	806,761
16 Robert Winston	66-485	14%	455,093
17 Paul Mulrennan	65-593	11%	463,936
18 Richard Kingscote	60-350	17%	481,380
19 Mickael Barzalona	57-369	15%	1,149,864
Hayley Turner	57-526	11%	577,574

Covers period from March 31 (first day of championship) to October 15

FOCUS ON RYAN MOORE

Moore has been dogged by bad luck in the three years since the last of his three title triumphs and this year's dose came when he broke his wrist in a fall at Warwick on August 21. He wasn't enjoying a vintage season – "if I was a golfer, I'd have been one over par" – but at the time he still held a narrow lead over Richard Hughes in the championship race and could look back on a daring 1,000 Guineas victory on Homecoming Queen and five winners at Royal Ascot. By the time he returned on October 5, Hughes had flown.

TOP FIVE APPRENTICES IN BRITAIN

	Wins-rides	Strike rate	Win and place prize-money £
1 Amy Ryan	39-314	12%	312,077
2 Darren Egan	38-382	10%	283,519
3 Raul Da Silva	32-289	11%	159,617
4 Sean Levey	31-276	11%	169,089
5 Harry Bentley	29-257	11%	240,361

Up to and including October 18

FOCUS ON AMY RYAN

Ryan, 22, has had plenty of help from father Kevin's powerful yard but there was no more impressive apprentice in 2012 and even after losing her claim in May she remained in the thick of the title battle with Darren Egan and Raul Da Silva. She had winners for more than a dozen trainers other than her father in 2012, which is an indication of her impact, and there are high hopes she can establish herself in the senior ranks alongside Hayley Turner and Cathy Gannon.

GB AND IRE CLASSIC WINNERS

4

O'Brien
Camelot
2,000 Guineas, Derby, Irish Derby
Power
Irish 2,000 Guineas

1 Moore
Homecoming Queen
1,000 Guineas

1 Heffernan
Was
Oaks

1 Barzalona
Encke
St Leger

1 Harley
Samitar
Irish 1,000 Guineas

1 Buick
Great Heavens
Irish Oaks

1 McCullagh
Royal Diamond
Irish St Leger

FLAT TRAINERS 2012

FLAT TRAINE

FOCUS ON JOHN GOSDEN

In terms of depth of quality, the balance of power in Newmarket has moved along Bury Road from Sir Michael Stoute's Freemason Lodge to Gosden's increasingly successful Clarehaven Stables. Gosden was second only to Aidan O'Brien for number of Group 1 winners in Britain and Ireland in 2012, with his team headed by Eclipse winner Nathaniel. But for Nathaniel's narrow defeat in the King George, Gosden's first title would have been sealed by late summer as he set a scorching pace ahead of O'Brien and Richard Hannon (the champion in the previous two years).

TOP 20 FLAT TRAINERS IN BRITAIN

	Wins-runs	Strike rate	Win and place prize-money £
1 John Gosden	110-585	19%	3,379,220
2 Aidan O'Brien	11-69	16%	2,859,196
3 Richard Hannon	205-1298	16%	2,677,395
4 Mark Johnston	207-1253	17%	2,174,346
5 Richard Fahey	141-1236	11%	1,962,725
6 Sir Henry Cecil	51-267	19%	1,883,717
7 Saeed Bin Suroor	73-373	20%	1,711,116
8 Andrew Balding	88-645	14%	1,311,155
9 Kevin Ryan	91-739	12%	1,196,308
10 Mahmood Al Zarooni	57-355	16%	1,151,593
11 William Haggas	77-391	20%	1,131,694
12 Tim Easterby	85-910	9%	1,022,842
13 Mick Channon	97-878	11%	976,415
14 Sir Michael Stoute	65-333	20%	936,519
15 Roger Varian	65-342	19%	818,612
16 Roger Charlton	36-230	16%	769,074
17 David O'Meara	67-507	13%	701,042
18 Clive Cox	38-354	11%	694,705
19 Jeremy Noseda	45-240	19%	666,422
20 David Simcock	61-428	14%	631,339

Covers period from Nov 6 2011 (first day of championship) to Oct 15

TOP 20 FLAT TRAINERS IN IRELAND

	Wins-runs	Strike rate	Win and place prize-money €
1 Aidan O'Brien	86-460	19%	3,419,115
2 Dermot Weld	55-390	14%	1,568,555
3 Jim Bolger	40-408	10%	1,311,406
4 John Oxx	32-181	18%	1,145,595
5 David Wachman	37-245	15%	1,000,993
6 Ger Lyons	31-209	15%	510,815
7 John Gosden	2-4	50%	509,900
8 Michael Halford	38-264	14%	507,621
9 Kevin Prendergast	22-215	10%	476,160
10 Andrew Oliver	22-219	10%	454,905
11 Ed Dunlop	1-1	100%	442,500
12 Jessica Harrington	19-214	9%	367,105
13 Ken Condon	18-154	12%	347,735
14 Tommy Carmody	16-64	25%	346,365
15 Tommy Stack	29-131	22%	324,375
16 Paul Deegan	18-178	10%	317,850
17 Eddie Lynam	17-175	10%	306,793
18 Pat Flynn	25-197	13%	242,475
19 Mick Channon	2-7	29%	234,750
20 Willie McCreery	13-177	7%	207,235

Covers period from March 25 (first day of championship) to Oct 15

FOCUS ON AIDAN O'BRIEN

O'Brien dominated the early Classics in Ireland and Britain and, although he was overhauled by John Gosden in the British standings, he was unbeatable again at home as he took a 14th consecutive championship. History beckoned in the St Leger at Doncaster but Camelot's defeat meant the trainer was denied a Triple Crown and a clean sweep of the British Classics. Excelebration, so often in the shadow of Frankel, joined O'Brien for 2012 and was Ballydoyle's top older horse with victory in the Prix Jacques Le Marois and QE II.

FLAT OWNERS 2012

FOCUS ON GODOLPHIN

Having not won the owners' title since 2007, Godolphin have gone through a period of renewal with the elevation of Mahmood Al Zarooni to top trainer and the recruitment of Mickael Barzalona as No.1 jockey in place of Frankie Dettori. Barzalona's victory on Monterosso in the Dubai World Cup was full of promise, although in Britain there were few highlights until Al Zarooni, Barzalona and Encke scuppered Camelot's Triple Crown bid.

TOP 20 FLAT OWNERS IN BRITAIN

		Wins-runs	Total prize-money £
1	Godolphin	131-716	2,942,422
2	Khalid Abdullah	59-330	2,078,774
3	Sheikh Hamdan Bin Mohammed Al Maktoum	13-648	1,272,326
4	Hamdan Al Maktoum	85-508	1,128,732
5	Derrick Smith	15-101	1,081,968
6	Dr Marwan Koukash	82-610	934,970
7	Mrs John Magnier	17-123	919,989
8	Michael Tabor	14-110	887,058
9	Lady Rothschild	26-75	739,889
10	George Strawbridge	17-62	576,890
11	Gestut Burg Eberstein & Teruya Yoshida	1-1	567,100
12	Mrs J Wood	12-86	531,209
13	Cheveley Park Stud	28-190	469,716
14	Niarchos Family	8-49	444,463
15	H R H Princess Haya of Jordan	24-129	424,672
16	Qatar Racing Limited	9-67	400,527
17	C H Stevens	9-60	399,890
18	David W Armstrong	11-79	390,144
19	Pearl Bloodstock Ltd	20-107	352,552
20	Andrew Tinkler	30-228	345,838

Covers period from Nov 9, 2011 (first day of championship) to Oct 13

TOP 20 FLAT OWNERS IN IRELAND

		Wins-runs	Total prize-money €
1	Derrick Smith	12-54	1,102,195
2	H H Aga Khan	36-145	826,895
3	Mrs J S Bolger	22-280	738,088
4	Mrs John Magnier & Michael Tabor & Derrick Smith	27-107	630,090
5	Anamoine Ltd	8-47	580,085
6	Khalid Abdullah	15-46	492,090
7	Michael Tabor & Derrick Smith & Mrs John Magnier	16-82	485,190
8	Derrick Smith & Mrs John Magnier & Michael Tabor	10-51	480,410
9	Andrew Tinkler	16-65	406,365
10	Moyglare Stud Farm	10-65	389,460
11	Michael Tabor	13-60	355,800
12	Christopher Tsui	0-4	300,500
13	Lady O'Reilly	11-105	285,430
14	Lady Rothschild	1-1	236,000
15	Helena Springfield Ltd	1-2	195,900
16	Hamdan Al Maktoum	9-74	189,360
17	A Oliver	10-85	183,100
18	Dr R Lambe	6-69	179,415
19	B Keswick	2-2	177,300
20	Martin S Schwartz	1-1	177,000

Covers period from March 25 (first day of championship) to Oct 15

FOCUS ON ANDREW TINKLER

The boss of the Stobart haulage firm is a new name high up the list of owners in Ireland, having had a successful first season with the 17 horses he has in training with Tommy Carmody at the yard owned by Johnny Murtagh. The highlight was the remarkable Irish St Leger triumph of Royal Diamond, although their highest-rated horse was Ursa Major, who won the Group 3 trial for the Irish Leger and then finished fourth to Encke in the St Leger at Doncaster.

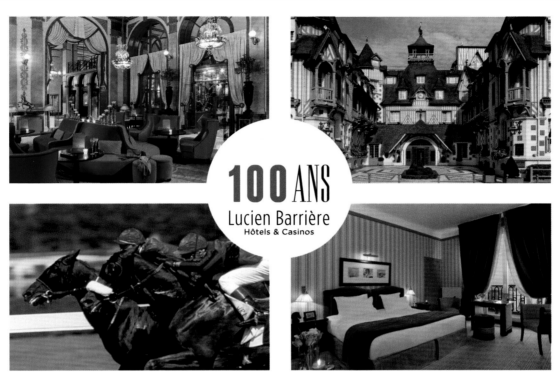

Some years are worth a celebration!

In 2012 Lucien Barrière Hôtels & Casinos is celebrating its 100th anniversary.

100 years already!! Lucien Barrière Hôtels & Casinos is celebrating in Deauville, and all over France,
the company's outstanding track record by offering customers exceptional accommodation packages.

100 years of constant innovation in gaming, 100 years of pampering at our hotels and spas, 100 years of gourmet flavours,
100 years of glamour and films, 100 years of shows, dreams and entertainment, 100 years of customer service…

Lucien Barrière Hôtels & Casinos has dreamt up an anniversary year
that pays tribute to our staff's talent and all our Deauville facilities.

Lucien Barrière
Hôtels & Casinos · Deauville

+ 33 800 15 00 00
deauville@lucienbarriere.com

www.lucienbarriere.com

THE
BIGGER
PICTURE

A fall with far-reaching consequences unfolds as Wishfull Thinking comes down at the fourth fence in the Queen Mother Champion Chase and hurtles through the inside rail. With rider Richard Johnson and photographer Jean-Charles Briens lying injured, the fence had to be bypassed next time round as Finian's Rainbow beat Sizing Europe in a close finish. Fortunately, nobody was seriously hurt in the incident, while Wishfull Thinking returned to action at Aintree in April
PATRICK McCANN (RACINGPOST.COM/PHOTOS)

JUMPS CHAMPIONS 2011-12

Two-mile chaser

SPRINTER SACRE

Trainer **Nicky Henderson**
Owner **Caroline Mould**

RACING POST RATINGS	
Sprinter Sacre	176
Finian's Rainbow	175
Sizing Europe	174
Sanctuaire	168
Somersby	169

The outstanding novice Sprinter Sacre put up the best two-mile performance of the season with his seven-length victory in the Arkle and, although that race is not directly comparable with the following day's Queen Mother Champion Chase, he ran the distance 1.11sec faster than the seniors. Finian's Rainbow just edged Sizing Europe, the

Tingle Creek winner, in the Champion Chase and his winning RPR of 175 was a big step up from his previous best of 167 when runner-up to Somersby in the Victor Chandler Chase in January.

Two-and-a-half-mile chaser

FINIAN'S RAINBOW

Trainer **Nicky Henderson**
Owner **Michael Buckley**

MASTER MINDED

Trainer **Paul Nicholls**
Owner **Clive Smith**

RACING POST RATINGS	
Finian's Rainbow	175
Master Minded	175
Riverside Theatre	172
Medermit	170
Albertas Run	169
Somersby	169

Finian's Rainbow, having achieved a career-best RPR of 175 to land the Queen Mother Champion Chase in March, ran to the same level over two and a half miles the following month with a seven-length victory from Wishfull Thinking in the Melling Chase at Aintree. He shared top spot with Master Minded, who set the early standard when conceding 4lb to Somersby in winning the Amlin Chase at Ascot but was retired after injuring a tendon in the King George.

Three-mile-plus chaser

KAUTO STAR

Trainer **Paul Nicholls**
Owner **Clive Smith**

RACING POST RATINGS	
Kauto Star	182
Long Run	181
Synchronised	175
The Giant Bolster	172
Burton Port	171

Kauto Star was the best chaser in Britain and Ireland for the fourth time in his illustrious career after an amazing resurgence that brought stirring victories in the Betfair Chase at Haydock and the King George VI Chase at Kempton. There was no dream ending in the Gold Cup, where he was pulled up as the ill-fated Synchronised went on to victory, but his RPR of 182 for his fifth King George was a remarkable 10lb higher than his best of the previous season.

Novice chaser

SPRINTER SACRE

Trainer **Nicky Henderson**
Owner **Caroline Mould**

RACING POST RATINGS

Sprinter Sacre	176
Grands Crus	168
Sir Des Champs	168
Sanctuaire	168
Cue Card	167

Sprinter Sacre stood head and shoulders above a strong group of novice chasers, with the next three in the list all bettering the RPR of 167 achieved by the previous season's champion, Wishfull Thinking. Sprinter Sacre was way ahead of that mark and came close to Gloria Victis's novice record RPR of 177 in 1999-2000. After three RPRs in the 170s and a high in the Arkle, the sky is the limit for Sprinter Sacre.

Two-mile hurdler

HURRICANE FLY

Trainer **Willie Mullins**
Owner **George Creighton**

RACING POST RATINGS

Hurricane Fly	173
Rock On Ruby	171
Binocular	170
Overturn	167
Grandouet	166

Hurricane Fly lost his Champion Hurdle crown to Rock On Ruby at Cheltenham, finishing five and a half lengths behind in third, but he was still the overall champion for the second season in a row. He matched his previous season's best RPR of 173 with a runaway win over

Oscars Well in the Irish Champion Hurdle on heavy ground at Leopardstown in January and rounded off the season with the 11th Grade 1 victory of his career at Punchestown (RPR 170).

Two-and-a-half mile-plus hurdler

BIG BUCK'S

Trainer **Paul Nicholls**
Owner **The Stewart family**

RACING POST RATINGS

Big Buck's	173
Oscar Whisky	167
Thousand Stars	165
Smad Place	164
Voler La Vedette	163

Big Buck's remained utterly dominant in stayers' hurdles, stretching his remarkable winning run to 17 by the end of the season as he landed

five more victories by a grand total of more than 30 lengths. His best RPR of 173 was achieved twice, both at Cheltenham in the World Hurdle and Cleeve Hurdle, but it was down from his career-high 178 the previous season and meant he had only a share of the overall hurdling title with Hurricane Fly.

Novice hurdler

SIMONSIG

Trainer **Nicky Henderson**
Owner **Ronnie Bartlett**

RACING POST RATINGS

Simonsig	162
Boston Bob	156
Darlan	156
Fingal Bay	156
Brindisi Breeze	154

Simonsig achieved an RPR of 162 not once but twice as he established a clear superiority over a good bunch of novices. Having already run to RPRs in the low 150s twice in the run-up to Cheltenham, he took the Neptune by seven lengths and followed up with a 15-length success in the Mersey at Aintree. The next-best of the Cheltenham Festival winners was Brindisi Breeze in the Albert Bartlett, while Boston Bob, Darlan and Fingal Bay all put up good performances elsewhere.

JUMPS WINNERS 2011-12

GRADE I WINNING TRAINERS IN BRITAIN

Nicky Henderson | Paul Nicholls | Donald McCain | Philip Hobbs | Alan King | Others

GRADE I WINNING TRAINERS IN IRELAND

Willie Mullins | Tony Martin | Dermot Weld | Colm Murphy | Peter Casey | Philip Fenton | Others

BRITISH GRADE I WINNERS 2011-12

Race	Distance	Course	Month	Age	Winner	RPR	SP
Betfair Ch	3m	Hayd	Nov	5+	Kauto Star	178	6-1
Fighting Fifth Hdl	2m	Newc	Nov	4+	Overturn	157	7-4
Tingle Creek Ch	2m	Sand	Dec	4+	Sizing Europe	172	11-8
Henry VIII Nov Ch	2m	Sand	Dec	4+	Al Ferof	154	4-11
Long Walk Hdl	3m1f	Asct	Dec	4+	Big Buck's	164	3-10
King George VI Ch	3m	Kemp	Dec	4+	Kauto Star	182	3-1
Christmas Hdl	2m	Kemp	Dec	4+	Binocular	166	5-4
Feltham Nov Ch	3m	Kemp	Dec	4+	Grands Crus	168	6-5
Champions Finale Juv Hdl	2m1f	Chep	Dec	3	Hollow Tree	140	13-8
Challow Nov Hdl	2m5f	Newb	Dec	4+	Fingal Bay	149	1-4
32red Hdl (nov)	2m1f	Sand	Jan	4+	Captain Conan	145	9-1
Victor Chandler Ch	2m1f	Asct	Jan	5+	Somersby	169	9-2
Betfair Nov Ch	2m4f	Newb	Feb	5+	For Non Stop	153	3-1
Ascot Ch	2m6f	Asct	Feb	5+	Riverside Theatre	172	13-8
Champion Hdl	2m1f	Chlt	Mar	4+	Rock On Ruby	171	11-1
Supreme Nov Hdl	2m1f	Chlt	Mar	4+	Cinders And Ashes	151	10-1
Arkle Challenge Trophy Ch	2m	Chlt	Mar	5+	Sprinter Sacre	176	8-11
Champion Bumper	2m1f	Chlt	Mar	4-6	Champagne Fever	142	16-1
Queen Mother Champion Ch	2m	Chlt	Mar	5+	Finian's Rainbow	175	4-1
RSA Ch	3m1f	Chlt	Mar	5+	Bobs Worth	166	9-2
Neptune Nov Hdl	2m5f	Chlt	Mar	4+	Simonsig	162	2-1
Ryanair Ch	2m5f	Chlt	Mar	5+	Riverside Theatre	171	7-2
Ladbrokes World Hdl	3m	Chlt	Mar	4+	Big Buck's	173	5-6
JCB Triumph Hdl	2m1f	Chlt	Mar	4	Countrywide Flame	145	33-1
Chltenham Gold Cup Ch	3m3f	Chlt	Mar	5+	Synchronised	175	8-1
Albert Bartlett Nov Hdl	3m	Chlt	Mar	4+	Brindisi Breeze	153	7-1
Liverpool Hdl	3m1f	Aint	Apr	4+	Big Buck's	159	2-9
Anniversary 4-Y-O Juv Hdl	2m1f	Aint	Apr	4	Grumeti	148	11-4
Betfred Bowl Ch	3m1f	Aint	Apr	5+	Follow The Plan	168	50-1
Manifesto Nov Ch	2m4f	Aint	Apr	5+	Menorah	164	3-1
Melling Ch	2m4f	Aint	Apr	5+	Finian's Rainbow	175	13-8
Sefton Nov Hdl	3m1f	Aint	Apr	4+	Lovcen	154	8-1
Aint Hdl	2m4f	Aint	Apr	4+	Oscar Whisky	165	9-4
Maghull Nov Ch	2m	Aint	Apr	5+	Sprinter Sacre	170	1-7

IRISH GRADE I WINNERS 2011-12

Race	Distance	Course	Month	Age	Winner	RPR	SP
Champion Ch	3m	DRoy	Nov	5+	Quito De La Roque	167	11-4
Morgiana Hdl	2m	Punch	Nov	4+	Thousand Stars	161	5-4
Hatton's Grace Hdl	2m4f	Fairy	Dec	4+	Voler La Vedette	156	7-4
Drinmore Nov Ch	2m4f	Fairy	Dec	4+	Bog Warrior	162	15-8
Royal Bond Nov Hdl	2m	Fairy	Dec	4+	Sous Les Cieux	151	6-4
John Durkan Ch	2m4f	Punch	Dec	5+	Rubi Light	167	5-2
Navan Nov Hdl	2m4f	Navan	Dec	4+	Boston Bob	153	9-4
Racing Post Nov Ch	2m1f	Leop	Dec	4+	Blackstairmountain	148	9-2
Dial-A-Bet Ch	2m1f	Leop	Dec	5+	Big Zeb	167	8-11
Future Champions Nov Hdl	2m	Leop	Dec	4+	Cash And Go	143	11-2
Fort Leney Nov Ch	3m	Leop	Dec	4+	Last Instalment	154	11-4
Lexus Ch	3m	Leop	Dec	5+	Synchronised	171	8-1
Istabraq Festival Hdl	2m	Leop	Dec	4+	Unaccompanied	153	10-3
Irish Champion Hdl	2m	Leop	Jan	4+	Hurricane Fly	173	4-5
Arkle Nov Ch	2m1f	Leop	Jan	5+	Flemenstar	164	6-4
Dr P.J. Moriarty Nov Ch	2m5f	Leop	Feb	5+	Last Instalment	149	8-11
Spring Juv Hdl	2m	Leop	Feb	4	Hisaabaat	139	15-2
Hennessy Gold Cup	3m	Leop	Feb	5+	Quel Esprit	160	5-4
Deloitte Nov Hdl	2m2f	Leop	Feb	5+	Beneficient	147	50-1
Powers Gold Cup Ch	2m4f	Fairy	Apr	5+	Flemenstar	164	11-10
Champion Ch	2m	Punch	Apr	5+	Sizing Europe	171	8-13
Champion Nov Hdl	2m	Punch	Apr	5+	Alderwood	148	5-2
Champion Nov Ch	3m1f	Punch	Apr	5+	Sir Des Champs	159	-7
War Of Attrition Nov Hdl	3m	Punch	Apr	4+	Marasonnien	144	12-1
Champion INH Flat Race	2m	Punch	Apr	4-7	Champagne Fever	142	11-4
World Series Hdl	3m	Punch	Apr	4+	Quevega	159	11-10
Champion Hdl	2m	Punch	Apr	4+	Hurricane Fly	170	4-11
Champion Nov Hdl	2m4f	Punch	Apr	4+	Dedigout	152	10-3
Ryanair Nov Ch	2m	Punch	Apr	5+	Lucky William	149	4-1
Punchestown Gold Cup	3m1f	Punch	Apr	5+	China Rock	168	0-1
Champion 4YO Hdl	2m	Punch	Apr	4	Hisaabaat	141	4-1

THE TOP GRADE I PERFORMERS IN BRITAIN AND IRELAND

Big Buck's | Champagne Fever | Finian's Rainbow | Flemenstar | Hisaabaat | Hurricane Fly | Kauto Star | Last Instalment | Riverside Theatre | Sizing Europe | Sprinter Sacre | Synchronised

BIG HANDICAP CHASE WINNERS IN BRITAIN 2011-12

Race	Distance	Course	Month	Value	Winner	RPR	SP
Grand National	4m4f	Aint	Apr	£547k	Neptune Collonges	157	33-1
Scottish Grand National	4m1f	Ayr	Apr	£103k	Merigo	134	15-2
Bet365 Gold Cup	3m6f	Sand	Apr	£85k	Tidal Bay	154	9-1
Hennessy Gold Cup	3m3f	Newb	Nov	£85k	Carruthers	146	10-1
Paddy Power Gold Cup	2m5f	Chlt	Nov	£85k	Great Endeavour	147	8-1
Spinal Research Gold Cup	2m5f	Chlt	Dec	£57k	Quantitativeeasing	145	6-1
Racing Plus	3m	Kemp	Feb	£57k	Nacarat	154	9-2
Becher	3m2f	Aint	Dec	£57k	West End Rocker	137	10-1
Topham	2m6f	Aint	Apr	£56k	Always Waining	138	11-1
United House Gold Cup	3m	Asct	Oct	£56k	Exmoor Ranger	137	12-1
Welsh National	3m6f	Chep	Dec	£51k	Le Beau Bai	131	10-1
Betvictor.com	2m6f	Asct	Jan	£44k	Tatenen	143	8-1
Sky Bet	3m	Donc	Jan	£43k	Calgary Bay	151	12-1
Grand National Trial	3m4f	Hayd	Feb	£43k	Giles Cross	138	4-1
JLT Specialty	3m1f	Chlt	Mar	£43k	Alfie Sherrin	129	14-1
Grand Annual	2m1f	Chlt	Mar	£43k	Bellvano	138	20-1
Byrne Group Plate	2m5f	Chlt	Mar	£43k	Salut Flo	137	9-2
Midlands Grand National	4m2f	Uttx	Mar	£37k	Master Overseer	126	11-1
Red Rum	2m	Aint	Apr	£34k	Edgardo Sol	143	9-2
Badger Ales Trophy	3m2f	Winc	Nov	£34k	The Minack	141	11-4
John Smith's Handicap	3m1f	Aint	Apr	£34k	Saint Are	137	11-1
Betfair Handicap	2m4f	Hayd	Apr	£33k	Auroras Encore	134	12-1
Betfair Series Final	2m6f	Hayd	Apr	£33k	Sound Accord	116	8-1
Classic	3m5f	Warw	Jan	£31k	Hey Big Spender	156	14-1
Ultima Business Solutions	3m3f	Newb	Mar	£31k	Ikorodu Road	134	4-1
32red.com	3m1f	Sand	Jan	£31k	Hold On Julio	133	5-2
Grand Sefton	2m6f	Aint	Dec	£31k	Stewarts House	134	11-2
Carey Group Handicap	2m1f	Asct	Nov	£31k	I'msingingtheblues	145	8-1
Fulke Walwyn Kim Muir	3m2f	Chlt	Mar	£30k	Sunnyhillboy	142	13-2

Breakdown of horses rated 140+ in the Anglo-Irish Jump Classification

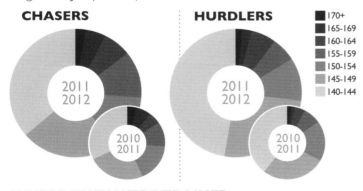

	170+
	165-169
	160-164
	155-159
	150-154
	145-149
	140-144

WHERE THEY WERE TRAINED

Britain — 2011-2012: 165, 2010-2011: 154
Ireland — 2011-2012: 75, 2010-2011: 75

Britain — 2011-2012: 107, 2010-2011: 120
Ireland — 2011-2012: 71, 2010-2011: 55

Breakdown of novices rated 140+ in the Anglo-Irish Jump Classification

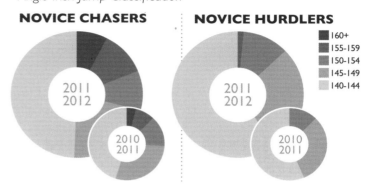

	160+
	155-159
	150-154
	145-149
	140-144

WHERE THEY WERE TRAINED

Britain — 2011-2012: 52, 2010-2011: 51
Ireland — 2011-2012: 27, 2010-2011: 22

Britain — 2011-2012: 39, 2010-2011: 38
Ireland — 2011-2012: 31, 2010-2011: 19

BIG HANDICAP HURDLE WINNERS IN BRITAIN 2011-12

Race	Distance	Course	Month	Value	Winner	RPR	SP
Betfair	2m1f	Newb	Feb	£87k	Zarkandar	151	11-4
The Ladbroke	2m	Asct	Dec	£84k	Raya Star	134	12-1
Greatwood	2m1f	Chlt	Nov	£57k	Brampour	149	12-1
"Fixed Brush"	3m	Hayd	Nov	£43k	Dynaste	141	7-1
Pertemps Final	3m	Chlt	Mar	£40k	Cape Tribulation	142	14-1
Coral Cup	2m5f	Chlt	Mar	£40k	Son Of Flicka	135	16-1
Vincent O'Brien County	2m1f	Chlt	Mar	£40k	Alderwood	139	20-1
Imperial Cup	2m1f	Sand	Mar	£34k	Paintball	128	20-1
Fred Winter Juv	2m1f	Chlt	Mar	£34k	Une Artiste	127	40-1
Betfair Series Final	2m4f	Hayd	Apr	£32k	Hada Men	122	4-1
Totescoop6 Levy ABoard	2m1f	Newb	Dec	£31k	Celestial Halo	160	12-1

BIG HANDICAP HURDLE WINNERS IN IRELAND 2011-12

Race	Distance	Course	Month	Value	Winner	RPR	SP
Galway	2m	Galw	Jul	£135k	Moon Dice	130	20-1
Boylesports.com	2m	Leop	Jan	£50k	Citizenship	118	10-1
Setantabet.com	2m4f	Punch	Apr	£41k	Drive Time	125	10-1
www.thetote.com	2m	Fairy	Apr	£33k	Vast Consumption	121	7-1

BIG HANDICAP CHASE WINNERS IN IRELAND 2011-12

Race	Distance	Course	Month	Value	Winner	RPR	SP
Irish Grand National	3m5f	Fairy	Apr	£118k	Lion Na Bearnai	135	33-1
Galway Plate	2m6f	Galw	Jul	£104k	Blazing Tempo	139	5-1
Paddy Power	3m	Leop	Dec	£92k	Cross Appeal	125	7-1
Guinness Kerry National	3m	Listo	Sep	£83k	Alfa Beat	148	20-1
Troytown	3m	Navan	Nov	£45k	Groody Hill	124	10-1
Thyestes	3m	GowP	Jan	£43k	On His Own	125	10-1
Munster National	3m	Limk	Oct	£42k	Muirhead	132	10-1
Guinness Handicap	2m4f	Punch	Apr	£41k	Foildubh	137	9-2
Leopardstown	2m5f	Leop	Jan	£41k	Seabass	131	7-1
Dan Moore Memorial	2m1f	Fairy	Apr	£41k	Bob Lingo	130	12-1

JUMP JOCKEYS 2011-12

FOCUS ON JASON MAGUIRE

Donald McCain's stable jockey made another big leap forward last season, less heralded than his 2011 Grand National triumph on Ballabriggs but significant nonetheless. This time it was more about the bread and butter than the cream as Maguire announced himself as a credible championship contender of the future, improving his score by almost 50 winners to 144. That put him only nine behind Richard Johnson, the eternal second, and more than halved the gap on 17-times champion Tony McCoy.

TOP 20 JUMP JOCKEYS IN BRITAIN IN 2011-12

		Wins-rides	Strike rate	Win and place prize-money £
1	Tony McCoy	199-727	27%	1,471,821
2	Richard Johnson	153-834	18%	1,296,401
3	Jason Maguire	144-625	23%	1,095,247
4	Daryl Jacob	83-455	18%	1,391,365
5	Tom O'Brien	83-536	15%	577,085
6	Paddy Brennan	82-477	17%	568,806
7	Sam Twiston-Davies	81-598	14%	629,579
8	Paul Moloney	70-547	13%	473,898
9	Tom Scudamore	65-450	14%	1,701,471
10	Barry Geraghty	63-220	29%	1,735,426
11	Aidan Coleman	58-381	15%	458,292
12	Ruby Walsh	55-221	25%	1,497,668
13	Denis O'Regan	55-428	13%	509,502
14	James Reveley	53-414	13%	419,645
15	Brian Hughes	53-492	11%	314,864
16	Robert Thornton	51-353	14%	683,902
17	Noel Fehily	49-351	14%	713,324
18	Andrew Tinkler	48-287	17%	290,601
19	Nick Scholfield	48-381	13%	335,804
20	Felix de Giles	44-299	15%	259,363

THE LIST

Jockeys who had their first Cheltenham Festival winner in 2012

Richie McLernon Alfie Sherrin *JLT Specialty Handicap Chase*

Nick Scholfield Hunt Ball *Pulteney Novices' Handicap Chase*

Jerry McGrath Une Artiste *Fred Winter Juvenile Handicap Hurdle*

Dougie Costello Countrywide Flame *JCB Triumph Hurdle*

Campbell Gillies Brindisi Breeze *Albert Bartlett Novices' Hurdle*

Harry Haynes Attaglance *Martin Pipe Conditional Jockeys' H'cap Hurdle*

TONY McCOY
British champion
Interview, page 66

HENRY BROOKE
British champion conditional

"The aim is the conditionals' title," Brooke told last year's Annual when he was picked as a rising star to watch in 2012, and the ambitious 22-year-old was as good as his word. Backed by the powerful Donald McCain stable, and only two years after riding his first winner, Brooke clinched the title with 42 winners. That was a big jump from his previous best of 17 and left him four clear of Lucy Alexander. He finished joint-22nd in the overall table.

DAVY RUSSELL
Irish champion

Michael O'Leary, rather than Willie Mullins, was the kingmaker for once as Russell took a well-deserved first championship. Russell, who has been No.1 rider for O'Leary's Gigginstown House Stud since 2007, finally made it to the top after finishing runner-up for the previous five seasons behind the Mullins stable jockeys Ruby Walsh and Paul Townend. Twice the margin of defeat could be counted on one hand but Russell was a clear-cut winner this time as he romped to a century, with the highlights including Grade 1 victories on Quito De La Roque, Last Instalment, Sir Des Champs and Dedigout.

TOP 20 JUMP JOCKEYS IN IRELAND IN 2011-12

		Wins-rides	Strike rate	Win and place prize-money €
1	Davy Russell	104-528	20%	1,801,246
2	Ruby Walsh	85-358	24%	1,878,043
3	Paul Carberry	64-416	15%	1,088,205
4	Barry Geraghty	56-304	18%	1,205,631
5	Paul Townend	46-308	15%	1,093,105
6	Andrew Lynch	45-395	11%	1,214,459
7	Mr Patrick Mullins	42-129	33%	419,137
8	Andrew McNamara	41-397	10%	545,843
9	Bryan Cooper	36-428	8%	661,877
10	Miss Nina Carberry	31-153	20%	262,305
	Eddie O'Connell	31-272	11%	348,535
	Mark Walsh	31-325	10%	483,555
	Tom Doyle	31-388	8%	642,321
14	Robbie Power	29-270	11%	660,611
15	Patrick Mangan	27-321	8%	438,495
16	Declan Bates	25-385	6%	284,190
	Phillip Enright	25-403	6%	385,336
18	Alan Crowe	24-302	8%	349,807
	Davy Condon	24-363	7%	436,794
20	Niall Madden	19-308	6%	310,270

THE MILLIONAIRES CLUB

Top ten jockeys on prize-money (£) in GB and Ireland in 2011-12

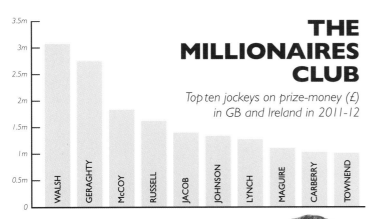

PATRICK MANGAN
Irish champion conditional

The 21-year-old son of Grand National-winning trainer Jimmy Mangan judged his challenge to perfection as he overhauled Eddie O'Connell's target of 26 to take the title by one. O'Connell rode out his claim in November 2011, which meant his subsequent winners did not count in the conditionals' championship and all he could do was watch as Mangan drew ever closer. The decisive moment was Mangan's victory on Fever Pitch in a handicap chase at Tramore, less than a fortnight from the end of the season.

WHO WON THE GRADE 1s?

Includes jockeys with at least two winners in the respective countries

JUMPS TRAINERS 2011-12

PAUL NICHOLLS
British champion

Helped enormously by Grand National winner Neptune Collonges, Nicholls broke through the £3m mark for the fourth time to clinch his seventh title in a row. He has now amassed more than £21m in total prize-money during his title-winning years. The Ditcheat trainer had three of the top eight earners in 2011-12 – Neptune Collonges (first), Big Buck's (fifth) and Rock On Ruby (eighth).

TOP 20 JUMPS TRAINERS IN BRITAIN IN 2011-12

	Wins-runs	Strike rate	Win and place prize-money £
1 Paul Nicholls	138-598	23%	3,297,804
2 Nicky Henderson	167-627	27%	2,741,454
3 Donald McCain	153-717	21%	1,248,262
4 Jonjo O'Neill	97-649	15%	1,144,901
5 Alan King	82-523	16%	1,135,082
6 David Pipe	101-632	16%	996,492
7 Philip Hobbs	73-512	14%	959,802
8 Nigel Twiston-Davies	70-579	12%	666,757
9 Evan Williams	88-579	15%	588,367
10 Tim Vaughan	102-592	17%	547,816
11 Colin Tizzard	46-320	14%	413,389
12 Lucinda Russell	57-454	13%	397,826
13 Charlie Longsdon	69-349	20%	382,761
14 Tom George	40-247	16%	356,574
15 Sue Smith	45-337	13%	356,412
16 Venetia Williams	52-401	13%	344,273
17 Nick Williams	20-132	15%	342,707
18 Peter Bowen	53-413	13%	340,139
19 Brian Ellison	37-230	16%	327,816
20 Willie Mullins	5-52	10%	327,672

The order of the top ten was shuffled but nobody broke into it

If it had been decided on wins …
Nicky Henderson would have been champion

TOP 20 JUMPS TRAINERS IN IRELAND IN 2011-12

	Wins-runs	Strike rate	Win and place prize-money €
1 Willie Mullins	138-498	28%	2,997,712
2 Noel Meade	59-254	23%	948,040
3 Edward O'Grady	25-224	11%	673,316
4 Jessica Harrington	34-350	10%	642,281
5 Gordon Elliott	40-354	11%	589,132
6 Dessie Hughes	34-400	9%	589,115
7 Tony Martin	33-277	12%	540,500
8 Colm Murphy	17-131	13%	523,010
9 Henry de Bromhead	34-181	19%	487,096
10 Charles Byrnes	24-161	15%	415,935
11 Thomas Mullins	15-71	21%	385,785
12 John Joseph Hanlon	23-240	10%	371,587
13 Christy Roche	25-183	14%	348,292
14 Mouse Morris	9-158	6%	323,710
15 Dermot Weld	16-44	36%	306,075
16 Paul Nolan	18-210	9%	296,765
17 John Kiely	21-85	25%	269,035
18 Michael Hourigan	19-217	9%	265,406
19 Ted Walsh	15-55	27%	255,115
20 Philip Fenton	14-105	13%	238,988

Breaking into the top ten
Tony Martin 13th to 7th
Henry de Bromhead 11th to 9th

If it had been decided on wins …
Willie Mullins would still have been champion

WILLIE MULLINS
Irish champion

Mullins remains utterly dominant in Ireland, clinching his fifth successive title and his sixth in all with a record prize-money haul. Even if the prize-money won by the next four trainers in the list had been combined, Mullins would still have finished on top. Mullins did not, however, have a monopoly on quality as only four of Ireland's top 15 earners were in his yard.

THE LIST

Leading trainers at the 2012 Cheltenham Festival

	Prize-money	Winners
Nicky Henderson	£778,888	Bellvano, Bobs Worth, Finian's Rainbow, Riverside Theatre, Simonsig, Sprinter Sacre, Une Artiste
Jonjo O'Neill	£427,963	Alfie Sherrin, Sunnyhillboy, Synchronised
Paul Nicholls	£412,646	Big Buck's, Rock On Ruby
Willie Mullins	£253,019	Champagne Fever, Quevega, Sir Des Champs
Donald McCain	£186,198	Cinders And Ashes, Son Of Flicka
David Bridgwater	£106,850	
Colm Murphy	£97,827	
Alan King	£94,929	
Henry de Bromhead	£70,232	
David Pipe	£69,120	Salut Flo
Malcolm Jefferson	£68,017	Attaglance, Cape Tribulation
Philip Hobbs	£58,420	Balthazar King
Lucinda Russell*	£56,950	Brindisi Breeze
John Quinn	£56,950	Countrywide Flame
Rebecca Curtis*	£47,650	Teaforthree
Thomas Mullins*	£39,865	Alderwood
Colin Tizzard	£38,481	
Mouse Morris	£34,801	
Keiran Burke*	£29,480	Hunt Ball *(right)*
Nick Williams	£28,441	
Paul Webber	£24,600	
Noel Meade	£23,007	
Edward O'Grady	£22,449	
Dermot Weld	£22,255	
Rodger Sweeney*	£20,986	Salsify

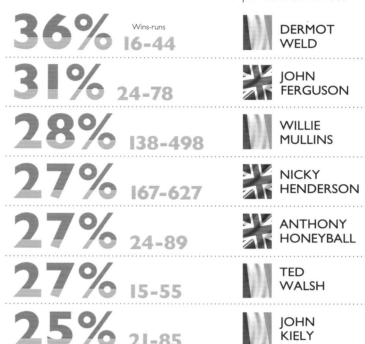

Includes all trainers with at least one winner. *Denotes trainer who won at the festival for the first time.

MONEY TRAIL
The most profitable trainers to follow in Britain and Ireland

MALCOLM JEFFERSON
+82.88

CHARLIE LONGSDON
+56.70

ANTHONY HONEYBALL
+53.88

KIERAN PURCELL	TIM WALFORD	JOHN QUINN	JOHN FERGUSON	THOMAS MULLINS	SARAH HUMPHREY
+40.17	**+40.00**	**+35.29**	**+32.04**	**+31.71**	**+31.11**

PLAYING THE PERCENTAGES

British and Irish trainers with at least a 25 per cent strike-rate

	Wins-runs		
36%	16-44		DERMOT WELD
31%	24-78		JOHN FERGUSON
28%	138-498		WILLIE MULLINS
27%	167-627		NICKY HENDERSON
27%	24-89		ANTHONY HONEYBALL
27%	15-55		TED WALSH
25%	21-85		JOHN KIELY

Includes trainers who had 30 or more runners

FOCUS ON **JOHN FERGUSON**

Until last season Ferguson's name was in the peripheral vision of most punters, if they were aware at all that he was a chief bloodstock adviser and buyer for Sheikh Mohammed. But he quickly made his mark in his own right as he fulfilled a long-held ambition to set up as a jumps trainer. Ferguson, who had his first winner in September 2011, became a trainer to follow as he built an impressive 31 per cent strike-rate with a £32.04 profit to a £1 stake. Fifteen of the 26 horses to represent him in 2011-12 were successful and the best of them was Cotton Mill (RPR 153), who gave the trainer his first Graded winner at Warwick in January and was challenging Simonsig when he ran out at the second-last in the Neptune at Cheltenham.

Includes trainers who had ten or more winners and a profit of at least £30 (€30) to a £1 (€1) stake

JUMPS OWNERS 2011-12

JP McMANUS
British and Irish champion

This was the fifth British-Irish double for McManus, who reclaimed the British title from Trevor Hemmings and retained his Irish crown after a tough battle with Michael O'Leary's Gigginstown House Stud. Gigginstown is now a major rival to his long-held position at the top of Irish racing, while in Britain he has been beaten only twice in the past seven seasons and both times that was by the Grand National-winning owner.

TOP 20 JUMPS OWNERS IN BRITAIN IN 2011-12

	Wins-runs	Strike rate	Total prize-money £
1 John P McManus	99-535	19%	1,394,654
2 J Hales	3-26	12%	543,951
3 The Stewart Family	16-60	27%	525,282
4 Michael Buckley	17-64	27%	419,591
5 T G Leslie	26-97	27%	411,078
6 Andrea & Graham Wylie	18-76	24%	345,554
7 Trevor Hemmings	22-186	12%	338,194
8 S Munir	12-50	24%	334,543
9 The Festival Goers	3-8	38%	256,742
10 Clive D Smith	4-17	24%	253,083
11 Jimmy Nesbitt Partnership	2-3	67%	232,548
12 John Wade	20-226	9%	216,720
13 Mrs Diana L Whateley	9-57	16%	206,552
14 Mrs T P Radford	6-35	17%	202,415
15 Walters Plant Hire Ltd	20-98	20%	200,243
16 Mr & Mrs Raymond Anderson Green	14-88	16%	183,425
17 Mrs Caroline Mould	7-28	25%	181,372
18 D A Johnson	16-65	25%	170,074
19 Robert Waley-Cohen	1-22	5%	163,394
20 Jared Sullivan	6-23	26%	159,186

TOP 20 JUMPS OWNERS IN IRELAND IN 2011-12

	Wins-runs	Strike rate	Win and place prize-money €
1 John P McManus	99-785	13%	1,701,245
2 Gigginstown House Stud	83-439	19%	1,611,745
3 Mrs S Ricci	24-61	39%	767,350
4 Barry Connell	19-112	17%	285,643
5 Ann & Alan Potts Partnership	40-354	11%	253,837
6 Graham Wylie	8-12	67%	251,210
7 Dr R Lambe	13-58	22%	245,100
8 Hammer & Trowel Syndicate	2-5	40%	193,600
9 Redgap Partnership	11-112	10%	181,535
10 Lock Syndicate	3-6	50%	177,400
11 George Creighton	2-5	40%	170,200
12 Stephen Curran	5-8	63%	158,790
13 Three Friers Cross Syndicate	1-2t	50%	158,600
14 W Hennessy	5-45	11%	152,495
15 John Corr	3-13	23%	145,075
16 Mrs M Brophy	3-5	60%	143,950
17 Red Barn Syndicate	3-4	75%	139,610
18 John Patrick Ryan	3-63	5%	136,815
19 Garden Kingdom Syndicate	4-7	57%	130,300
20 D Cox	4-22	18%	127,205

FOCUS ON GRAHAM WYLIE

Apart from double champion JP McManus, Wylie was the only owner to appear in the top 20 of both the British and Irish lists at the end of a season that marked a fresh beginning for the technology tycoon. Forced to disperse his horses following the disqualification of Howard Johnson, Wylie opted for the best in Paul Nicholls and Willie Mullins. The move paid off handsomely and he finished sixth in both lists. Nicholls got the old rogue Tidal Bay to win the Bet365 Gold Cup on the final day of the British season and Mullins won with all five of his Wylie-owned runners, including Cheltenham novice runners-up Boston Bob and Felix Yonger.

TOP 5 EARNING HORSES IN 2011-12

Neptune Collonges
£574,674
Owner John Hales
Trainer Paul Nicholls

Synchronised
£372,947
JP McManus
Jonjo O'Neill

Finian's Rainbow
£328,736
Michael Buckley
Nicky Henderson

Sizing Europe
£298,439
Ann & Alan Potts
Henry de Bromhead

Big Buck's
£292,648
The Stewart family
Paul Nicholls